Reshaping National Intelligence in an Age of Information

The world of intelligence has been completely transformed by the end of the Cold War and the onset of an age of information. Prior to the 1990s, U.S. government intelligence had one principal target, the Soviet Union; a narrow set of "customers," the political and military officials of the U.S. government; and a limited set of information from the sources they owned, spy satellites and spies. Today, world intelligence has many targets, numerous consumers – not all of whom are American or in the government – and too much information, most of which is not owned by the U.S. government and is of widely varying reliability.

In this bold and penetrating study, Gregory Treverton, former Vice Chair of the National Intelligence Council and Senate investigator, offers his insider's view on how intelligence gathering and analysis must change. He suggests why intelligence needs to be both contrarian, leaning against the conventional wisdom, and attentive to the longer term, leaning against the shrinking time horizons of Washington policy makers. He urges that the solving of intelligence puzzles taps expertise outside government – in the academy, think tanks, and Wall Street – to make these parties function as colleagues and co-consumers of intelligence, befitting the changed role of government from doer to convener, mediator, and coalition-builder.

Gregory F. Treverton is Acting President and Director of Studies at the Pacific Council on International Policy and Senior Consultant at RAND. He has also served as Vice Chair of the National Intelligence Council in Washington, DC, as a staff member of the National Security Council, and as a professional staff member of the Senate Select Committee on Intelligence. Dr. Treverton headed RAND's International Security and Defense Policy Center from 1995 to 1998 and served as Senior Fellow and Director of the Europe-America Project and the Project on America's Task in a Changed World at the Council on Foreign Relations in New York from 1988 to 1992. He has also been a Lecturer in Public Policy and Senior Research Associate at the Kennedy School of Government (1982–87) and Director of Studies at the International Institute for Strategic Affairs in London (1978–81). Dr. Treverton is author or coeditor of more than a dozen books on international relations and American foreign policy, including *Making American Foreign Policy* (1993), *America, Germany, and the Future of Europe* (1992), and *Rethinking America's Security* (1992, coedited with Graham T. Allison).

RAND Studies in Policy Analysis

Editor: Charles Wolf, Jr., Senior Economic Advisor and Corporate Fellow in International Economics, RAND

Policy analysis is the application of scientific methods to develop and test alternative ways of addressing social, economic, legal, international, national security, and other problems. The RAND Studies in Policy Analysis series aims to include several significant, timely, and innovative works each year in this broad field. Selection is guided by an editorial board consisting of Charles Wolf, Jr. (editor) and David S. C. Chu, Paul K. Davis, and Lynn Karoly (associate editors).

Also in the series:
David C. Gompert and F. Stephen Larrabee (eds.), *America and Europe: A Partnership for a New Era*
John W. Peabody, M. Omar Rahman, Paul J. Gertler, Joyce Mann, Donna O. Farley, Jeff Luck, David Robalino, and Grace M. Carter, *Policy and Health: Implications for Development in Asia*
Samantha F. Ravich, *Marketization and Democracy: East Asian Experiences*

Reshaping National Intelligence in an Age of Information

Gregory F. Treverton
RAND

CAMBRIDGE
UNIVERSITY PRESS

PUBLISHED BY THE PRESS SYNDICATE OF THE UNIVERSITY OF CAMBRIDGE
The Pitt Building, Trumpington Street, Cambridge, United Kingdom

CAMBRIDGE UNIVERSITY PRESS
The Edinburgh Building, Cambridge CB2 2RU, UK
40 West 20th Street, New York, NY 10011-4211, USA
10 Stamford Road, Oakleigh, VIC 3166, Australia
Ruiz de Alarcón 13, 28014 Madrid, Spain
Dock House, The Waterfront, Cape Town 8001, South Africa

http://www.cambridge.org

First published 2001

Printed in the United States of America

Typeface Sabon 10/13 pt.   *System* MS Word   [AU]

A catalog record for this book is available from the British Library.

Library of Congress Cataloging in Publication Data

Treverton, Gregory F.
Reshaping national intelligence in an Age of Information / Gregory F. Treverton.
p. cm. – (RAND studies in policy analysis)
Includes bibliographical references and index.
ISBN 0-521-58096-X
1. Intelligence service – United States. 2. Military intelligence – United States. 3. World
politics – 1989–   I. Title. II. Series

UB251.U5 T74 2001
327.12′0973 – dc21
00-068863

ISBN 0-521 58096 X hardback

Contents

Foreword   *page xi*

Preface   *xiii*

Note on sources   *xvii*

1   The imperative of reshaping   1
        Failing in India   3
        The legacy of hot war and cold   5
        Open sources vs. secrets   8
        Puzzles vs. mysteries   11
        Aiding war-fighters   13
        The intelligence of policy   15
        A guide for readers   18

2   The world of intelligence beyond 2010   20
        Redefining America's interests in the world   20
        Forms of power   25
        Global processes   28
        "New old threats"   35
        "Threats without threateners"   43
        The coming of the market state   46
        Changing public and private roles   51
        The intelligence of the market state   54
        What kind of America?   56

3   The militarization of intelligence   62
        What mission for intelligence?   63
        Retargeting the Cold War legacy   65
        Plus ça change, or forward to the past   70

Cold War reconnaissance: who controls?   74
National and tactical: new missions for old systems   79
NIMA: creating an imagery stovepipe   81
Which systems, at what cost?   84
Owned by whom?   89
Serving intelligence's national purposes   91

4   Designated readers: the open source revolution   93
America's Cold War intelligence   98
Intelligence for an age of information   102
Distributed intelligence?   104
Open sources and secrets   108
Learning to read: using open sources   113
Processing information, not secrets   119
Organizing for tactical support   120
The tactical franchise   123
And the strategic franchise   125
Addressing mysteries: national intelligence estimates   127
Doing well at addressing mysteries   129
Bringing outsiders inside   132
Estimating as process   134

5   Spying, looking, and catching criminals   136
The range of clandestine operations   137
Shaping America's clandestine service   138
Framing an assessment   141
The culture of spying   145
To spy or not   150
Reshaping the clandestine service . . . in service
  of NSA?   152
Spying for money   157
Hiring lookers   161
Law enforcement   167
The Bureau and the Agency   170
The question of covert action   173

6   The intelligence of policy   177
Analysts and policy-makers   179
The messenger and the message   185
Questions not asked and not answered   191
Questions asked   195

The bright line   197
Commanders and assessments   202
Changing the culture   205
Challenging mind-sets   208
Erasing the line?   211
Intelligence for whose policy?   213

7   A reshaped intelligence   216
Retargeting the Cold War legacy   220
A new paradigm   225
The rise of the market state   229
The role of the DCI   234
The collection "market"   240
The split franchise of analysis   243
Collecting what is free   246
Points of leverage: a practical agenda   248
Making the case publicly   253

Index   257

Foreword

This book is a happy collaboration between RAND and the Twenti-eth Century Fund, now The Century Foundation. In fact, it became a tripartite collaboration, including Cambridge University Press, with which RAND inaugurated a new book series of policy analyses, a series edited by Charles Wolf, Jr., just as Greg Treverton joined RAND. Greg had left the vice chair of the National Intelligence Council during the Clinton administration to come to RAND to run the International Secu-rity and Defense Policy Center. At the same time, he joined a Twentieth Century Fund task force on intelligence that produced a report several years ago, *In From the Cold.* Greg contributed a background paper to that report, a paper that began to develop the issues treated in this book, and he played a major role in pushing the report to conclusion.

Our premise in this collaboration is the same as Greg's: Not only has the world of American intelligence been upended by the end of the Cold War, but the necessary reshaping of intelligence will itself have to result from a more open discussion of it than has been the norm in the American democracy. RAND and The Century Foundation share an interest in that reshaping of intelligence as an important part of America's capacity in foreign affairs. For RAND, U.S. intelligence is a client and an increasingly important one. As intelligence strives to adapt to a changed world, a range of RAND capacities — from regional analysis, to budgeting and manpower planning, to thinking about costly systems against an uncertain future — is more and more relevant. For its part, The Century Foundation's task force on intelligence followed an earlier one, focused on the question of covert action. The Foundation continues to foster discussion of the adequacy of current governmental arrangements in light of the changed world, and intelligence is an important part of those arrangements.

This book by Greg Treverton is fine policy analysis, enriched by his own experience and his examples, drawn from his various angles of vision on intelligence — Senate investigator, White House consumer, and intelligence community manager. His central propositions are the basis for the discussion of intelligence that ought to happen but hasn't, despite several blue-ribbon panels during the late 1990s. He argues that intelligence is no longer in the secrets business but rather in the information business; that it now has too much information, not too little; that it now has many consumers, not few, and that many of those new consumers are non-Americans and people from the various private sectors; and that while collection used to be the problem, selection now is the central task for intelligence. His own bias is that intelligence needs to be both contrarian, leaning against traditional wisdom, and attentive to the longer term, leaning against the time horizons of Washington, which seem shorter and shorter.

It is a pleasure for our two institutions to join with Cambridge University Press in publishing this book. We can only hope that it will help provoke the serious discussion of reshaping intelligence for which it calls. That discussion is both necessary and long overdue.

James Thomson   Richard Leone
President, RAND   President, The Century Foundation

Preface

When I took over the national estimates process as vice chair of the National Intelligence Council (NIC) at the beginning of the first Clinton administration, I had been a Senate investigator of intelligence, a White House consumer of intelligence, and an academic student of intelligence. But this was my first time in what is called, slightly quaintly, the "intelligence community." As with other such locutions in life, the word *community* describes precisely what it is not; it is somewhere between a fiction and an aspiration.

I vowed that I would stay only as long as I could laugh at aspects of the organizational culture in which the NIC worked — we took bed and board from the Central Intelligence Agency (CIA) at its headquarters in Langley, Virginia — that struck me as Cold War throwbacks, such as the fact that my daily schedule, neatly typed and frequently revised each day, was classified "secret." I never did figure out why it was so classified, but I did leave, for other reasons, about the time I stopped laughing.

More to the point, I felt like the candidate member of a priesthood, with both the positive and the negative connotations of that label. Positively, the CIA analysts who were my most immediate colleagues and helpers reinforced the impression I had formed of them in earlier executive programs I had taught: they made me proud of the public service. They were, and are, person for person, the match of any American organization, public or private. Their savvy and dedication belied all the tired, unfair chestnuts about Washington bureaucrats. Theirs was a true calling.

Yet the other connotation of *priesthood* was also apt. Intelligence analysts thought of their calling as one apart, with whiffs of superiority and condescension in their view. A lot had changed over the previous decade or so — those changes are a theme of this book — but there were still hints of the view that said we're in the business of speaking truth, and if those policy types downtown don't listen, the hell with them. There are books to be written about the organizational culture of the CIA — about the organizational culture*s*, really, because the CIA's three main directorates, for operations, analysis, and science and technology, are worlds apart. My Harvard colleague Ernest May described them as about as integrated as the military services, and sometimes he would add, "in 1947"! Organizational culture is not the subject of this book but is its theme, for the revolution confronting intelligence ultimately is one of mission and culture.

The aim of my teaching and writing about intelligence had been to better connect it, and especially analysis, to the needs of policy. So when I had the chance to try my ideas out not on my students but on myself, I could hardly resist. It was a happy irony that the person who offered me that chance was Bob Gates, the director of central intelligence in the Bush administration and an old friend from government service. Bob knew I had been helping Bill Clinton's campaign against his president but made me, in the months before the election's outcome was apparent, a nonpartisan offer rare in these days: "Come to the NIC. If President Bush is re-elected, you'll have some years to see if your ideas can make intelligence estimates better. If he's not, I'll be a lame duck, and you can decide whether to serve the new administration at the NIC or elsewhere." In the event, my old friend and colleague Joe Nye became chair of the NIC, and I stayed, happily.

But I owe Bob a debt for giving me the chance to try my ideas on myself. I also owe a clutch of intellectual debts, ones I eagerly acknowledge without tarring any of those creditors with responsibility for this book's shortcomings. Joe Nye and I had known each other since my days in graduate school, but we had never worked closely together. Doing so became a treat for me. Joe gave me enough discretion in managing the national estimates process, and, more important, he gave me the example of a mind that is clearer at framing issues than any I have known.

I owe debts both pecuniary and substantive to the Twentieth Century Fund, now The Century Foundation. The fund's 1991 task force on covert action gave me a chance to try my ideas, already formed, on interested colleagues; their 1995 task force on intelligence gave me the opportunity to begin to assemble the ideas that became this book, with financial support from the fund. I am grateful for both, and especially for the criticism and encouragement of the Fund's president, Richard Leone, and his colleagues, Morton Halperin and Janne Nolan. My recent professional home, RAND, has been a fortunate one in many respects. RAND's book series with Cambridge University Press was an ideal place to publish this book, and I appreciate the flexibility of the three institutions — RAND, the Foundation, and Cambridge Press — in making this tripartite collaboration a reality.

RAND was good enough to regard writing this book as part of its broader public service, and it has supplied me with both interested colleagues and able graduate students. Among my colleagues, I am particularly indebted to Kevin O'Connell and to Dick Neu. As always, Robert Klitgaard — happily a colleague again, at RAND — helped me think through the framing of central issues. Loch Johnson, with whom I first became interested in intelligence while working for the first Senate Select Committee on Intelligence, often called the "Church committee" after its chair, Senator Frank Church (D-Idaho), gave me characteristically insightful comments. I also appreciate the wise comments I've received from David Gompert, Dick Kerr, and John Koehler. Of graduate students, I particularly thank Lorne Teitelbaum, who served as both research assistant and intellectual sparring partner; and Brett Neely, who was enormously helpful in tracking down all those final details.

As a condition of my employment at the NIC, I had agreed to a CIA review of any manuscript on intelligence. The review of this manuscript was more arduous than I expected, although the officials of the CIA Publications Review Board were unfailingly helpful and good natured. The problem was that my subject is broad, so the manuscript had to be farmed out to a number of agencies. Some of the first responses were so sweeping as to underscore the need for a dramatic change of culture in intelligence; in two cases, I was asked to delete material that agency heads had discussed publicly. In the end, though, we agreed on a score of changes, all of which affected details and not major points of analysis or conclusions. Most of the changes were quite minor, but in several cases, I do indicate in footnotes that deletions were made, lest the reader think that bland or convoluted prose is the result of my or my editor's falling down on the job.

Finally, this book is dedicated to my wife, Karen. Pursuing her to California may have delayed finishing the book, but it surely enriched my life in the interim.

Note on sources

This book assesses recent history to suggest the future shape of American intelligence. The "age of information" in the book's title is a purposive double meaning. It is meant to connote the rush of developments, mostly technological, that is now regularly described by the label "information age." At least as important, though, is that the phrase is intended to call attention to another dramatic feature of the future world in which intelligence will operate: Technology, but not just technology, is producing overwhelming amounts of information. Intelligence's future world is both an information age and an age of information.

The book is analysis. To sharpen the analytic points and make them more vivid, it uses anecdotes from my various vantage points on intelligence — Senate investigator, White House consumer, outside student, and, most recently, National Intelligence Council producer. In that respect, the book is like intelligence, for I have come to believe that most people, including most policy officials, grasp analytic points more readily if they come tethered to a fact, or caselet or anecdote.

Analyzing intelligence has become easier over the last generation, but it is still not easy. It is not so much that information is in short supply (though that is true in critical particulars). The last few years have produced not only memoirs but histories and cases, and intelligence remains fascinating enough to induce a steady stream of investigative journalism.

Rather, all these sources have their defects. The temptations of memoir writers are all too well known. Current history, written in the absence of documents, is vulnerable to reproducing errors just because they were ferreted out of *Aviation Week and Space Technology* or uttered in an interview. Journalism is all the more vulnerable. Even case-writing has recently turned competitive, with insiders selectively declassifying documents to prove their points.

I try to hedge my judgments appropriately. About intelligence processing and analysis, I am confident. I have used, produced, and studied intelligence analysis. I am less confident in two other areas, and I try to point that out.

One is espionage, clandestine collection. There, it is not so much that I lack experience — for I have been a consumer of espionage in several jobs — as that I am, to some extent, surely the prisoner of my own perspective. I outline my judgments in chapter 5, and they are harsh. But that harshness no doubt reflects my own preoccupation with broad strategic mysteries, not specific tactical puzzles. If I had been working on, for instance, the Hamas terrorists or the Cali drug cartel, my judgments about espionage might be gentler. As I suggest in chapter 5, a first step in any serious restructuring of the clandestine service would be a retrospective evaluation of U.S. spying, including eminent outsiders, in order to develop a record of where the United States has done well and where poorly, and why.

The other area is technical collection, and here I feel still less confident. My situation is not so different from that of intelligence's senior managers and congressional overseers: We generalists can hardly know enough about the systems to begin to connect what we'd like to know about Iran with where to fly or point a satellite, much less about which new system to build. I am like the ballistics expert I describe later; I have strong hunches but cannot justify them in a fully analytic way. Those who do know the technical details well enough are very far from the policy officials they are trying to help and may, to boot, have acquired deep stakes in "their" collection systems. The first need here, one I discuss in chapter 3, is for something like the Pentagon's Policy Analysis and Evaluation (PA&E) shop to give decisions about major intelligence systems the same analytic scrub that major weapons decisions receive.

For both human and technical collection, as well as for the rest of intelligence, the margin of what is debated publicly needs to be dramatically widened. Only if they know more about what they are buying will the American people be prepared to pay for it. In any event, that is the premise of this book.

1

The imperative of reshaping

When India tested nuclear weapons in May 1998, and Pakistan quickly followed with tests of its own, Washington was immediately abuzz with the familiar bemoanings over the latest intelligence failure. Why hadn't the United States known in advance about the tests? George Tenet, the director of central intelligence (DCI), immediately set in motion an investigation, chaired by former vice chairman of the Joint Chiefs of Staff, Admiral David Jeremiah. Tenet himself admitted bluntly: "We did not get it right. Period."[1]

The case displayed all but one of the challenges that U.S. intelligence confronts. The exception is providing intelligence to support military operations around the world by the United States and its coalition partners. Known by its acronym, SMO, this support to military operations has become intelligence's primary new business in the world beyond the Cold War. In other respects, though, Jeremiah's report, which remains secret but whose conclusions were briefed publicly, echoes this book's themes. Intelligence is drifting, unsure of what it does and for whom. It remains mired in institutions, processes, and habits of mind that may have been appropriate to the Cold War but manifestly are not now. It badly needs to be radically reshaped for an age of information. This is a time to reexamine first principles, which are now open to question in a way they haven't been for a half century.

---

1 For reportage on the case and the Jeremiah report, see *Washington Post*, June 3, 1998, p. A18, and *New York Times*, same date and page.

Most obviously, the United States didn't have a single spy worth his (or, less likely, her) salt in India, the Jeremiah report apparently concluded. That is a shame but not a surprise, given the record of America's clandestine service, the Central Intelligence Agency's (CIA's) Directorate of Operations (DO). The United States needs to build a new clandestine service on the remains of the DO, one that would focus entirely on a few closed potential foes, such as North Korea, on closed and dangerous programs of open societies, such as India's nuclear weapons, and on terrorists or other enemies who may not have nation-state names attached to them.

Intelligence now confronts not one overwhelming target, the Soviet Union, but a myriad of targets: Witness India, which is a democracy and a friend but was also a target. Intelligence also has, much more so than in the past, a range of customers, some of which, such as other governments or private actors such as nongovernmental organizations (NGOs), are unusual ones with which intelligence has little experience in dealing. It needs to fashion new arrangements for organizing itself and, particularly, for getting close to these customers. The old dogma that intelligence should not get too close to policy lest it be politicized is no longer helpful guidance — quite the contrary.

The final set of challenges is the most fundamental. Cold War intelligence lived in a world where information was scarce; it relied on "secrets" not otherwise available. Its business was those secrets. Now, though, it faces an era of information. Information and its sources are mushrooming, and so are the technologies for moving information rapidly around the globe. Given these circumstances, the business of intelligence is no longer just to provide secrets; rather, its business is to produce high-quality understanding of the world using all sources.

The clearest warning of India's impending test came a few days before the test in an obscure anti-India newsletter, *Charhdi Kala International*, which circulated within the Sikh community in British Columbia. The letter reported in its May 7 edition: "Preparations for an Indian nuclear blast have been confirmed by our sources in India (who so far have never been wrong having millions of pairs of eyes and ears fixed to the ground) who report all kinds of feverish activities in the vicinity of Pokharan. . . ."[2]

2   Quoted in *New York Times*, May 17, 1998, p. A5.

FAILING IN INDIA

As usual in Washington's blame wars, the India story was more complicated than it seemed, but that fact made it little the less damning for intelligence. In one sense, the entire fuss was beside the point because the Indians eventually became determined to test a bomb in any case. So whether intelligence could give the United States warning in advance didn't matter very much; Washington would have appeared either feckless if it knew but failed to dissuade New Delhi from testing, or ignorant if it didn't know. If there were real failings, they were less those of intelligence than of a policy that presumed India had little reason to test and so would be easily deterred from doing so. Tenet was being a good soldier by carrying the blame for the administration.

The case underscored that successful spying is both a patient business and a target-of-opportunity one. Spies not recruited as young people a generation ago won't be in a position to know of sensitive matters now. India's 1974 nuclear test had put the United States on notice about the country's nuclear ambitions, so there had been reason to try to recruit spies from within India's nuclear agency. Those efforts, however, might not have succeeded. Or if they did, the spy might have retired or moved on by 1998. A spy in the right place might not have been privy to the exact deliberations of interest. In this case, there seems to have been no spy, but the Indians also tried hard to deceive and so, no doubt, restricted the circle of those who knew the tests were coming. Even had a spy been in a position to know, he or she might not have been able to pass the information in time.

The lack of information on the ground left intelligence reliant on photographs and other imagery acquired by spy satellites in space. There, the shortcomings were two. In 1995 and 1996, U.S. intelligence analysts had detected what appeared to be preparations for Indian tests. Armed with that information, U.S. diplomats had persuaded India not to test. In the process, India had learned about what the United States knew and something about how it knew it. Tracking imagery satellites is not all that hard, and in earlier years, the Soviet Union had provided its friends and allies with the tracks of U.S. satellites. Knowing where the United States was looking, and when, and having some idea of what it was looking for made India's efforts at deception easier. The test site was, for instance, kept in a continual state of high readiness, thus masking increased activity in the run-up to a test. In addition, India's nuclear program was to a considerable extent homegrown, so U.S. intelligence's understanding of Chinese or Russian patterns did not help much in assessing it.

Moreover, the United States takes so many more images than analysts can examine that key signals can be lost in a flood of unexamined "pictures" (actually, it is "dots" that go unexamined, because all U.S. imagery except that from the old U-2 spy planes is now digitized). In the India case, only one imagery analyst at the National Imagery and Mapping Agency (NIMA) was responsible full-time for the Indian nuclear program. While that analyst had colleagues at the CIA, the Defense Intelligence Agency (DIA), and the State Department, they did not cooperate well enough, Jeremiah argued. That ragged cooperation is a feature of U.S. intelligence as old as the attack on Pearl Harbor, which came as such a surprise more than a half century ago.

The lack of priority attention to India is linked to the crucial failing of the case, that of mind-set. As Jeremiah put it, analysts and policy officials alike "acted as if the BJP would behave as we behave."[3] The Hindu nationalist party, BJP, had come to power in 1996 but fell after only thirteen days. It returned to power again in March 1998. According to the Jeremiah report, one 1996 CIA memorandum did call for more focus on India and Pakistan. But for policy and intelligence officials alike, thinking they understood the BJP made it seem unnecessary to pay more attention to it. The party's bluster about nuclear weapons was only campaign rhetoric designed for the Hindu faithful: "To ensure the security, territorial integrity and unity of India we will take all necessary steps and exercise all available options. Towards that end we will re-evaluate the nuclear policy and exercise the option to induct nuclear weapons."[4] The party would moderate in government, especially since it would have to govern in coalition. And so on. Thus ran the mind-set, one that had come to be almost impenetrable.

This mirror imaging was convenient because it spared the need to ask "What if?" In this case, the "what if?" was "what if the BJP meant what it said?" for it had made no secret of its intention to make nuclear weapons part of India's arsenal. As Senator Daniel Patrick Moynihan (D-New York) put it with characteristic puckishness: "The State Department said 'Why didn't the CIA tell us?' To which the answer is, 'Why doesn't the State Department learn to read?'" In that sense, Tenet

3   Quoted in *Washington Post*, June 3, 1998, p. A18.
4   BJP *National Agenda for Governance*, March 18, 1998.

did the State Department, and also the White House where the mind-set was just as impenetrable, a favor by taking the blame.

To be fair, India's America handlers at the foreign ministry and elsewhere purred reassurance, saying that no test was imminent. Whether those reassurances represented deception or simple ignorance remains unclear. In any case, Indian diplomats, who were suave internationalists attuned to India's image abroad, were likely to have had nearly as much trouble understanding the Hindu nationalists for whom they now worked as did the Americans.

The convenience was reinforced by the view in American officialdom that testing would be a disaster *for India*. That view was strongly held in Washington officialdom both before and after the tests, and it is eminently sensible. India had already tested a bomb once, in 1974, so no one, least of all Pakistan, could be in doubt that India was a nuclear power. Yet by not moving overtly to build nuclear weapons and by not testing again, it had avoided international opprobrium and sanctions. India could have its cake and eat it too. It could frighten Pakistan and perhaps deter China with its nuclear weapons in the closet; meanwhile it could get on with India's real business of making itself richer. Why risk that happy state of affairs by testing?

Getting at that "why?" meant getting into the heads of the Hindu nationalists. It meant asking: Why might they be telling the truth? Why might nukes in the closet not be enough for them? It meant challenging mind-sets that were more comfortable for policy than for intelligence. Yet getting into the heads of those who are different is the ultimate task of intelligence. Intelligence is supposed to have the people who understand Bonn and Delhi better than they do Washington. Being contrarian is also part of their job description. On occasion, they are joyfully contrarian, happily kicking the props of premise on which their policy counterparts have erected policy. This time, though, they were as guilty of conventional wisdom as anyone else in government. If intelligence doesn't challenge prevailing mind-sets, what good is it?

THE LEGACY OF HOT WAR AND COLD

The world of intelligence has been upended by both politics and technology. The demise of the Soviet Union and the end of the Cold War are what get the attention, but the underlying transformation is longer and deeper. The history of the first stage of U.S. intelligence,

1945 to 1990 or so, is the history of the last stage of the industrial age. The onset of an age of information has enabled dramatic changes that encompass the end of communism, the onset of the "market state," with accompanying transformations in the roles of government and of private actors, the rise of emerging states, and the proliferation of non-state actors. Intelligence now has many targets, not one; many consumers, not just a few; and vast amounts of information that is to a great extent unreliable, not a scarcity of information that mainly comes from satellites or spies and is therefore regarded as accurate.

The nation's existing intelligence, about $27 billion per year in size,[5] was shaped in World War II's wake and the Cold War's shadow. Centralization was a legacy of Pearl Harbor and fears of another surprise attack, this time from the Soviet Union. Pearl Harbor's lesson for intelligence was that critical puzzle pieces of warning had been present in the system but were never assembled by the separate Army and Navy intelligence organizations. A central intelligence agency, with access to everything, would hedge against that happening again.

The bright white line that separated intelligence from policy during the Cold War was not so much a reflection of wartime lessons. Rather, it resulted more from the CIA's growing standing in Washington and from the beliefs of the founders of postwar intelligence, in particular Sherman Kent, who was first the deputy director and then the director of the CIA's prestigious Office of National Estimates (ONE). The operating agencies of government were bound, so Kent's logic went, to want intelligence judgments cut to suit the cloth of ongoing policies. It took no accusations of wrongdoing to worry that the U.S. Air Force, charged with building American missiles, would incline toward higher estimates of the threat posed by Soviet weapons, for instance. Intelligence separated from policy, as the CIA was separated, would serve as a check on such tendencies.

By the early 1950s, the main contours of America's Cold War intelligence were in place. The CIA had moved from coordinating intelligence

5   This and every other number or detail about intelligence capabilities here are derived from published sources. The total budgets finally were officially released in 1997: $26.6 billion for FY97 and $26.7 billion for FY98. For more details, see, for instance, *Washington Post*, June 13, 1994, p. A8, or *New York Times*, November 5, 1994, p. 54.

to collecting and analyzing it. While the CIA was more and more dominated by its clandestine service, it had come to be a major producer of analysis in its own right. The original intention was for the CIA to be the centralizer, the hub of a wheel of intelligence production. In fact, it came to centralize by dominating, especially with regard to the overarching target, the Soviet Union. In the early years, the CIA was also the prime mover of technical collection systems such as the U-2 spy plane.

In the circumstances of the high Cold War, there were powerful arguments for targeting intelligence tightly on the Soviet Union, for giving pride of place to secrets, especially those collected by satellites and other technical means, and for centralizing intelligence and separating it from the stakes of policy agencies. None of these arguments, however, is so compelling today.

To use a business analogy, intelligence then had one main target, the Soviet Union, and essentially one consumer, in form the president but in fact the National Security Council (NSC), encompassing the State and Defense departments, and the NSC staff. Intelligence knew what its business was, and that business was secrets. In that sense its "technology" was stable. To be sure, the particular technologies that made possible spy or eavesdropping satellites were anything but static; the technical achievements of the intelligence in the first Cold War decades were dazzling. But the advances were better ways of doing the job. They did not change the basic task.

So, too, the broader "operating environment" of intelligence was relatively stable. Measuring the extent of the Soviet threat was no mean feat, but the Soviet Union was not about to be supplanted as the main threat to the United States and, as such, the principal target for U.S. intelligence. The hierarchy of U.S. interests, putting Europe in first place, was held over from hot war to cold, and when Europe evolved into a grinding stalemate, new issues or threats that arose in the Third World could be calibrated — sometimes oddly, at least in retrospect — against the U.S.-Soviet competition. And no other information sources were about to break into the franchise that secrets conferred on intelligence.

With one target and one preeminent consumer, there was a certain logic to the way intelligence was — and is — organized. It was structured according to the different ways intelligence is collected: the National Security Agency (NSA) for intercepting signals, the CIA's DO for spying, and so on. These "INTs," or "stovepipes" in the language of insiders — SIGINT for signals intelligence and HUMINT for human intelligence, or spying — could each concentrate on the distinct contribution it could make to understanding the Soviet Union. In the process, though, the INTs became formidable baronies in their own right.

Now, however, no corporation would organize itself this way given its business, its production processes, and its market. The old structure just has to be wrong. Now there are many targets and many consumers, though there are some consistent alignments among targets, customers, and collectors. In these circumstances, a firm would organize around lines of business, establishing a distributed network or a loose confederation in which the different parts of intelligence would endeavor to build very close links to the customers each served.

OPEN SOURCES VS. SECRETS

No matter how often it is said, it is still difficult for outsiders to grasp what intelligence's focus on the Soviet Union meant, and thus just how big a change its demise represents. To be sure, Russia's fate still makes a difference, not least because of all its nuclear weapons that have not disappeared. Russia will weigh heavily on the prospects for peaceful futures in both Europe and Asia, but it will not again soon threaten America's existence.

During the Cold War, what, literally, could be learned about the United States from the Government Printing Office had to be pieced together painstakingly about the Soviet Union. Take the work on the Soviet economy, work that was later criticized for not appreciating how weak that economy had become by the 1980s. In the 1950s, basic data either didn't exist or were suspect; moreover, because prices were determined by administrative fiat and the ruble wasn't convertible into any other currency, there was no way to calculate Soviet gross national product (GNP).

The CIA's response was to examine Soviet goods and price them by Western standards. The "what price?" question meant, again literally, taking apart Soviet goods. The "how many?" question required vacuuming tidbits of information from everywhere — first, published Soviet sources, and later, intercepted conversations or satellite photos of Soviet factories. The CIA reconstructed the Soviet economy from the ground up. It may have been, said one outside observer, "the largest single project in social science research ever undertaken."[6]

If the Soviet Union was secretive about its economy, it was still more so about its military might. There, virtually everything had to be pieced together from information that was collected if not secretly, then at least by unusual means, such as intercepting the telemetry from Soviet missile tests. What could be seen or read openly provided at best hints of corroboration. And so the pride of place to secret sources was natural. In the process, the United States built expensive national collection systems matched to *the* national purpose: understanding the Soviet Union. The agency titles reflect that national focus: the National Reconnaissance Office (NRO), whose name remained an official secret until a few years ago, for building, launching, and operating satellites; NSA for code making and breaking and for turning intercepted signals into useful intelligence, or SIGINT; and the Central Imagery Office (CIO), which became the National Imagery and Mapping Agency (NIMA), both of which were experiments of the 1990s intended to mimic NSA by building an efficient stovepipe for imagery, or IMINT.

Now, however, most of the world does not have to be photographed from thousands of feet in the sky. It can simply be looked at directly — what might be called "eyeball INT," not IMINT. Of course the lookers need to be trained to see a factory's output, technology, and morale where the rest of us would perceive only noise. During the Cold War, much of the globe was a "denied area"; now, in this age of information, only North Korea and a few similar states are truly closed.

Now, surfing the Internet provides access to an exploding amount of information. By one estimate, stored information is doubling every two years.[7] The challenge for intelligence — sorting fact from fiction, or signals from noise — is new only in magnitude. But the change in magnitude is awesome. There is so much more information out there, and so much more of it is misleading because, in effect, anyone with a computer can now produce or "publish" anything. The risk that hackers, who may be simply curious kids but who also may have more evil

6   Quoted in "Sunshine and Shadow: The CIA and the Soviet Economy," Case C16-91-1096.0, Kennedy School of Government, Harvard University, 1991, p. 2.
7   The estimate is of the total capacity of all the world's computer hard drives. See John L. Simonds, "Magnetoelectronics Today and Tomorrow," *Physics Today*, April 1995, pp. 26–32.

motives, can enter restricted databases is well known if not yet well addressed. But in some respects, the harder problem for intelligence arises simply from volume, not evil intent: As "publishing" gets easier, standards of verification go down. Collecting information is less of a problem, and verifying it is more of one.

This means that policy-makers will be more, not less, reliant on information brokers. The images that are sometimes evoked of policy-makers surfing the Net themselves, in direct touch with their own information sources, are very misleading. Most of the time, as their access to information multiplies, their need for processing, if not analysis, will go up. If collection is easier, *selection* will be harder. There will also be more brokers and more competition among them. Intelligence analysts will be one set of brokers, but others, the competition, will range from CNN anchors (and their producers), to Bloomberg and Oxford Analytica, to journalists and academics.

The more-open world is blurring the distinction between collection and analysis. The best looker is not a spymaster, much less an impersonal satellite, but someone steeped in the substance at hand — in short, an analyst. By the same token, while reference librarians used to be able to point scholars toward reliable sources, the sources on the Net are many, but their reliability is dubious. So consumers need to beware of those who surf the Net but are not themselves experts: Who knows what such people might make of the Net's mix of fact, fancy, and pure error?

To be sure, those who do the surfing or the looking need to be connected to the rest of intelligence. For example, the bombing of China's embassy in Belgrade during NATO's air war over Kosovo in 1999 almost defies explanation — and for that reason the Chinese could be forgiven for believing it had to have been done on purpose. But the awful accident derived, in part, from the gap between spying and looking. Those who analyze spy photos look for telltale signatures such as antennas, and for them, almost any map will do as long as the structure of the buildings hasn't changed. In this case, the imagery analysts used a 1992 map, and because the building looked the same in the satellite photos, they did not know that it had ceased being a war office and become a foreign embassy. They did not know Yugoslavia, and more to the point, they did not routinely talk to those who did. They were disconnected from the "lookers" who, from walking Belgrade's streets, might have told them that the building was now an embassy.

PUZZLES VS. MYSTERIES

The U.S. government's need for information, and the possible roles for intelligence in providing it, can be conceived along several dimensions — secret sources or open ones, tactical purposes or strategic ones, and questions that are puzzles or ones that are mysteries. In those terms, the Cold War legacy of intelligence was a vast capacity to solve strategic puzzles, primarily about the Soviet Union, with a high secrets content.[8]　Then, the pressing questions that preoccupied intelligence were puzzles, ones that could, in principle, have been answered definitively if only the information had been available: How big was the Soviet economy? How many missiles did the Soviet Union have? Had it launched a "bolt from the blue" attack? These puzzles were intelligence's stock-in-trade during the Cold War.

Different from a puzzle is a mystery, which is a question that cannot be answered with certainty even in principle. Russia's inflation rate this year is a mystery. Interrogating Russia's president in detail would not answer it, because he does not know the answer. No one does. The mystery is real. The puzzles were more important during the Cold War than they are now, but there were plenty of mysteries then, too, and intelligence probably was mistaken in making puzzle solving its principal business. Would the Soviet Union close Western access to Berlin? Would China intervene in Korea if the United States attacked to the Yalu? Would West Germany go nuclear?

Likewise, today's chaotic world still throws up plenty of puzzles to be solved. Whether China sold M-11 missiles to Pakistan is a puzzle. So is whether France bribed Indonesia to give a contract to a French company. Yet most of the critical questions facing American foreign policy are mysteries: Will North Korea fulfill its nuclear agreement with the United States? Will Iraq again misbehave? Looking further ahead, will China continue to grow rapidly, or will it fragment? Will reform and democracy take hold in the former Soviet Union — or in South Africa?

Collecting secrets was and is crucial to solving foreign policy puzzles. Indeed, the special franchise conferred by secrets is at the root of why U.S. intelligence made puzzle solving its principal Cold War business.

8　Joseph S. Nye, Jr., and I both found this distinction useful when we were colleagues at the National Intelligence Council. See his "Peering into the Future," *Foreign Affairs*, 77, 4, July/August 1994, pp. 82–93.

The Soviet Union did not advertise its military capacity, but neither do today's potential foes of the United States. Nor do would-be proliferators of nuclear weapons or other weapons of mass destruction. Nor, for that matter, do nations advertise their bribes or their positions in trade negotiations.

For the mysteries, however, information collected secretly may be helpful, but it is seldom as critical as it was to solving Cold War puzzles. Then, information was scarce; now it is overwhelming. Then, hints of Kremlin politics had to be guessed from pieces of previous puzzles that had been solved; now, Russia's politicians talk as much as any other. Then, it was not hard to see what secrets contributed to framing mysteries; if the value added was often small, the ignorance to which it added something frequently was large.

Mysteries also differ from puzzles in that, by definition, puzzles have already happened. The result has occurred, though it may not yet be known. The missiles have been built, with warheads and accuracy that may remain unknown even though they are knowable. War plans have been framed, and the attack started, though it may still come as a surprise. Thus, any opportunity by the United States to influence the outcome has been lost. The United States may influence the next round; it may deter the conflict from escalating further or negotiate constraints on the next generation of missiles.

By contrast, many of the most interesting mysteries — for example, Will North Korea keep its nuclear agreement with the United States? — are not only unknowable at this time, but their eventual answer is intertwined with what the United States government does. We often care most about events we hope to influence, or we hope to influence them because we care about them. And so, as for the North Korea problem, trying to understand "them" is impossible without knowing in detail what "we" are up to. The Cold War's separation of intelligence and policy becomes a barrier.

Many mysteries also frustrate another, related distinction of Cold War intelligence, that between "foreign" and "domestic."[9] Treating

---

9   The mischief in both of these distinctions is discussed in Willmoore Kendall's wonderful review of Sherman Kent's book, *Strategic Intelligence.* See "The Function of Intelligence," *World Politics,* July 1949, pp. 542–552. See, also, Donald P. Steury, ed., *Sherman Kent and the Board of National Estimates,* Washington, D.C.: Central Intelligence Agency, 1994.

the Soviet Union as a *foreign* intelligence problem was fair enough. To the extent we mattered to what "they" did; the "we" was the U.S. government; Soviet outcomes were not much affected directly by the actions of Americans outside the government. The same may be said of North Korea today, though even in that case, nongovernmental actors are becoming more important; the authority that is building power reactors and supplying oil to North Korea is a private entity, and private humanitarian relief organizations are becoming active in the country.

The actions of Americans outside the government manifestly matter to Mexico's future, where the Americans in question range from New York bankers to California voters. In the case of Russia, actions taken by George Soros, the financier and philanthropist, count for almost as much as those of the U.S. government. Yet if American intelligence is disinclined by professional norms to turn its attention on U.S. policymakers, it is barred by law from snooping on private Americans. These limitations apply in spades to the agenda of issues, such as terrorism or law enforcement, that intelligence will confront even more directly in the future.

AIDING WAR-FIGHTERS

In one crucial area, supporting military operations, puzzles will remain. You can buy commercial models of Japan's economy, but you couldn't buy them of Saddam Hussein's forces. Enemy units do not send public announcements of their positions. Americans and their allies that venture into harm's way will depend on puzzle solving where secrets matter. They will depend on intelligence providing SMO.

During the Cold War, if the big national collection system could help U.S. military war fighters who were engaged in conflict, that was a spillover benefit. Anyway, until technology improved, it took too long to produce pictures or process signals from national satellite systems and to communicate them to the war fighters on the ground, who needed to know where the enemy tank or plane was *now*. The turnaround times for IMINT and SIGINT were measured originally in days, later in hours, and only more recently in minutes, and as a result, until the 1980s and 1990s, war fighters weren't much interested in the big national collection systems. Now, they are very interested.

Imagine American "info-warriors" of the 21st century.[10]   The "eighth Gulf war," of 2015, might not be fought in the Persian Gulf. But wherever it was fought, it would be a far cry from Desert Storm in 1991. Desert Storm was a war on sand that the United States and its NATO allies had prepared for on the north German plain: heavy armor divisions fighting along continuous fronts. Instead, in 2015's war, lightly armed mobile cavalry units would seek to control territory in overlapping zones. Their control would depend not on the firepower they carried but on what they could command.

They would call down fire from afar — from ships offshore, missiles, or planes stationed out of harm's way, perhaps from space, all guided precisely to moving targets. If foes leaked through the outer perimeter of their zones, the info-warriors would first flee, standing and fighting only as a last resort.

Desert Storm was a dim foreshadowing of these future wars; NATO's air campaign in Kosovo in 1999 was a somewhat brighter one. The mission, not to mention the lives of those future U.S. and allied warriors, would depend on the 21st century's form of what now drives the American intelligence budget — precise geolocation of foes and friends, accomplished by satellites triangulating intercepted signals or by satellites, planes, and unmanned drones observing. By 2015, the observing, now available as snapshots in real time, would be continuous, like CNN but monitoring foreign forces instead of foreign crowds. That puzzle solving for warriors depends on technical collection, primarily SIGINT and IMINT — satellites and other sensors intercepting signals and taking pictures (or radar or infrared images). Already, technical collection accounts for the bulk of the money intelligence devotes to collecting information, which in turn consumes about two-thirds of the total intelligence budget. To the extent money is at issue in the future of intelligence, the money is here, in SMO.

Money is the first issue posed by SMO because the mission is open-ended; more is always better. The second issue is authority, which is intertwined with the role of the DCI. DCIs are regarded by all and sundry, including official Washingtonians, as the directors of the CIA. And so they are. But DCIs wear a second hat, that of coordinator of all the intelligence agencies. However, the budgets of the big technical collection agencies, such as NSA and NRO, are in the defense budget;

---

10   This scenario derives from work by my RAND colleagues Daniel Fox and Samuel Gardiner.

indeed, more than four-fifths of the entire intelligence budget is part of Defense. So the DCI's coordinating role always has been awkward because it means trespassing on the defense secretary's authority. If intelligence is to be mostly in the business of supporting warriors, then perhaps secretaries of defense, not DCIs, should do the coordinating.

In an important sense, the renewed emphasis on SMO represents a movement forward toward the past; it marks a return to intelligence as primarily tactical after the long Cold War interlude when intelligence was preoccupied with the strategic imperative, understanding the Soviet threat. The ultimate issue SMO raises is one of mission and priority: Should intelligence primarily support military planning and operations? Or should it also serve the entire U.S. government — and, perhaps, the broader American society as well — much more of which is engaged with the world beyond America's borders?

THE INTELLIGENCE OF POLICY

Intelligence and policy are such different cultures that it is a surprise that they ever connect at all. Intelligence analysts still work in a world of paper, while policy is mostly an oral culture. Analysts think analytically of what can go wrong, while policy officials tend to think wishfully of what might go right. Analysts, focused on events abroad, take a long view and tend to presume that the world is largely impervious to U.S. actions. Policy officials, by contrast, have a perspective that is dominated by the short term and by their own personal stakes. The average tenure of assistant secretaries is little more than a year, and they go to Washington to accomplish something. They are prone to overstate how much of a difference official Washington can make.

For the CIA, physical separation from the policy agencies compounds the difficulty of connecting to policy. So do sheer size and the inertia of a settled bureaucracy. It can be so time-consuming for a CIA analyst to get an assessment cleared through the internal bureaucratic daisy chain that the ultimate point of the exercise, affecting the mind-set of someone downtown in the executive branch or on Capitol Hill, is almost lost. Moreover, because the CIA in principle works for everyone in the government, there is the risk that it will wind up working for no one.

More tellingly, given current norms and practices, intelligence pays little price for being irrelevant, but it does, by contrast, pay a price for being "politicized" — for crossing or being pulled across the line from objectivity to advocacy, for "joining the policy team." It is little wonder, given that bias, that intelligence is so often not very relevant to the making of policy. The issue of politicization was vivid in Robert Gates's confirmation hearings to be DCI in 1991. Gates, who was then the deputy national security advisor, was accused of having politicized the CIA's analysis of the Soviet Union. In particular, he was charged with having stacked the deck by authorizing analysts to make the best case they could that the Soviet Union had been behind the 1981 attempt to assassinate the Pope.

In fact, the paper in question was unusual but not unprecedented; it asked just how good a case could be made. In the intelligence culture, though, it looked as if a policy answer was being imposed. And in trying to sharpen analyses and perhaps make them more relevant to the policy agenda as he saw it (Gates had served several times in senior positions on the policy side of the house), Gates was vulnerable to the charge of politicization. A person's editing can easily be seen as politicizing by a recipient of that editing whose ego is bruised. It is nevertheless striking how far intelligence tilts toward avoiding the charge of politicization. There is still little price to be paid for irrelevance.

In the circumstances of an age of information, perhaps it is time for intelligence to "split the franchise" and dramatically change how it is organized. Tactical puzzles where secrets matter are both fewer and more varied today than they were in the Cold War, but they are still important. For instance, according to press accounts, the CIA analysis of ethnic cleansing in Bosnia was classic puzzle solving, using information from secret and open sources to make clear who were the cleansers and who the cleansed.[11] For solving puzzles, analysts need to be close to the collectors of secrets. In a world of too much information, policymakers will want to "pull" up what they need, not have information "pushed" upon them; they will want to pull up puzzle solutions when they need them, not receive a torrent of information whether they ask for it or not. Yet solving the puzzle is often important enough that getting policy officials to pay attention is not a problem.

Mysteries are surely more abundant now. For them, Washingtonians would be served (whether or not they always realize it) by strategic warning and by frames of reference. When, for example, has yesterday's vanishingly small chance of upheaval in Turkey become today's

11   See *New York Times*, March 12, 1995, sec. 4, p. 2.

greater risk, still small but worth elevating Turkey to the agenda for active concern? This warning is strategic, not tactical; it is shaping a mystery, not solving a puzzle. No one knows the answer, not least the Turks themselves.

When turmoil engulfs Zaire, do events amount to a humanitarian crisis to be succored, a conflict that can be mediated or separated at small cost, or a bloodbath that now, though perhaps not earlier, can be stanched only by serious U.S. forces on the ground? What, in short, is the "story" that makes sense out of the various facts? This is mystery shaping of the highest order. It is intelligence as understanding, the second meaning of "intelligence." It is the kind of understanding that might have convinced official Washington that India's BJP might actually have meant what it said, that it might be serious about nuclear weapons.

In Somalia in the early 1990s, the United States thought it was providing humanitarian relief when it was also entering a fight for power, one of long standing. Then, it slid from giving relief to taking sides without quite realizing what it was doing. Through years of bloodshed, the United States could not decide what to do in Bosnia or how much the conflict mattered, because it could not decide which frames of reference applied in what measure — civil war, aggression, genocide, or humanitarian crisis. In 1995, President Clinton decided to take the country into active involvement in Bosnia's tragedy, and both Congress and the public went along, yet the questions about purpose and frame of reference remained.

This franchise of framing strategic mysteries is very different from puzzle solving. For it, analysts need access to secrets, but their crucial partnerships are those with colleagues outside intelligence and outside government, in the academy and think-tank world, in NGOs, and in the world of private business. Intelligence needs to be opened wide, not cosseted in secret compartments. For these purposes, a kind of governmentwide designated reader, a version of the Congressional Research Service, could help. So could an intelligence version of the special relationships the Pentagon has with private think tanks such as RAND. New government institutions are not much in fashion these days; nor are new connections of public and private, at least not in what is still called the "national security" realm, though that will change in the era of the market state.

This franchise is based on the recognition that intelligence's business is information, not secrets, and that its product is people, experts, not paper. The Pearl Harbor argument for centralizing analysis is not so plainly imperative today. The problem is as likely to be that no one is looking at the next Somalia (or the next bizarre sect seeking revenge) as that everyone is looking but only at his or her parochial puzzle pieces. On the surface of the India case, it appeared that intelligence was paying too little attention and was not well coordinated. The fundamental problem, however, was mind-set, and with regard to that problem, there was not too much competition, but too little. What was needed was a band of analysts, close to and empowered by a relevant policy agency, that was out to make the case that the Indians might just mean what they said.

In a world where both structures and U.S. interests are up for grabs, policy-makers would be better served by intelligence brokers close at hand, down the hall, not out at Langley. In this confused world, Senator Daniel Patrick Moynihan may be right for the wrong reasons.[12] He wondered if a CIA that couldn't notice the signs of impending Soviet collapse deserved to exist. Perhaps the CIA should be not abolished but dispersed, its analytic pieces assigned to State, Treasury, Commerce, and elsewhere around official Washington.

A GUIDE FOR READERS

The changes in the world that are already apparent are more than enough to require a complete reshaping of intelligence, and the extension of those changes into the future of the market state will only sharpen that need. The next chapter sketches the features that will form the world beyond 2010 and their implications for intelligence.

Chapter 3 turns to the retargeting of the big technical collection systems, from keeping tabs on the Soviet Union to supporting military operations. Advances in technology are permitting those systems to help war fighters in ways that were impossible during the Cold War, yet the growing importance of SMO for intelligence, and vice versa, raises issues of how much the United States should spend on intelligence and who should control the big collectors. The larger question, though, is

---

12   See his "Our Stupid But Permanent CIA," *Washington Post*, July 24, 1994, p. C3.

what the mission for intelligence should be: Where and how should intelligence strike the balance between supporting war fighters, on the one hand, and, on the other, providing information and analyses to a range of "civilian" policy-makers?

Chapter 4 explores the implications for intelligence of a more open world, with its multiplying of information sources. That world confronts intelligence with the need to understand that the nature of its business has changed: It is no longer in the secrets business but rather in the information business. While the world of the market state will be a much more open one, it will continue to present the United States with dangerous, secretive adversaries, and the United States will want to employ espionage against them. If it is to do so, however, it needs to completely rebuild its clandestine service. Moreover, in the world of the market state, espionage and traditional intelligence for foreign policy purposes will become entangled with law enforcement more and more often. These issues are the subject of Chapter 5.

Chapter 6 turns to the connection, or lack thereof, between intelligence and policy. Given the gap that separates the two cultures, analysts and policy officials need to find ways to calibrate each other. Intelligence still thinks of its products as discrete analyses on paper or computer screens. In fact, especially for the strategic franchise, its product is people, experts in a position to be helpful to the making of policy. The line between intelligence and policy needs to be purposefully blurred.

The concluding chapter begins with a vision of intelligence a decade hence. The consumers, sources, and coalition partners of intelligence might change roles from day to day, and the coalitions that intelligence helped to build would range across Americans and foreigners, government officials and private citizens. Intelligence's secrets would be fewer and more fleeting. A more immediately practical agenda for reshaping intelligence departs from the change in doctrine — intelligence as information, not just secrets — and would encompass a variety of experiments in connecting to the world beyond intelligence. Finally, if intelligence is to be supported by the American public, it must make its case much more openly. It needs to look for ways to build public understanding, not avoid them.

2

The world of intelligence beyond 2010

Intelligence is in an exquisitely awkward position in adapting to a changed world. It is a "service" industry, one designed to serve American foreign policy, but how can it do so when the definitions of American interests and policy are themselves in flux? It is charged with providing information for its "customers" in both the executive branch and Congress, but those customers are in the process of redefining their objectives. Intelligence, however, will not have the luxury of waiting for the changes to solidify.

Despite the swirling changes, enough is known of the world that intelligence will confront beyond 2010 to begin the reshaping. That world will require intelligence to be dispersed, not concentrated; open to a variety of sources, not limited to secrets; sharing its information and analyses with a variety of would-be coalition partners, including foreigners and people outside government, not guarding its "secrets" tightly. And the America for which it works will be different — less cohesive and less focused, with a government that is less the regulator or doer and more the convener of coalitions of the willing.

REDEFINING AMERICA'S INTERESTS IN THE WORLD

The redefining of America's purposes and policies will take time. In the wake of World War II, as hot peace turned into cold war, it took nearly a decade to establish the doctrine of containment as the primary focus of American foreign policy, despite an increasingly apparent Soviet threat. Without such a clearly defined threat, the process this time around will take even longer. Another great event might ensue, or a great rival emerge, that would again force clarity on the debate, but intelligence would not be wise to expect it.

Nor would the effect necessarily be as sharp as the one that ensued in the Cold War. Then, the Soviet threat and the national security perspective turned out to be the organizing principle not just for the U.S. government but, to a considerable extent, for American society as well. *Foreign* and *domestic* had clear meanings, and pride of place went to the former. Indeed, domestic initiatives paid foreign policy the compliment of that priority, as illustrated by the names of programs such as the National Defense Highway Program and the National Security Education Act.

Policy attention concentrated where the Soviet threat seemed most urgent, in Europe, though the prevailing U.S. conception of the early Cold War linked the Soviet Union and China, so Asian events such as the fall of nationalist China affected judgments about the urgency of the threat in Europe. In the process, though, attention to the Western Hemisphere waned, to be revived only at the end of the 1950s by Fidel Castro.

While the Cold War was no golden age, there was a shape and clarity to how the United States conceived its role in the world then. Because the basic decisions had been made, perhaps as early as 1950 with the commitment of American forces to Europe, many of the debates that raged later look marginal in retrospect.[1] And, of course, the Cold War was won, and in just about the way the architects of containment had envisioned — with external pressure on the Soviet system causing it to collapse from its own internal contradictions.

Now, the logical first step in redefining policy would be to ask about the world in which the United States will operate; a second would be to inquire into the nature of American interests. In practice, though, intelligence will be reshaped, or not, while the debate about America's role, about the boundaries of what used to be called "domestic" and "foreign" or "public" and "private," ambles along. The changed world has drained both familiar concepts and customary vocabulary of meaning. Neither will be replaced soon. Fighting the Cold War was foreign and public, and it was a government monopoly; private citizens and

---

1   How decisive the early choices were struck me in writing about U.S. policy toward Germany and Europe. By the end of 1946 the basic outline of policy was discernible. See my *America, Germany and the Future of Europe*, Princeton: Princeton University Press, 1992, p. 35ff.

private actions mattered, but there was no doubt where ultimate responsibility lay.[2] But now, for instance, concern has been growing about the vulnerability of U.S. infrastructures — telecommunications, electric power, finance, and air traffic control.[3] Yet these are all multinational, if not global, so "domestic" measures alone cannot protect them. And the infrastructures, which are a public interest, are mostly in private hands.

Logic notwithstanding, intelligence cannot be a mere bystander to the debate about American purposes while it waits for its own role to be clarified. It will, or should, be a participant, because the crux of the debate over interests lies at the junction where what is vital meets what is desirable. Stakes cannot be defined apart from the ease with which they can be protected. If the cost is small, then important but secondary stakes — such as sustaining U.S. leadership, building international institutions, and trying to set norms for tolerable behavior — can shape America's interest. If, for example, a future Bosnia or Kosovo can be pacified at small cost in American life and treasure, the body politic may decide that pacifying it is a U.S. interest. If the cost is high, then the question becomes "What *in Bosnia* justifies the price?" And the answer may well be "nothing." In either case, intelligence's stock-in-trade — understanding the foreign reality well enough to judge the cost of any action and also to help reckon the benefits — is a necessary part of the answer.

Policy-making toward Bosnia in the 1990s drives home that need. Bosnia was my biggest disappointment at the National Intelligence Council (NIC) during the Clinton administration. It was precisely the interchange between intelligence and policy over interests and their cost of achievement that did not happen. The fall of the Berlin wall in 1989 had also been the death knell for communist Yugoslavia's uneasy federation. Its most cohesive ethnic pieces, first Slovenia, then Croatia, sought independence from the Serbian-dominated rump Yugoslavia, and the international community had neither arguments against inde-

2   This is a theme of Graham Allison and Gregory F. Treverton, eds., *Rethinking America's Security: Beyond Cold War to New World Order*, New York: W.W. Norton and Co., 1992, especially chapter 1.

3   See *Critical Foundations: Protecting America's Infrastructures*, Report of the President's Commission on Critical Infrastructure Protection (PCCIP), Washington, D.C., October 1997, available at www.pccip.gov/report_index.html.

pendence nor the stomach for preventing it. However, Yugoslavs had not sorted themselves into tidy ethnic states; the signal success of Tito's federation had been to keep an uneasy peace among the various groups.

Independence for Croatia was nasty enough, for its Krajina region was home to ethnic Serbs who chafed under Croat rule and looked to Belgrade and mother Serbia for protection. Independence for Bosnia was a predictable disaster, for neither Bosnia's Serbs nor its Croats would tolerate being governed by Muslims, who were a slim plurality of Bosnia's population. Those Muslims had no ethnic homeland as a protector or refuge. For both Serbs and Croats, the Muslims were, in the words of one European diplomat, "in the way." And so the world relearned the horror of ethnic strife in the Balkans, "ethnic cleansing" this time around. By 1993, Serbian militias had harassed Bosnia's Muslims into isolated enclaves, most visibly in the capital, Sarajevo, where they were scarcely protected by lightly armed United Nations (UN) peacekeepers, the UN Protection Force (UNPROFOR).

I was committed to a more activist, interventionist approach to Bosnia and former Yugoslavia, and Bill Clinton had seemed during the campaign to embrace that approach, too. Yet it was also apparent that he wanted to remain focused on his domestic agenda; remember "It's the economy, stupid!" In the circumstances, I thought a pause in Bosnia policy-making was required while the administration asked itself hard questions: What could it do in Bosnia? At what cost? Policy would have pressed pointed questions about interests, while intelligence judged costs of alternative courses.

Why the exchange never happened is instructive, and intelligence bore part of the responsibility. The administration plunged immediately into the details: How much foodstuff was getting through the Serbian blockade to Sarajevo? Intelligence was good at these details; by contrast, with regard to the larger, "iffier" mysteries — what would it cost to coerce Serbian leaders into abandoning ethnic cleansing? — it had little fresh information to put forward.[4] The closest that the govern-

---

4   In 1993, the CIA did produce one intriguing analysis, one I sent to NSC colleagues. It used a method called factions analysis to aggregate analysts' subjective judgments. In this case, the question was what it would take to affect Serbian behavior. The midpoint judgment was that inducing Serbia to change its goals in Bosnia would require air attacks on critical institutions *in Serbia proper* — a step well beyond anything on the U.S. agenda

ment came to asking hard questions about interests was a Pentagon memorandum months later in the summer of 1993.[5]

The resulting American policy during 1993 and 1994 bordered on hypocrisy. It pretended that the United States was doing something when it wasn't, and it pretended that the Europeans could handle Bosnia when we knew they couldn't (though, to be fair, they wanted to try, at least initially). The administration opposed giving some formal recognition to Bosnia's de facto ethnic partition — in particular a proposal worked out by David Owen, former British foreign secretary, and Cyrus Vance, former U.S. secretary of state — but was not prepared to face what might be required to avert partition. The combination of fulsome rhetoric about Bosnia's survival with little engagement on the ground also, it seemed to me, tended to stifle any broader discussion of U.S. interests and instruments. Those, like me, who thought Bosnia an important interest could hope the inflated rhetoric might one day be matched by action, while those who deemed Bosnia relatively unimportant could take comfort from knowing that day was not yet.

What induced a more honest judgment about costs and interests was less intelligence analysis than the sheer press of events in 1995. The UN force, UNPROFOR, drawn mostly from European NATO allies of the United States, was classic UN peacekeeping, lightly armed and thus dependent on the consent of the combatants. As Bosnia spiraled downward in ethnic violence, however, there was the real risk that UNPROFOR would have to be rescued from the Serb militias with the force of American arms. The NATO alliance itself was at stake, and so was America's credibility as the leader of that alliance. And so, President Clinton reckoned, if the United States was to pay the cost of putting its troops in harm's way to rescue Europeans, why not take the risk for some positive purpose?

UNPROFOR became IFOR, i.e., the protection force became the intervention force; peacekeeping by consent, led by the UN and accomplished by Europeans, became muscular peacekeeping, run by NATO and the United States with tanks and firepower enough to coerce the Bosnian factions into stopping the killing. The eventual result was the Dayton accords of 1995, which recognized the reality of partition but

and a clear indication that the policy ends sought were well beyond the means contemplated.

5   The debate, though not the memo, is discussed in *Washington Post*, July 30, 1993, p. A1.

also included not only expanded safeguards for the Muslims but institutions and incentives for the ethnic factions eventually to begin to mend the ripped fabric of their cooperation.

FORMS OF POWER

The only safe prediction about the world of 2010 or 2015 is that it will surprise us in some respect. Yet 2010's major powers are tolerably clear. So are the global processes that will shape the world beyond 2010, if not how those processes will play out. If specifics lie beyond prediction, broad contours do not.

Global military power

The United States is indeed the sole superpower in the sense that only it has the whole panoply of military instruments and the capacity both to combine arms in complex, joint operations and to project those operations over long distances. It will remain so beyond 2010, after which a Russian resurgence or, more probably, the emergence of an Asian peer, most likely China, is conceivable. However, in purely military terms, the American lead is lengthening. According to the most recent U.S. government statistics, the U.S. defense budget now is more than the combined totals of the next five countries — and several of these are American allies.[6] This goes well beyond the 19th century British standard for its navy — a navy as large as the world's next two.

Moreover, the United States seems poised for another leap forward in both technology and, more critically, new concepts about how to integrate that technology in battlefield operations.[7] The war against Iraq in 1991, Operation Desert Storm, was only a tepid foretaste of those

6 Arms Control and Disarmament Agency, *World Military Expenditures and Arms Transfers*, Washington, D.C., 1996. The methodological complications of comparisons across countries and currencies make this no more than a vivid metaphor.

7 A good introduction to these changes, the so-called revolution in military affairs (RMA), is Jeffery Barnett's *Future Warfare: Assessment of Future Aerospace Campaigns, 2010*, Birmingham, AL: Air War College, 1996. Official discussions of the RMA and the related need to "transform the force" can be found in the Department of Defense's 1997 *Quadrennial Defense Review* and the Joint Staff's *Joint Vision 2010*.

concepts; the air war over Kosovo in 1999 gave a clearer hint about the future. Both suggested how much damage precision-guided weapons could inflict on U.S. foes and how safe they could be for the United States and its friends if delivered from the air. What remained for the future was integrating those precision strikes from afar with new ways of controlling the battle on the ground.[8] Still, America's European allies had reason to fear that they were lagging so far behind the United States in military technology that they would soon cease being attractive partners. Would-be American adversaries had still more reason to fret.

Despite American dominance, keeping tabs on the military power of major nations will continue to be a task for intelligence. In most ways, this task will be easier than it was during the Cold War, because many of those powers are open and friendly and because the same trends that are making Russia more transparent will do the same for China over the next decade. In one sense, though, the task will be harder. During the Cold War, Soviet military expenditures could safely be presumed to march steadily upward almost no matter what economic or political conditions prevailed in the country. As a result, assessing the Soviet military became a bean-counting exercise, albeit a sophisticated one because the beans were hard to locate and characterize.

For the future, though, the political and economic context of military power will be decisive. The hollowness of the Soviet Union's economic and political base caused the collapse of its military power. Whether Russia again becomes a formidable military power, let alone a threat, will depend on whether it manages to construct an information-age economy that is able to support that military. Whether China becomes a military peer of the United States will turn not just on the progress of its economy. It will also depend on whether China can remain a cohesive state as it grows or whether it decentralizes, perhaps even fragments, in ways that would make it, militarily, less than the sum of its economic parts.

8   The debate will long rage about how to employ airpower and whether it alone was decisive in either case or could be in the future. For a nice inside account of the debate over Kosovo, see Dana Priest, "The Commanders' War: The Battle Inside Headquarters," *Washington Post*, September 21, 1999, p. 1.

Political and economic power

Most of the major powers beyond 2010 will be large, rich, and relatively homogenous. The list is almost certain to include the United States, Japan, and Europe; Russia or China may be on it as well.[9] From this vantage point, it is less certain that Russia will deserve a place on the list than that China will. It is also possible to make a case that nations such as India and Brazil might make the list, though the arguments supporting them would be weaker.

While Europe will be on the list, it is hard to know what Europe will *be*. It will be an economic power, but will it also be a cohesive political actor? That is the question mark. Its Economic and Monetary Union (EMU) is a leap into the unknown, creating a single monetary policy without a common fiscal policy to match. In trade, the European Commission now speaks for the European Union (EU) countries, but aspirations toward a common foreign and security policy, much less a European security and defense identity (ESDI), have remained just that. Europe's future shape will depend on how successful EMU and the expansions of the EU are, and how much its leaders summon the will, or are driven by external events, to work more closely together.[10]

Intelligence's role in tracking the politics and economics of these major powers will be both smaller and different than it was in the Cold War. On one hand, if current trends continue, by 2010 America will have neither a foreign service nor traditional print and electronic media that do in-depth reporting on foreign states — friends, let alone foes. On the other hand, the information revolution will make available vast, messy riches of information through what intelligence labels, rather quaintly, as "open source" — the World Wide Web, visitors and travelers, and "gray" sources, such as communications within political or ethnic groups, which are neither fully open nor secret. Already, the Economist Intelligence Unit, Oxford Analytica, DRI, and a dozen other entities constitute a thriving industry providing in-depth analyses of foreign states for a fee. If intelligence has a niche, it will be to add

9   Charles Wolf, Jr., et al., *Long-Term Economic and Military Trends, 1994–2015: The United States and Asia*, MR-627.0-OSD, Santa Monica, CA: RAND, 1995.

10 See Gregory F. Treverton and Marten van Heuven, *Towards the 21st Century: Trends in Post–Cold War International Security*, MR-1038.0, Santa Monica, CA: RAND, 1998, p. 14ff.

understanding by being open to those riches and by being in touch with the best experts outside government.

GLOBAL PROCESSES

The global processes in motion are also tolerably clear, though exactly how they will play out is only dimly visible. These processes are undermining, slowly or not so slowly, the hegemony of the nation-state, which has been the dominant fact of international politics since the Treaty of Westphalia in 1648.

Economic globalization

Global transactions are multiplying with dizzying speed, and in the process, distances matter much less. The right image for the future is the World Wide Web, private and driven by the needs of commerce, rather than Radio Free Europe, information supplied by government. Nations are learning, sometimes to their regret, that the only factor endowment that really matters is human capital, people. In the short run, natural resources make for riches, but beyond the short run, those riches seem as likely to tempt nations to make foolish decisions as to guarantee long-term success.

Economic trends are both integrating and disintegrating. They integrate in that national borders and distances matter less. Sitting in California, it doesn't make much difference to me whether a bit of data or a physical product is made in San Diego or Helsinki. Those of us with an interest in the data or product are drawn together to become intellectual collaborators or business partners. At the same time, though, in a world where people skills are really the only factor endowment that matters, economics integrates only those who can be integrated. Thus, the gap between the haves and have-nots is growing, not just between nations, but within nations, including the rich ones. Anecdotal evidence for this proposition, such as for India's high-tech enclaves, is abundant, though rigorous evidence in national income accounts or across them, for instance, is not yet available.

It also appears, though again without rigorous confirmation yet, that this period of technological growth is contributing to growing disparities in income. Compared to the period after World War II, the current premium on knowledge is higher; poor countries (or poor citizens of rich ones) find it harder to use cheap, unskilled labor to create a niche.[11] Surely, the competition for niches in the global economy is intense. It may be, though, that part of the apparent effect is, for the United States at least, simply an artifact of World War II. In the immediate aftermath of that war, the U.S. economy was so dominant by comparison to its destroyed competitors that its huge domestic market was virtually insulated.

As a result, the image of the 1950s in which two high school graduates had nearly equal earning potentials despite one going to college and the other to the local factory may have been true, but only for a while. Over time, foreign competition pressed American firms to improve quality and raise productivity — imagine how bad American cars might still be but for the pressure of Japanese imports. That, in turn, put an increasing premium on skill and knowledge, so outcomes for those two high school graduates came increasingly to diverge.

Communications revolution

The information revolution is the key enabler of economic globalization. It was the information revolution that undid the Soviet Union; planning and brute force could produce roads and dams but could not induce innovation in computer chips. However, communications also makes it possible, for instance, for drug traffickers to encrypt their communications or for would-be Haitian boat people to learn within a day what fraction of their predecessors have been screened into the United States. When guerrillas of the Zapatista National Liberation Army challenged the Mexican government in Chiapas in the 1990s, for instance, they used e-mail and the Internet to organize and plan operations; they set up Web bulletin boards to build support for their cause. Several of the pitched battles that were reported through nongovern-

---

11   The consensus on this point is broad enough to make one nervous. It is, for instance, the theme of Robert Reich's work. For a terse popular formulation, see Peter F. Drucker, "The Age of Social Transformation," *The Atlantic*, November, 1994.

mental organizations (NGOs) in touch with the guerrillas were "virtual" events, not real ones. They never happened.[12]

The information revolution also contributes to the segmenting of populations, both within and across states. Earlier communications technologies — radio, telephone, and television — were easy to use and thus diffused rather rapidly from the more educated through the rest of society. In contrast, computers and their associated technologies are harder to use. The entry cost in skill is higher, so their diffusion from richer, better-educated users throughout society has, so far at least, been much slower. As telephone, computer, and television converge, using them will become easier. But it remains a question whether, despite more user friendliness, there will continue to be a high payoff to those who can employ the more advanced technologies that are less friendly. At a minimum, it is hard to foresee anything like the long periods of stability in technology that characterized radio, telephone, and to a lesser extent, television until quite recently.

The information revolution has several more specific driving implications. One is that the power of states to control information seems to be waning, for good or ill. A generation ago it was feared that computers would abet dictators; Big Brother seemed closer at hand. Now, the opposite seems true. Administrations in Washington cannot control the "spin" on a news story; European governments could not control capital flows if they tried; and China seems less and less able to control what its citizens read and hear. While the effect is starker in some places than others, governments face a Hobson's choice: They can cut their states off from international communications but not easily and only at a high price. They may be able to have isolation but only at the price of poverty; they cannot be both isolated and rich.

The information revolution also powerfully influences expectations all around the globe. The "CNN effect" seems to shorten time horizons; governments find it harder to plead for time to deliberate when correspondents report the latest unfolding tragedy minute by minute. Governments are expected to react, and to react to events as shaped by the media. In the autumn of 1998, for instance, President Clinton's national security advisor, Samuel ("Sandy") Berger, alerted the president

12   See John Arquilla and David Ronfeldt, *The Advent of Netwar*, Santa Monica, CA: RAND National Defense Research Institute, 1996, pp. 72–73.

one hour short of war that Iraq was offering a settlement to the crisis; he did so on the basis of a CNN report from Baghdad.[13]

Those same communications technologies also shape expectations of citizens. Just as former East German citizens acquired their images of life beyond communism from West German television, so Bosnians today and Rwandans tomorrow will frame expectations about what other states will or won't do from what they see on TV or the Web, or what their kinsman report from cell phones.

Rising belief in the nonmaterial

People seek to differentiate "us" from "them," in religion, ethnicity, and other ways. In that sense, the driving forces behind the tragedy of former Yugoslavia and the revival of Islam that is visible around the world look like two sides of the same coin, and what motivates the American militias does not seem very different. Perhaps partly in alienation from processes of global integration, peoples seek some form of transcendental association. One manifestation is the quest of ethnic groups for smaller units, often for states of their own, a trend that is not just a result of the death of the Soviet Union's deadening hand. Borders are now in question. Of the world's 170 states, only about half are populated by ethnic groups making up more than 75 percent of the population.

Another manifestation is the rise of belief in the nonmaterial. Men and women don't lay down their lives for the free market; if they ever did for Marxism, that ended long ago. The loss of community in modernizing societies may propel the search for something in which to believe; the anomie of being marginalized may sharpen the search. Today, religion most visibly provides such a purpose. But it is not beyond imagining that, beyond 2010, other such motivations will arise. Francis Fukuyama argued that with the end of the Cold War, history's long dialectic of alternating ideologies had come to an end. Liberal democracy had won.[14] He did not mean that history had stopped, only that there had proved to be no rival, in principle, to liberal democracy as the way to organize national political life. Yet it is sure that pretenders to the

---

13   See *Washington Post*, November 16, 1998, p. A1.
14   See his *The End of History and the Last Man*, New York: The Free Press, 1992.

throne will arise, perhaps especially among groups of people that feel dispossessed by states or are left behind as state power wanes.

Communications technology is facilitating connections among those who feel dispossessed, now mostly in the richer countries but soon in the poorer ones as well. Yesterday's communications technologies, such as radio and television, were "broadcast" — one sender transmitted the same message to many receivers. Americans who watched the network news on television saw the same national news whether they lived in California or South Carolina. By contrast, today's technologies are "narrowcast" — one sender transmits to one receiver, or many senders to one receiver. Those on the Web can seek out the chat rooms that appeal to them, whether the subject is sports or Bosnia or the UN conspiracy to impose a global government. They can then be in touch with kindred spirits.

There is room for debate about how much religion is, and will be, a factor leading to conflict.[15] Samuel P. Huntington evokes the "clash of civilizations" as the shaper of the future world.[16] His clashers are civilizations, not religions, though religion is a key definer of the civilizations. The civilizations thus defined are broad and internally heterogeneous; the variations within them seem as large as those among them, so their coherence as units of analysis, much less clashers, is questionable. Still, conflict does seem most likely where the civilizations intersect — in central or southwest Asia, or across the Mediterranean, or in Southeast Asia where the clashing civilizations exist within states as well as across them. The perspective is thus another lens for viewing mysteries, one that may reveal features that are less prominent when looked at some other way.

Changing demographics

Over time, enormous disparities in north-south growth rates will sharpen emigration pressures. Years ago, I asked a colleague, the dis-

15   For a thorough analysis of the idea of religion-based threats, one that concludes by rejecting it, see Mark Juergensmeyer, *The New Cold War? Religious Nationalism Confronts the Secular State*, Berkeley: University of California Press, 1993.

16   See his "The Clash of Civilizations?" *Foreign Affairs*, 72, Summer 1993, pp. 22–49; and *The Clash of Civilizations and the Remaking of World Order*, New York: Simon & Schuster, 1996.

tinguished economist Thomas Schelling, what he thought the world would look like in a few decades. Chillingly, he said he thought it would resemble South Africa then — enclaves of rich people, mostly white, literally fencing themselves off from multitudes of poor people, mostly dark. If his vision has not quite come true, it is because migrating is difficult for most people, often dangerous, and because border controls remain pretty effective.

Still, the disparities in populating growth rates between rich and poor countries are striking: Egypt and Tunisia are growing at over 5 percent per year, and Turkey at over 7 percent; by contrast, growth rates in the richer countries are in the 2 to 4 percent range, and Japan is growing at less than 1 percent.[17]

These high growth rates run the risk of creating youth "bulges" — that is, cohorts, especially of young men, much too large to be integrated into the job force. Those bulges may be sources of dissatisfaction, and so of instability, in key developing countries, such as Egypt and Turkey.

Environmental concerns

Like demographic shifts, environmental concerns are also chronic, not acute: From one year to the next, an environmental indicator may simply worsen gradually, almost imperceptibly, and then come to a sharp crisis once some tipping point is reached. These concerns will become more and more salient. For instance, if China continues to grow as fast as it has been growing, it will produce not just awful local pollution in China, but also dramatic increases in global warming, not to mention possible upward pressure on prices of fossil fuels. And the chronic environmental processes will be punctuated by acute episodes. Imagine what two nuclear meltdowns, two Chernobyls, within a year would do to the international agenda — or to intelligence's.

The outbreak of major regional fires in the late 1990s, from Southeast Asia to Mexico, was another example. Land-clearing fires in Indonesia got out of control during the country's prolonged drought. The smoke from the fires respected no national borders and eventually closed the airport in neighboring Singapore. When it did so, not only

17   Figures are from *CIA World Fact Book*, available at www.odci.gov/cia/publications/factbook/.

did the environment surge to the top of the agenda, but "foreign" and "domestic" ceased to have much meaning. The Asian fires also underscored how far institutions lagged behind the need for them, for the countries affected had no forum for beginning to turn Indonesia's crisis into a matter for regional action.

The processes afoot on the way to 2010 and beyond are subjects more for academia and think tanks than for government, let alone intelligence. But some of their implications for intelligence can be foreseen. The communications revolution indicates new possibilities and new competition for intelligence; the CNN factor is already a fact of life. The intelligence world of the Cold War was one of small amounts of information regarded as reliable — spy reports and satellite photos. The intelligence world of tomorrow is the Web — enormous amounts of unreliable information. And that world will permit easy communications, or quick transfers of images, between policy officials (or intelligence analysts) and people on the ground anywhere in the world. The gap between what information is available and what can be processed will grow.

Communications that increase expectations, plus demographic shifts that produce youth bulges, plus increasing ethnic conflict suggest that the United States will become engaged, including with its military forces, in places not easily predicted in advance. As a result, intelligence will need to be flexible enough to quickly support those engagements. By one count in 1994, there were some 50 ethnic conflicts under way. By the same count, 13 to 15 of those had caused more than 100,000 deaths, 20 others had been responsible for more than 10,000 deaths, and fully half of the conflicts had produced refugee streams of more than 100,000.[18] At century's end, there were 1.5 million Kalashnikov automatic rifles scattered around Mozambique alone.[19]

Supporting U.S. forces in far-flung peace and humanitarian operations is a major change, little noticed, in intelligence's role since the Cold War's end. Supporting U.S. military operations will also blur the line between capacities inside the government and those outside. As is the case for broad mysteries, this role too will require reaching out be-

18   The data are from Ted Robert Gurr, "Peoples Against States: Ethnopolitical Conflict and the Changing World System," *International Studies Quarterly*, 28, 3, September 1994, pp. 347–377.

19   This estimate is from Terry Gander, ed., *Jane's Infantry Weapons, 1996–97*, Alexandria, VA: Jane's Information Services, 1996.

yond the government, for when crisis comes to, say, the Congo, it will turn out that international relief organizations and perhaps a few academic anthropologists are the best sources about what is going on. James Clapper, then director of the Defense Intelligence Agency (DIA), described for the Senate how his intelligence analysts were called upon to provide not just targeting data, order of battle, and other classical intelligence, but also information on 40 clans and subclans in Somalia, on the risk of tuberculosis and malaria in that country, and on infrastructure and geography in Zaire and Rwanda.[20]

These peace and humanitarian operations also suggest another far-reaching implication for intelligence. Like it or not, the United States and its intelligence will continue to operate in coalitions. In addition to putting the politics of partners on the intelligence agenda, that will continue to stretch intelligence's conception of *who* are its customers. So far, U.S. intelligence has been creative in finding ways to share its wares with partners, even somewhat dubious ones, without compromising sources. Yet that sharing so far has been concessive, us helping them; intelligence, like the U.S. military, is only starting to venture into operations that are fully cooperative. The challenge beyond 2010 will be to extend that sharing of intelligence to private actors, to NGOs but also to private companies that are parts of the coalition. It will be sharing, not providing, and so verifying information received from private sources will be a necessity.

"NEW OLD THREATS"

For some developments that emerge from these global processes, the old-fashioned language of threat is appropriate.

Rogue states

The 1990s demonstrated how awkward it can be for the United States and its partners to deal with rogue states, even ones with but a fraction of America's military power. North Korea, Iraq, and Iran top today's lists. The list beyond 2010 no doubt will be different, but the

---

20 See Lieutenant General James R. Clapper, Jr., director of DIA, before the Senate Armed Services Committee, January 17, 1995, in *Defense Issues*, 10, 5, cited at www.defenselink.mil/speeches/1995/di005.html.

characteristics of those on it will be much the same: Rogues will be alienated from international life but determined, relatively cohesive, controlled by ruthless leaders, and advanced enough to aspire to dangerous weaponry.

For these threats, our existing armory — both real and conceptual — is more or less apt. Deterrence and its means are relevant. Yet notice that the United States fought Desert Storm against Iraq with an eye on the bond markets: It passed the begging bowl afterwards lest the war's cost increase the American deficit. And the instruments for dealing with most possible rogues — whether blocking North Korea's path to nuclear weapons, containing Iraq's weapons of mass destruction, or preventing Russia's slide to autocratic enmity — are not strictly military. They are more political and economic.

American military predominance gives rise to a paradox: Because the United States is so predominant in conventional war, it is not likely to fight another one. Only a fool, or a desperate man, would repeat Saddam Hussein's mistake by taking on the United States where it is strong. Future foes will try to find where the United States is weak. They will not confront American power *symmetrically*. Rather, they will reach for *asymmetric* strategies and tactics, in which weapons of mass destruction, especially chemical and biological weapons, will loom large. Future regional conflicts will be fought under the shadow of such weapons and thus must be planned for under that shadow.[21] Would-be foes will threaten to use such weapons against U.S. forces where they mass, or against the long lines of communication over which the United States must move forces.

Foes will also pursue other asymmetric strategies. Desert Storm was the Cold War's European war transplanted to Arabia's sands; it was, on wide-open sand, the tank war for which the United States and NATO had prepared on the north German plain. No serious adversary would try that again. Rather, enemies might seek to draw the United States into messy, urban fighting, where standoff weapons are much harder to bring to bear and the chances of U.S. casualties much greater. Those foes would hope to induce the American body politic to dismiss the conflict as far away and of little consequence.

21   This emphasis on asymmetric threats was a theme of the Pentagon's 1997 *Quadrennial Defense Review*. See, also, Gregory F. Treverton and Bruce Bennett, "Integrating Counterproliferation in Defense Planning," RAND Issue Paper, 1997.

The American mood at the new century's beginning continues to prefer self-reliance to coalitions. At the same time, though, there is little inclination to pay the price of unilateral military endeavors in blood or treasure. When the United States sends forces abroad, it looks to others for company, for help, as in former Yugoslavia, or for both help and money, as in Desert Storm. Little by little, defense planning will catch up with the facts of coalition warfare. However, because U.S. reliance on coalition partners will be apparent to would-be foes, those foes will also target the coalitions. They will probe for weak links, seeking to deny the United States bases and ports of entry for its forces if they can, or they will try to deny the United States the moral high ground, for instance by forcing it to kill many civilians in order to attack military targets.

Or, those foes will pursue several kinds of asymmetric strategies at once. Not much more than intimations of a threat to use biological weapons against Saudi Arabia might be enough to detach it from a U.S.-led coalition in the Gulf. Nor might it take much to detach Japan from a coalition in northeast Asia, especially if the Korean contingency that gave rise to the coalition were ambiguous, perhaps internal disarray in North Korea more than a determined intent to attack the South. If allied governments held firm, their populations might not. The United States depends on local laborers to unload ships and planes at ports; it might not take much to induce them to stay home or to flee. In current circumstances, evacuating Americans and other foreign civilians from Korea is already a daunting planning task: Imagine if the evacuation had to be done under the shadow of chemical threats.

The case for an intelligence role will be strongest for those states that are most secretive and whose future orientation toward the United States is most in doubt. Some of those will be rogues, such as North Korea or Iraq, third-rate powers but secretive ones with the capacity to do the United States and its allies harm. The world beyond 2010 will also contain rogue pieces of stronger states, such as India's nuclear program, or rogue behaviors by states that are not otherwise hostile. The key question about Russia's rump biological weapons program, for instance, was whether it was a rogue piece or a rogue behavior, the answer turning on how much Moscow's leaders were willing or able to control that program.

For these threats, intelligence's secrets will continue to matter, as will the patient puzzle solving about armies and weapons that has been the hallmark of intelligence. As the United States approaches an armed conflict, the will and vulnerabilities of possible coalition partners will be critical questions whose answers will lie mostly, but not entirely, in the domain of information that is available openly.

In assessing asymmetric threats from lesser military powers, the challenge will be to move beyond bean counting. For all the talk of such threats, there has been little serious thinking about how, for instance, Saddam Hussein might actually use threats of chemical or biological weapons. Much of what passes for analysis has been a simple toting of capabilities, with perhaps some mirror imaging of the sort that plagued U.S. analysis of India's nuclear program: If we were Saddam, what would we do? A deeper understanding will require getting inside the heads and strategies of would-be foes. For that purpose, insights from open sources, such as military writings, can help, as can what spies might learn about thinking inside militaries or what satellites might pick up about exercises. Intelligence can add value by "red teaming," simulating potential foes and how they might threaten U.S. interests or respond to U.S. moves against them.

Terrorism

A gruesome string of bombings has reminded Americans that they are vulnerable to terrorism, including in the United States itself and including from American terrorists — the World Trade Center in 1993, the federal building in Oklahoma City in 1995, the air force housing in Saudi Arabia in 1996, the U.S. embassies in Kenya and Tanzania in 1998. If there is good news, it is not much better than the bad news. It is that technology has not dramatically lengthened the menu of terror weapons.

There was and remains concern that the Soviet Union's demise might result in nuclear bombs, materials, or know-how spilling into rogue states or terrorist groups. So far, however, this fear has been the dog that didn't bark. There have been plenty of tales of would-be deals in nuclear materials, but the large seizures of such materials have not been bomb grade, and the bomb-grade seizures haven't been large. Many have been law enforcement "stings." In 1996, for example, there were no seizures of nuclear material in the United States, but there were two cases involving conspiracies to import radioactive material into this country.[22] The Russians themselves surely have reason not to encourage nuclear-armed groups in their neighborhood, and nuclear know-how may be harder to transfer than was imagined in 1990. U.S. programs to work with Russia in eliminating nuclear stocks and employing nuclear scientists also have played a role in limiting the spread of nuclear wherewithal.

Or it may be that terrorists have little need for nuclear weapons simply because they long have had plenty of violent material. The basic design of atomic weapons themselves hasn't been a secret for a long time, so building such a weapon has been a fissile material and engineering problem for terrorists. Terrorists might assemble fuel rods into crude "radiation bombs" instead of nuclear weapons. More to the point, the Tokyo subway gassings by the mysterious Aum Shinrikyo group demonstrated that lethal biological weapons have been and are within reach of almost any terrorist group. And U.S. intelligence did not know Aum was a terrorist group until after the attack.[23] Building biological weapons is not much more difficult than brewing beer (though the biological brew-masters do risk death if they make a mistake).[24] If

22 From Statement of Louis J. Freeh before the Senate Appropriations Committee, Subcommittee on Foreign Operations, Hearings on International Crime, March 12, 1996, cited at www.fas.org/irp/congress/1996_hr/s9603.

23 See the collection of statements presented at Global Proliferations of Weapons of Mass Destruction, Hearings by the Permanent Subcommittee on Investigations of the Senate Committee on Government Operations, November 1, 1995.

24 Former Director of Central Intelligence (DCI) John Deutch chaired a 1999 commission that looked at the adequacy of U.S. government arrangements. See its report: Commission to Assess the Organization of the Federal Government to Combat the Proliferation of Weapons of Mass Destruction (Deutch Commission), *Combating Proliferation of Weapons of Mass Destruction,* July 14, 1999, available at www.senate.gov/~specter/. See, also, Richard A. Falkenrath, Robert D. Newman, and Bradley A. Thayer, *America's Achilles' Heel: Nuclear, Biological, and Chemical Terrorism and Covert Attack,* Cambridge, MA: MIT Press, 1998; Gideon Rose, "It Could Happen Here: Facing the New Terrorism," *Foreign Affairs,* 78, 2, March/April 1999, pp. 131–137; John M. Deutch, "Terrorism," *Foreign Policy,* 108, Fall 1997, pp. 10–22; and Ashton Carter, John Deutch and Philip Zelikow, "Catastrophic Terrorism: Tackling the New Danger," *Foreign Affairs,* 77, 6, November/December 1998, pp. 80–94.

terrorists seek to kill on a vast scale, they have no reason to go to all the trouble of building atomic or radiation weapons. They could use biological ones instead.

If terrorists have not used atomic or biological terror thus far, that has been because conventional explosives have been lethal enough for their purposes. For downing airplanes or otherwise killing large numbers of people at once, conventional explosives are more than enough. Indeed, the truck bomb that destroyed the U.S. Marine barracks in Lebanon in 1983 was, at the time, the largest nonnuclear explosion the Federal Bureau of Investigation (FBI) had ever seen. The suicide bomber who drove it into the barracks didn't have to go to meet his maker to accomplish his mission; he could have achieved nearly the same result by parking the truck several hundred yards from the barracks and exploding it by remote control. The same was true of the bomber who attacked the U.S. complex in Saudi Arabia in 1996.

If anything is new, it may be motivation, a point hinted at in the World Trade Center bombing. Most previous terrorists have been rational, if extreme; they have sought specific political ends. Thus, they have had to reveal their role, opening the possibility of retaliation against them or their state sponsors.

Ominously, however, future terrorists might be anomic, their terror pure revenge, their behavior beyond calculations of deterrence and retaliation. While few places are strangers to terrorism and while yesterday's sponsors of terror may be tomorrow's targets, the United States will continue to be the target of choice for these avengers. Its sheer size and dominance of the international system will make it the "Great Satan."

The other new face of terrorism is the possibility of mass disruption rather than mass destruction. The industrial economies depend more and more on critical infrastructures — power, air traffic control, banking, and telecommunications — and information lies at the core of all of them.[25] Thus, an adversary state or terrorist group might seek to disrupt those networks either physically by destroying particular stations or nodes, or indirectly by getting inside the information systems.

25   For early thinking about these threats, see Roger Molander, Andrew Riddile, and Peter Wilson, *Strategic Information Warfare: A New Face of War*, Santa Monica, CA: RAND, 1996; and John Arquilla and David Ronfeldt, *In Athena's Camp: Preparing for Conflict in the Information Age*, Santa Monica, CA: RAND, 1997.

Mother Nature provided North America a preview of those vulnerabilities during the winter of 1997–98 when ice storms broke power lines, which in turn disrupted water supplies; Canada came within hours of evacuating Montreal.[26]

The infrastructures, especially information, are global, so protection can be only as good as the weakest link. The policy problem is compounded because the infrastructures are increasingly in private, not public, hands. In the United States, moreover, those private sector managers, especially in telecommunications, have spent their careers breaking free of government regulation. They will not easily accept government intervention to safeguard their networks even if they might privately acknowledge that competition drives them to invest too little in protection.

The rogues without a state name attached to them will be obvious targets for intelligence. The lists produced by blue-ribbon panels studying intelligence tend to lump all evildoers together, from terrorists to drug traffickers to other international criminals. Terrorists plainly need to be on the lists, and while projections of future worlds do not settle the question, a betting person would, alas, imagine that the terrorist threat to America and Americans will grow. Terrorists are both secretive and seriously threatening; they are purposive rogues who mean to do us harm. Moreover, as the government seeks to draw private managers of infrastructure into initiatives to better safeguard the public interest, one of the things it will have to offer will be information about the threat — a natural role for intelligence.

Organized crime

The form of organized crime represented by drug trafficking long has been at the edge of the traditional security agenda. It has been there because the drug problem is serious and because military instruments can be used to locate crops or traffickers, interdict supplies, and destroy drug laboratories or crops. It has also been there because dealing with the problem's "domestic" manifestation, drug use, is frustratingly slow in displaying visible effects, so the apparent logic of trying to get at the

26   *The Economist*, "Canada: After the Storm, the Clearing-Up," January 17, 1998.

problem abroad, "cutting off drugs at their source," continues to appeal.[27]

Now, drug trafficking plus economic integration and communism's disintegration create a new threat, one that puts the governance of key countries such as Russia at risk. Aspects of that threat, the Russian mafia for instance, already stretch inside U.S. borders. Economic transition, especially in the former Soviet Union, has created lucrative opportunities for organized crime. Black markets arise when old structures have collapsed but not been replaced, and when rules are weak and enforcement weaker. Members of the old regime may use special knowledge or access to derive economic rent. "Protection rackets" flower. Drug money provides capital for new illicit ventures, along with incentive for criminal alliances across nations. Thus far, there is little evidence that organized crime has trafficked in nuclear materials — it has other, richer product lines — but the possibility cannot be ruled out.

For the world of 2010 and beyond, the question is how much of international crime's recent growth is the result of economic transition. If its transition proceeds, will Russia become more like Italy or the United States, where organized crime prospers but does not threaten national governance? Or will Russia come to resemble Colombia or worse, where new, uglier elites displace traditional leaders and the nature of governance is up for grabs? In any event, crime, the underside of economic globalization, is likely to seem a greater and greater threat, all the more so if more-traditional security threats do not reemerge.

The "domestication" of threats such as terrorism and crime will blur the line between intelligence and law enforcement, between what John Le Carré calls "pure intelligence" and "enforcement."[28] In one sense, it is only natural that as traditional threats wane, pure intelligence should turn to new purposes such as catching criminals. Yet that turns intelligence to purposes for which it was expressly *not* designed: Not only has domestic practice separated intelligence and law enforcement, lest the two together become Big Brother, but intelligence is avowedly national, its purpose to get a leg up on other nations, while future law enforcement will be inherently cooperative. Law enforcement also blurs

27   For a discussion of crime as a security issue, see my "International Organized Crime, National Security and the 'Market State,'" in Tom Farer, ed., *Transnational Crime in the Americas*, New York: Routledge, 1999.

28   See his *The Night Manager*, New York: Knopf, 1993.

the other distinctions on which American intelligence has been based, between public and private and between foreign and domestic.

The cultures of intelligence and law enforcement are worlds apart. For intelligence, the purpose is policy, and the standard is good enough to serve as a basis for making that policy. For law enforcement, the purpose is convicting criminals, and the standard is that of a court of law. Intelligence takes pains to protect sources, and so stays out of the line of evidence. Law enforcement has to trade off protecting sources against convicting criminals, and its officers need to be prepared to testify publicly. This clash of perspectives and the challenge of finding new missions will be a primary shaper of U.S. intelligence in the years ahead; the disagreements will be sharper because the history of two main organizations, the CIA and the FBI, is one of ragged cooperation at best.

"THREATS WITHOUT THREATENERS"

While law enforcement will strain intelligence's role, the familiar concepts and language of threat, deterrence, and punishment will still remain relevant. For other results of global processes beyond 2010, however, the old language is misleading, and the old concepts do not suffice. These developments can be thought of as *threats without threateners*. If they are a threat, the threat results from the cumulative effect of actions taken for other reasons, not from an intent that is purposive and hostile. They might also be called *systemic* threats. Those who burn the Amazon rain forests or try to migrate here or who spread pandemics here, or even those who traffic in drugs to the United States, do not necessarily wish Americans harm; they simply want to survive or get rich. *Their* self-interest becomes a threat to *us*.

They differ sharply from the Cold War's nominal threat:

They are chronic and long term, not acute and short term. Human beings, with their adrenal systems, are optimized to deal with acute threats, such as war, not with chronic problems whose causes are today but whose consequences are tomorrow or the day after. We are galvanized by the "stun effect" of dramatic developments. During the Cold War, a nuclear exchange between the United States and the Soviet Union always was highly improbable, almost assuredly so after the early 1960s. But the image of that risk had a stun effect that mobilized the American public and its Congress. By contrast, the threats without threateners are like New York City bridges whose maintenance can be deferred from year to year without visible effect until, all of a sudden, they are on the verge of falling down.

They are not necessarily "zero sum" in the way traditional threats were. In war, one state's loss is usually another's gain. By contrast, action against environmental degradation can produce gains for all. But notice the limits of this difference: The United States and the Soviet Union were military competitors, even adversaries, but they shared an interest in not blowing up the planet. By about the mid-1960s, that positive-sum dimension came to outweigh the zero-sum competition in their nuclear relations.

By the same token, while states may all stand to gain if environmental problems are addressed, they will still be competitors over who pays and how much. The cutting down of the Amazon forest is almost pure loss for most of humankind; it is not, however, for those who do the cutting. Addressing some of these threats without threateners will give rise to classic "public goods" problems. All nations, for instance, have a stake in containing global warming by burning fewer fossil fuels, but all would prefer that other nations take the cuts. Indeed, the more others reduce, the greater the incentive for any given state to defect, for then it receives the benefit both of the reductions and of its own consumption. Since all states face similar incentives, all will be tempted to defect, and too little of the public good — in this case, reductions in fossil fuel burning — will be produced.

They may not be reversible. The effects of wars are reversible within a generation or two. Societies recover. Not so, perhaps, for global warming, whose effects might be permanent, or for some kinds of pandemic which might, like AIDS, rob societies of several generations of leaders.

They may be less susceptible to unilateral approaches than traditional security issues. During the Cold War, the United States made alliances and other such arrangements, in economics as well as security, but Americans still felt many of the levers of their security were in their hands. That seems less so for many of the "new" issues. Containing migration or environmental degradation inherently requires cooperation with other states. In that sense, the United States is coming to be less different from other nations than it was.

They may lie beyond the domain of government. National security during the Cold War was a government monopoly. The threat was political and military, and most of those levers were in the hands of government, particularly the federal government. That is much less so with the newer challenges, for which many of the levers are in the hands of companies or private citizens. American assistance plays a role in Egypt's development (Egypt is one of only several large recipients of U.S. aid left), but in the end, whether Egypt grows fast enough so that its youth bulge does not threaten its stability turns more on the actions of private capital than government assistance.

They may be neither so cheap nor so unifying as traditional security threats. It is now for historians to argue how close the United States and Soviet Union ever came to striking each other with nuclear weapons. Yet whatever the answer, the image of the nuclear danger was both stunning and unifying; nuclear war, one student put it, would have united in death all Russians — men, women, children, and the KGB. The nuclear danger was equally unifying for Americans. At the same time, for most Americans, responding to the Soviet threat meant paying taxes; their daily lives were not otherwise much affected. Given the economic conditions of most of the postwar period, buying insurance through defense spending was relatively cheap.

By contrast, addressing some "new" problems may be neither so unifying nor so cheap. Polls consistently record that poorer Americans are more concerned about immigration than are richer ones, and for good reason: For the rich, new immigrants are a source of cheap labor, but for some poor Americans, those same immigrants are competition. For instance, a 1999 poll found that only 18 percent of the "elite" sample thought that immigration and refugees posed a threat to vital U.S. interests, while 55 percent of the public sample thought so.[29] Doing something about environmental degradation or coping with a global economy may require Americans — or at least some of them — to drive less or work harder or otherwise change their behavior in more than trivial ways.

For intelligence, the challenge of these threats without threateners will be to assess motivation and so help policy-makers frame responses. The distinction between threats without or with threateners is not a di-

---

29   John E. Rielly, ed., *American Public Opinion and U.S. Foreign Policy 1999*, Chicago: Chicago Council on Foreign Relations, 1999, p. 15.

chotomy but a continuum. Amazon peasants burning the rain forest in order to subsist might be at one end, and determined, anti-American terrorists at the other. In between are international criminals or drug traffickers, who want mostly to make money but may do us harm in the process. Viewing them through the lens of threats without threateners can be instructive; efforts against drug traffickers, for instance, have been improved by so-called "linear strategies" based on conceiving of trafficking from crops to customers by analogy to legitimate businesses.

These issues will pose questions about how far intelligence's writ should run, and in particular about how much it should design its collectors with, for instance, environmental issues in mind. An intelligence task force on the environment in 1992 led to an agreement between then DCI Robert Gates and then Senator Al Gore to make available dated wide-area imagery to environmental scientists. In 1995, 800,000 images were released. In the short run, that was good policy and good public relations: The images were taken and processed, so the marginal cost of providing them to scientists was small. In the future, there will be plenty of imagery available commercially, but suppose a series of environmental crises pushed the issue up the agenda. Then, new technologies developed by intelligence — for instance, hyperspectral imagery capable of detecting fine differences in shading or texture — could be put to different purposes.

THE COMING OF THE MARKET STATE[30]

Intelligence's world beyond 2010 will be the world of the market state. That world is the political total of the global processes that are under way, especially in information and economics. The age of information is also the coming of the market state, which will dramatically change the roles of government and of private actors — and of intelligence.

30   This discussion owes much to my conversations with Philip Bobbitt, and the term *market state* is his. Bobbitt currently has a book in preparation on the coming of the market state. Richard Rosecrance speaks of the "virtual state," and Jessica Mathews also writes of technology breaking government monopolies on collecting and managing information. See Richard Rosecrance, "The Rise of the Virtual State," *Foreign Affairs*, July/August 1996, pp. 45–61; and Jessica T. Mathews, "Power Shift," *Foreign Affairs*, 76, 1, January/February 1997, pp. 50–66.

The demise of the Soviet Union and the end of the Cold War did not usher in the market state. Rather, those changes were themselves results of the forces that are shaping the world of the market state. The transition from what might be called the "territorial state" to the market state has been going on for a century at least. That transition, however, was obscured by this century's preoccupation with particular, and particularly fearsome, territorial states — Germany, Japan, and the Soviet Union.

It is not that competition among nation-states is shifting from politics to economics, what Edward N. Luttwak called "geoeconomics" supplanting the Cold War's "geopolitics."[31] Rather, power is dispersing around and through the nation-state, and the role of nation-state governments is changing.[32] The broad shape of the international system beyond 2010 may reflect the interactions of the major nation-states, but by then it will be apparent that the drivers of that system are elsewhere. What lies behind both old threats and new, and the uneasy interplay of the two, is a transformation of international politics.

The change in the role of the state is inseparable from the economic transformation. The territorial state was born in the period of agrarian economics, but it was the industrial revolution that gave it the iron and steel. It was only then that state power began to be measured by economic output, not territorial size or the wealth of the sovereign's purse. The postindustrial economy, by contrast, cuts across territorial states, devaluing the icons' power.[33] Lord Keynes was right in 1919 in his foreboding about the Treaty of Versailles:

> Political considerations cut disastrously across economic. In a regime of Free Trade and free economic intercourse it would be of little conse-

---

31 See his *The Endangered American Dream*, New York: Simon & Schuster, 1993. He was writing at a time of fretting over the Japanese challenge — the Japan that "could say no." See Shintaro Ishihara, *The Japan That Can Say No*, Simon & Schuster, 1991. This translation omitted some of the more inflammatory passages from the Japanese book of the same name by Ishihara and Akio Morita.

32 For early discussions of other actors on the world stage, see Robert O. Keohane and Joseph S. Nye, *Power and Interdependence,* Boston: Little Brown, 1973; and Robert O. Keohane, *After Hegemony: Cooperation and Discord in the World Political Economy*, Princeton: Princeton University Press, 1984.

33 See, for instance, Alvin and Heidi Toffler, *The Third Wave*, New York: William Morrow and Co., 1980.

quence that iron lay on one side of a political frontier, and labor, coal, and blast furnaces on the other. But as it is, men have devised ways to impoverish themselves and one another; and proffer collective animosities to individual happiness.[34]

It did matter where the factories were located. In the era of the market state, it matters much less.

To be sure, traditional issues among states remain, but they too are conditioned by the economic context.[35] Witness the Russian debate over NATO's enlargement eastward during the 1990s: That debate was intense but almost entirely confined to specialists and politicians inside the Russian "ring road," Moscow's equivalent of Washington's beltway. For most Russians, polls showed, the real issues were much closer to home, in their economic situations and how Russia's insertion into the global economy affected their lives and prospects.

Yet existing habits of thought and institutions remain powerfully conditioned by the concept of the nation-state that was enshrined in the Treaty of Westphalia — the sovereignty of nations and the principle of nonintervention in their internal affairs. There is thus a mismatch between what drives international issues and how we address them. Take immigration as an example. War aside (a large aside), economics is the main force behind migration, as people seek better lives elsewhere. Yet policy approaches to it derive from the older vision of international politics, one dominated by notions of border controls, citizenship, and sovereignty. Their mismatch is almost a complete one. Beginning to rectify it would imply recognizing that the market state requires people to move freely across borders to work, perhaps temporarily, but not necessarily to acquire the benefits of citizenship where they live. "Sojourner rights" might permit people to work where they need to but not to acquire health care, social security, or other specific benefits of citizenship.[36]

34   John Maynard Keynes, *The Economic Consequences of the Peace*, New York: Harcourt, Brace and Howe, 1920, p. 99.

35   For a provocative argument that the nation-state and national interest are alive and well, even in western Europe where they seemed most superseded, see John Mearsheimer, "Why We Will Soon Miss the Cold War," *Atlantic Monthly*, August 1990.

36   James C. Bennett, *The Anglosphere Century: The Future of the English-Speaking Nations in the Internet Era*, Lanham, MD: University Press of America, the Rowman & Littlefield Group, forthcoming October 2000.

While governments still are the most important actors in international politics, their power is being challenged from both above and below. As the traditional politics of interstate rivalries cedes place to the global market, governments lose unique attributes of their power. Armies and territory count for less. The world has not seen the end of armed conflict; on the contrary, warring seems built into the human species. But for the market state, any threat to go to war is, like nuclear threats made by the rival superpowers during the Cold War, a threat to cut off the nose to spite the face. It may be credible to make but not to carry out, for the cost surely exceeds the benefit.[37] If the threat is not credible to carry out, then making it credible before the fact depends on visibly leaving something to chance . . . or to passion. The logic of war is not the logic of the market state.

From above, international commerce is eroding what used to be thought of as aspects of national sovereignty: States are hard-pressed, for instance, to sustain controls on their currency. Of large states, only China has continued to do so with some success, but it is still poor. States that strive to be prosperous face sharp constraints on their monetary and fiscal policies: Witness France under François Mitterrand in the early 1980s, which sought to run an expansionary fiscal policy but found it could not. The French franc depreciated dramatically, and France was forced back to a more orthodox "German" policy of tight money and modest fiscal stimulus. What was graphic for France is only a little less true for other countries. Major Latin American states peg their currencies to the dollar; the aim is monetary stability, but the price is interest rates high enough to keep their currencies from devaluing.

Critical levers, many of which used to be in the hands of government, are passing to the private sector. Each of the ten largest companies in the world has an annual turnover larger than the GNP of 150 of the 185 members of the UN, including countries such as Portugal, Israel, and Malaysia.[38] More subjectively, at least 50 NGOs have more legitimacy than 50 UN member nations. Official government aid to developing countries now is trivial by comparison to private capital flows, though governments and their institutions, such as the World Bank and the International Monetary Fund (IMF), may continue to have some leverage because of their official status. During the 1983–88 period, the

---

37 This point is made compellingly by John Mueller, *Retreat from Doomsday: The Obsolescence of Major War*, New York: Basic Books, 1989.
38 I am grateful to Nicholas Butler for this statistic.

ratio of public to private flows of capital to the poorer countries averaged just under 2:1; over the course of 1989–1995, the ratio switched to almost 5:1 in favor of *private* flows.[39]   Later, just before the Asian economic debacle of 1997–98, it approached 10:1.

The market respects neither the borders nor the icons of the traditional Westphalian state. It does not care whether the worker is Filipino or American, Chinese or German, man or woman, homosexual or military veteran. If the person can do the job, he or she is rewarded, and if not, not. "Made in America" is not a label of interest to the market. Nor are national cultural symbols of interest except as marketing devices: Ask any American who has traveled and seen sweatshirts with "random English" on the front, or ventured to ask a foreigner wearing a Harvard t-shirt which class she was in and received only a blank stare in return.

If bankers and international finance are eating away at states from above, terrorists and drug traffickers challenge state power from beneath.[40]   They make use of technology and of international networks to act around and through states, pursuing their objectives by trying to compel states to acquiesce or by eluding the control of states. In 1996, the Tupac Amaru guerrillas in Peru set up their own home page on the Web, Rebel Voice. A loose network of sympathizers (including one site at the University of California, San Diego) grew up and began to channel propaganda back into Peru. Peru's government could not stop the inflow without cutting off the country's communications with the outside world.[41]

These challenges to the state, particularly in poor countries, gave rise to the notion of "failed states." Public commentary links Rwanda, Zaire, Haiti, Somalia, and Bosnia as "failed states," where governance has all but collapsed under the weight of poverty, population, corruption, crime, and disease.[42]   It is consequential, however, to be careful about cause and effect. On closer inspection, only Somalia, Zaire, and,

---

39   IMF, *World Economic Outlook,* 1997, p. 29.
40   See Jessica T. Mathews, "Power Shift," *Foreign Affairs,* 76, 1, January/February 1997, pp. 50–66.
41   See *Wall Street Journal,* January 6, 1997, p. A8.
42   Robert D. Kaplan's evocative article contributed to the attention to failed states — and perhaps also to the misunderstanding of them by seeming to lump different causes. See "The Coming Anarchy," *The Atlantic,* February 1994.

more provisionally, Haiti fit that description of failed states. In Bosnia, the problem was not weak "states" but surprisingly strong ones — Muslim, Serbian, and Croatian — that, alas, wished to occupy the same geographic area. And Rwanda seemed an old, and old-fashioned, civil war between tribal factions, either of which might have made a state.

Rather, state failure is best conceived along a continuum. At one end lie the industrial democracies. Hardly any of them, however, exercise all the attributes of state power everywhere — an example is the lawlessness of America's inner cities. Somalia at its worst was perhaps at the other end of the continuum. In between, the most obvious partial failures are territorial — for instance, Peru ceding control of much of its territory to Sendero Luminoso insurgents in the 1980s. But more-arresting partial failures are probably those related to the capacity to satisfy societal expectations — for instance, the periodic near-riots by French students and others when governments, pressed by global economics to restructure the economy, are perceived to be upsetting the existing social compact by limiting subsidized jobs for graduates.

CHANGING PUBLIC AND PRIVATE ROLES

The circumstances of the market state will transform the role of government. The government of the territorial state was a doer; students of public administration and, later, public policy learned that government's choice was "make, buy, or regulate." For tomorrow's public managers, the choice will be "cajole, incentivize, or facilitate" — a very different task (one perhaps rendered in punchier prose as "carrots, sticks, and sermons"[43]). What the government, and particularly the American federal government, will have is infrastructure and, perhaps, legitimacy. The government exists, with taxpayers providing buildings and secretaries and travel budgets. It *may* also have the legitimacy conferred by its custodianship of the public interest. It may be that private organizations will talk to it or will talk through it to other private organizations in ways those organizations could not or would not talk to each other.

At the NIC, we did yearly estimates of projected humanitarian needs and thus of possible relief operations. Our primary customer was the U.S. Air Force Transportation Command (TRANSCOM), which would

43   I owe this rendition to Robert Klitgaard.

wind up providing the airlift and so, wisely, thought it might try to plan ahead. In preparation for the estimate, the NIC invited representatives of the dozen largest humanitarian NGOs, such as CARE, to prepare short papers and attend a conference. To my surprise, they all agreed, most of them eagerly. For them, the taint of "intelligence" was an obstacle but not an overriding one. Taint aside, they welcomed the fact that *some* part of the U.S. government was paying attention. And I also had the impression that in convening them, we did them a favor: They may have found it easier to respond to an invitation from a neutral, official institution than to be convened by any one of their number.

More and more, the role of government will be to convene groups of the willing. Operation Desert Storm against Iraq in 1991 was an early example. In the future, those groups will bring together public institutions and private entities; like Desert Storm's partners, they will come from more than one nation. What the government will provide is its power to convene, its infrastructure, its legitimacy, perhaps, and its information — or intelligence. The shift in mind-set this will require of intelligence can hardly be overstated. Intelligence only slowly came to the realization that it worked for Congress as well as the U.S. executive branch. It will not come easily to the idea that it works with, and sometimes for, CARE and Amnesty International, not to mention Shell and Loral.

The market state implies dramatic changes in "private" responsibilities, a transformation that is the other side of the changing role of government. Traditionally, private actors were objects, not subjects, of international politics. States or groups of states acting through international institutions might try to regulate their behavior, but the private groups had little responsibility for setting norms. To that extent they were free riders on the international order. Of course, private efforts to influence state policies are a familiar feature of democratic politics, and those efforts also included the international policies of states. Such efforts were apparent in the U.S. debate over according most-favored-nation (MFN) trade status to China; major U.S. companies with stakes in China trade became more and more vocal advocates of MFN. Occasionally, private companies would act more creatively, for instance in Dupont's role in rallying chemical companies to support, not oppose, the 1996 Montreal Protocol's ban on damaging fluorocarbons. But those instances were rare.

The transition to the market state implies a vast increase in the responsibility of private actors, from companies and individuals to so-called NGOs (notice that the NGO label is itself a remnant of the old order!). They are becoming, in ways hardly realized let along charted, not the objects of the international order but its subjects, its architects. They are becoming the setters of international norms, not free riders on rules set by states. The IMF was discredited during Asia's crises as an after-the-fact fire brigade at best, and at worst as a brigade whose presence might have tempted governments to be careless with fire before the fact. In the event, private international banks negotiated with and through local governments, helping to begin the process of establishing norms of more transparency in Asian finance.

The logic of the market state also devalues international organization. At least, international institutions are orthogonal to the market, since those institutions are creatures of states, rooted in notions of state sovereignty. This observation has as much force for NATO as it does for the UN. It leaves international economic institutions, such as the World Bank or the World Trade Organization (WTO), in a tenuous middle ground. On the one hand, they may be less devalued by the market state than are international political or security institutions, for they have value as rule setters for international commerce. Yet, on the other hand, not only are they swamped by private international transactions — what the IMF or World Bank does is more and more overshadowed by private capital flows — but the status of those institutions is itself ambiguous. They too are creatures of governments, not of the forces that are coming to drive international politics.

To some extent, law is also devalued by the logic of the market state. After all, law itself is rooted in the traditional state, and thus to the extent that the traditional state is called into question, so is the legitimacy of law. Charles V of Spain could simply order a criminal's head chopped off. American presidents can hardly come close. President Clinton could sign, and the Senate could ratify, a treaty banning chemical weapons, a treaty which contains provision for challenge inspections of suspected private production facilities, but neither he nor the Senate could promise to deliver on that promise. They could only promise to try; whether the Constitution would permit such a government reach into the private sector was unclear. As the market state erodes distinctions between citizens and noncitizens, older notions of civil liberties or of law enforcement, which accorded greater protection to the sovereign's subjects than to mere foreigners, pass away.

In these circumstances, the status of international law is buffeted by cross currents. From one perspective, it is more relevant. Traditional international law always sat uneasily with U.S. traditions, for it too was based on Westphalian notions of state sovereignty and nonintervention in the affairs of sovereigns — just those attributes the Founding Fathers had sought to escape. States, not people, were the concerns of traditional international law.[44] Now, though, international law is moving in a very "American" direction: People are coming to matter, and what happens inside national borders is more and more regarded as a legitimate concern of the international community. To the extent that sovereignty, borders, and all the trappings of the Westphalian state are becoming less important in international law, that law should be more relevant.

Yet from another perspective, the world is still far from having any real alternative to states and state action, particularly when it comes to enforcement. It took a coalition of willing *states*, however covered by the legitimacy of international law and UN resolutions, to impose peace on Saddam Hussein, decency on the Bosnian Serbs, and minimal orderliness to Zaire's succession. There is still a mismatch between the forces that are driving international politics and the forces of international law.

THE INTELLIGENCE OF THE MARKET STATE

The plainest implication for the intelligence of the market state is that the agenda for American policy-makers, and thus for intelligence, will be more dispersed. Nations of not much interest will rush to the top of the agenda when humanitarian crises cannot be overlooked. Economic

44   These changes in international norms about intervention are richly debated in volumes of *Ethics and International Affairs*. In particular, see Thomas G. Weiss, "Principles, Politics, and Humanitarian Action," Vol. 13, 1999; Michael J. Smith, "Humanitarian Intervention: An Overview of the Ethical Issues," Oliver Ramsbotham, "Islam, Christianity, and Forcible Humanitarian Intervention," and Nancy Sherman, "Empathy, Respect, and Humanitarian Intervention," all in Vol. 12, 1998; Amir Pasic and Thomas G. Weiss, "The Politics of Rescue: Yugoslavia's Wars and the Humanitarian Impulse," Vol. 11, 1997; and Jeff McMahan, "Intervention and Collective Self-Determination," Vol. 10, 1996.

matters and private groups will claim attention. Absent the Soviet Union as both focal point and overarching threat, there is no immediate measure by which to reckon events. The meaning and import of those events is up for grabs, and none can be immediately dismissed or downgraded because it is isolated from the Soviet threat. Policy-makers have to deal with them all — a large number of snakes, if no big dragon, in former DCI R. James Woolsey's metaphor.

In the confusing world ahead, sorting out the link between events abroad and American interests will become more challenging. Intelligence's role in that sorting will be critical, for understanding what is going on *over there* is the first step in apprehending *whether* and *why* it matters to the United States. In Somalia, for instance, the United States first thought it was feeding hungry people. Only later did it understand that food was but a weapon in a long-standing power struggle. In Bosnia, the United States couldn't decide whether it was containing an inevitable war, succoring innocent victims, or punishing an evil aggressor. It did some of all of those, but the confusion of purposes, while perhaps understandable, still bordered on the tragic.

Drug trafficking and international crime will pose hard issues for intelligence because international concern over organized crime is likely to grow just as international capacity to deal with it diminishes. Law enforcement is rooted in the authority of the state and generally defined by geographic units; as a result, international institutions always have been weak. Crime will offend the pocketbooks and values of more and more of the planet's citizens, but for a time at least, national and international institutions for dealing with it will be devalued. For instance, there seems to be growing awareness that bribery in pursuit of international contracts is ultimately bad even for the nations whose officials are bribed, so it is possible to imagine something like the U.S. Foreign Corrupt Practices Act becoming a norm for international commerce. Yet acceptance of the norm is likely to run ahead of the capacity to enforce it, which will remain in both national and international institutions that are parts of the nation-state order.

That might change, and U.S. intelligence might, in effect, fill the gap between international norms and the international capacity to enforce them. When the United States seeks to "level the international economic playing field," that involves secrets, for nations do not advertise the bribes or side payments they make in trying to capture large foreign contracts for "their" firms. Now, the United States looks to the world as if it is trying to enforce the Foreign Corrupt Practices Act unilaterally, but as attitudes change, what is now a pure intelligence task, based on secrets, might come to be more accepted internationally.

For U.S. intelligence to play that role, however, would require a dramatic blurring of the bright white line between foreign and domestic. Already, understanding the Mexican economy, for instance, is impossible without knowing about what "domestic" American investors are up to. To push the example, major financial panics, such as the Mexican devaluation of 1994–95 or the Asian debacle of 1997–98, might be to the next century what the great politico-military crises of the Cold War were to the last. They might evoke "national security," broadly defined. Anticipating those crises would require knowing what millions of investors will know next week: Which government's reserves are lower than it has admitted? Which respected finance minister is about to resign? Which government doesn't have the stomach for raising interest rates to defend its currency? Secrets are relevant to answering these questions, many of them puzzles. They are good targets for intelligence.

More dramatically, the NSA's vast capacity to monitor signals is as close as the world has to a capacity to monitor the movements of money across borders. It might do so not just in the interest of the American state but for the sake of global transparency in capital movements. However, that task would upend every distinction on which U.S. intelligence is based — the movers of money have, in general, not committed a crime and do not pose a specific "national security" threat to the United States, many of them would be Americans, and NSA would be hard-pressed to share its take without revealing its capacity. Its international purposes would conflict directly with its national ones.[45]

WHAT KIND OF AMERICA?

The other change for intelligence will be the America in which it operates. For the United States, a strong nation but a relatively weak state, that change may be the most profound and the hardest to predict.

45   As Michael Herman puts it: "There is no complete escape from the paradox that intelligence knowledge tends to contribute to international security, while some of its collection is liable to detract from it." See his *Intelligence Power in Peace and War,* Cambridge: Cambridge University Press, 1996, p. 375.

America emerges from the 20th century's long war against fearsome territorial states with a capital, Washington, that would seem, in Ernest May's words, "to those sage, naive Orientals favored by the philosophers: 'Yes, a city. But, at heart, a military headquarters, like the Rome of the Fabians or the Berlin of the Hohenzollerns.'"[46] In 1935 or even 1945, it was not so obvious that it would turn out to be so. In the 1930s, the Agriculture and Commerce departments would have been thought weightier than State and War, and the Treasury Department, on its side of the White House, was literally as weighty as State, War, and Navy, all three then housed in what is now the Old Executive Office Building.

After World War II, it took the Soviet Union and its buildup, and U.S. elections, McCarthy, and nuclear weapons to produce the dominance of military and security issues in American governance. The domestic departments, preeminent in the 1930s, declined into New Deal husks. The creation of the National Security Council (NSC) did what its originators intended and what President Truman feared, giving the military a role in political matters and surrounding presidents with national security professionals.

In the context of the nuclear danger and the Soviet threat, the National Security Act's other creation, a secretary of defense, had paradoxical effects: It appeared to strengthen but in fact weakened civilian control of the military. Presidents after Truman were loath to take on powerful military figures directly. Meanwhile, senior flag officers came to be not just tank drivers or jet jockeys; they became technically proficient and politically astute. To these changes the Goldwater-Nichols reform of the mid-1980s contributed, for real jointness among the services also necessitated a real chairman of the joint chiefs, a military figure with legitimacy whose arguments could not easily be turned aside.

Whatever America ensues, and whatever Washington symbolizes it, the results seems most unlikely to resemble what Americans and intelligence have known. The Pentagon, the CIA, and the NSC were creatures of the hot and cold wars, tinkered with but not fundamentally changed since. They are odd creatures for addressing trade policy, population issues, terrorism, migration, or disease. The Clinton administration's creation of the National Economic Council (NEC) as a counterpart to the NSC is testimony to that fact; that the NEC seems to have

46   See his charming and provocative "The U.S. Government, a Legacy of the Cold War," *Diplomatic History*, 16, 2, Spring 1992, p. 270.

been stillborn speaks to the depth of the change that ultimately will ensue. Reshaping of the wartime institutions, including intelligence, more dramatic than can be imagined would still leave those institutions preoccupied with military or politico-military matters.

The safest bet about the circumstances looking beyond 2010 is that something like the current muddle will continue. No peer military competitor will emerge, and lesser nastiness abroad, while continuing, will not be so nasty as to push the United States toward decisive choices. The market state will be more and more visible, but from that military headquarters, Washington, the imperium's military might will still look impressive. The United States will continue to be sitting in the crossroads scratching its national head.

Perhaps, though, the tensions in the body politic will be more evident. They might be brought to a point by any of a number of misfortunes, from a war in Korea that will have occurred despite accumulating evidence that it would not, to a string of terrorist attacks killing lots of Americans, to the collapse of a major trading partner, such as the European Union. Americans will continue to become more engaged abroad, but it is not beyond imagining that crises will push them to turn their government's attentions inward. Already, "homeland defense" is on the agenda, and terrorist attacks inside the United States might turn that language into real action. Or a collapse in Mexico that threatens to turn the stream of migrants northward into a torrent would make plain what is already the case: Mexico is a "domestic" matter for the United States.

One tension is as old as the republic, that between America's isolationist and its messianic strain. The hope to keep the world at bay — isolationism by whatever name — is again in America's air. Isolation and activism, though, have alternated in American history, the will to retreat exchanging pride of place with the will to lead. Sometimes the "city on the hill" is to be insulated, to serve at most as a model; at other times, it is to be spread.

In many respects, the globe has been primed to be reshaped in America's image if the United States had the will to do so. The United States is not only the dominant military power, it is also the state most identified with democracy and free markets, both of which now reign virtually unchallenged. International law, as suggested above, used to be uncongenial to the American spirit but is now moving in an "American" direction, toward recognizing people, not just states, as the constituents of law. The United States has a number of potential partners depending on the tasks and no real competition in coalition building.

Not least, while the world remains dangerous, it is not, as it was for most of this century, existentially so. The United States could afford to take risks and be selective or experimental in building international order. The appropriate analogy is policing: Because crime cannot be stopped everywhere does not imply efforts should not be made anywhere. From that perspective, the record of the years since the fall of the Berlin wall is not so bad. Not all regions or states have been given international help in restoring order or decency, but some have, though probably not more than once.

If what connects the alternating American visions of the world is the desire to control the national destiny, that control seems more elusive now. In the transition of the 1920s and 1930s after World War I, as now, the United States was strong but not able to work its will alone; it needed to be selective about its engagements and to act with partners. Then, though, there seemed to be the option of opting out, seeking control by remaining aloof. That option proved tragic. Whether international arrangements in which the United States was a full partner might have prevented World War II is one of history's unknowables. We do know, however, what ensued *without* America. Now, the quest for control through aloofness seems more obviously futile, though it still tempts some Americans.

A second tension is the role of government. In the longer sweep of history, much more than institutional tinkering is occurring, for the depression, hot war, and Cold War gave Americans more government, including more federal government, than had been the custom. The United States, a strong nation but a weak state, came to acquire many of the trappings of the European territorial state with which America's founders had broken. It acquired that imperial military headquarters. At the same time, immigration was making the American nation more and more heterogeneous.

And so there are in this third transition real questions about both "state" and "nation," all of them sharpened by the rise of the market state. Much more is afoot than a rebalancing of roles among levels of the federal structure. To be sure, the emerging United States is not apt to opt for centralized state solutions on the model of European social democracy. That much was indicated by the recent history of welfare reform or the debate over health care. While federal budget deficits ended by century's end, the aging of baby boomers looms, with their claims on Social Security and Medicare. If any governments have budgetary room for maneuver, it is the states, but they are burdened with aging infrastructure and schools, the result of the last generation's voter initiatives to limit property taxes.

Approaches, rather, will emerge piecemeal and locally, more as private initiatives than government programs — in part a return to older, more "normal" American practice but also a circumstance of the market state. Private citizens or nongovernmental actors will act around and through government, often in ad hoc alliances. Those coalitions are evident with regard to "threats without threateners." One set of private actors, environmental NGOs, now negotiates with another set, major corporations, over carbon saving in Latin America. In economics, such coalitions are everywhere. They will be more and more present in the realm of what used to be regarded as high foreign policy. That much is suggested by Jimmy Carter's diplomatic interventions over Haiti and North Korea in the 1990s.

The third tension is more ominous, for it concerns not just the role of the state but also the role of the nation — who is "us." The bombing of the federal building in Oklahoma City in 1995 raised that question in gruesome caricature. The logic of those homegrown bombers defied our understanding as much as that of the World Trade Center bombers. The American militias have plenty of antigovernment antecedents in American history; yet, like a photograph's negative, their backlash against the global market outlines the devaluation of law. Their way of separating "them" from "us" is not primarily religious; rather it is a cocktail of populism and local nationalism, sometimes tinged with religion. In their gruesome contortion, the federal government and its law was not "us" but "them," the enemy whose officials were seen in bizarre cahoots with sinister forces of internationalism. They were not fellows but foes to be killed.

Who is "us" also arises, if less dramatically, in protests over immigration or when urban school districts spend a third per pupil what suburban ones do. It comes as little surprise that polls record people in the street as more concerned about immigration than elites. What looks like inexpensive labor to the latter appears as competition to the former, even if the competition is more apparent than real. Perhaps Americans, too, are seeking identification in smaller units. And the attraction of the immaterial seems to be on the rise here too.

At a minimum, the challenge for those who would make "foreign" policy — and for the intelligence that would support it — is to be as careful in understanding local effects as in assessing external trends. In particular, it will be crucial not to *assume* national interest but to *examine* it, for in this third transition the effects of particular issues will fall differently on different Americans. For intelligence, that will mean more engagement in questions that it has formerly taken for granted, such as what is the national interest. It will also mean dealing with a variety of Americans — those in states and localities, and private citizens — that it used to regard as beyond its ken.

3

-◼-

The militarization of intelligence

Imagine again those info-warriors of the 21st century, for if there is anything certain about the world beyond 2010, it is that U.S. soldiers will be sent into conflicts somewhere in the world. Wherever they fight, their "battlefield" will be radically transformed. The density of soldiers and formations on the battlefield has been diminishing for centuries, and that trend will be dramatically visible by 2010. Given the precise targeting of modern weapons, massed formations will only become tempting targets. And if the battlefield beyond 2010 is less dense than the battlefields of the past, it will also be broader. The distinction between the battlefield and the rest of society has also been eroding for some time, as industrial capacity has become critical to the ability to wage war. This trend, too, will accelerate by 2010, both as particular installations (such as communications nodes) become more and more critical to fighting wars and as the "military" and "civilian" purposes of those installations become more intertwined.

Most of 2010's info-warriors will be far from the battlefield as it used to be conceived, far from the violence and destruction. They will be operating sensors capable of seeing and weapons capable of striking over long distances. They may fly airplanes, but they will do so by remote control, not by sitting in the planes' cockpits. Some of the sensors they employ may be housed in satellites, but not many, for satellites are too far away and pass too quickly to be of real help to the info-warriors. Instead, the sensors will be closer, on unmanned airplanes or drones and on the ground. In Desert Storm, Special Forces infiltrated Iraqi territory to establish secret watching posts in order to keep track of Iraqi military movements. By 2010, that task will be done by "brilliant pebbles" dropped from the air and able both to sense move-ments and report the information back.

Kosovo in 1999 was a better foretaste of these future wars than Desert Storm was a decade earlier. In the future, as in Kosovo, the United States will seek to prevail through violence inflicted from the air, without putting troops on the ground. If ground troops are needed to control territory, they will fight in lightly armed mobile cavalry units. They would seek to control territory in overlapping zones, and their control would depend not on the firepower they carried but on the fire-power they could command from afar — from ships offshore and mis-siles or planes stationed out of harm's way, including in space, which will be heavily militarized by 2010. That firepower would be guided precisely to moving targets. The responses to their calls would be all but immediate — by 2015, measured in seconds, not minutes. If foes leaked through the outer perimeter of their zones, the info-warriors would first flee, standing and fighting only as a last resort.

WHAT MISSION FOR INTELLIGENCE?

Supporting these info-warriors is intelligence's biggest change since the end of the Cold War, and it poses the most important issues for the future, especially how much money the United States spends on intelli-gence. Yet the change has been out of the public eye despite a clutch of blue-ribbon panels that studied intelligence during the 1990s.[1] Instead, what grabbed the headlines were spying, the misbehavior of the CIA's spymasters, the Directorate of Operations (DO), and accusations of intelligence "failure": CIA spymaster Aldrich Ames committed treason,

---

1   The four most prominent to report recently are the executive-congressional Commission on the Role and Capabilities of the United States Intelligence Community (often and herein called the "Aspin-Brown commission" after its two chairmen), *Preparing for the 21st Century*, Washington, D.C., March 1, 1996; the House Intelligence Committee, *IC21: The Intelligence Community in the 21st Century*, Washington, D.C., March 4, 1996; and two private panels, the Council on Foreign Relations Independent Task Force, *Making Intelligence Smarter: The Future of U.S. Intelligence*, New York: Council on Foreign Relations, 1996, and the one I was most asso-ciated with, the report of the Twentieth Century Fund Task Force on the Future of U.S. Intelligence, *In From the Cold,* New York: Twentieth Cen-tury Fund Press, 1996, hereafter referred to as the "Twentieth Century Fund report."

followed by another CIA officer; the CIA's Guatemala station withheld crucial information about one of its sources, while the agency knowingly passed to the U.S. president information perhaps tainted by Soviet disinformation; intelligence failed to predict the Indian nuclear tests; and a Chinese-American was accused of passing nuclear secrets to China.

During the Cold War, that mission was *national* — finding out about and keeping tabs on the Soviet Union. Now it is becoming *tactical* — especially supporting American warriors around the globe. The change is most striking in the collection of information by what, for diplomatic reasons, was called "national technical means" during the Cold War — the vast network of spy satellites and other sensors. The network was built to learn about the Soviet Union but now is turning to support for military operations (SMO, as it is called). In one sense, the shift toward SMO and the tactical is only natural: The Soviet Union is gone, but the huge investments in collection systems remain, and technology has changed enough to permit those systems to render real service to tactical military commanders. The cost is sunk, so finding new purposes for existing systems is only logical.

Yet the shift raises issues that are hardly noticed, issues that return to first principles: What should intelligence *do?* And for *whom?* How should the obvious need to support military operations be squared with intelligence's mission to make sense of the world for all parts of the government (and perhaps for people outside the government)? Money is important but is only part of the issue. Analysts, even spies, are cheap, but new satellites are not. About half of what the United States spends on intelligence goes to the big technical collection systems. It is those systems that have driven up the nation's intelligence bill. The last time the defense budget was about the same size as today's in constant dollars, about $250 billion, was in the late 1970s. Then, intelligence was about $17 billion, again in constant dollars; now it is $27 billion.[2]

"National" purposes for intelligence remain. These purposes will be reconfigured but not made entirely obsolete by the rise of the market state. If the world beyond 2010 remains less existentially dangerous than that of the Cold War, it will still be more confusing. It is thus time to recognize that there are several purposes and several sets of consumers of intelligence. For a generation, reformers of American intelli-

2   The earlier estimate is an extrapolation from published figures.

gence have sought to centralize intelligence. If that ever made sense, it does not now. Intelligence's future should be a loose confederation, overlapping networks connecting sources, producers, and consumers. Military planners and operators will be prominent consumers. The task, though, is to ensure that national purposes — those of the secretary of state or trade representative — are not lost in intelligence's reversion to support for the military. It is a task without an easy solution.

RETARGETING THE COLD WAR LEGACY

When the Soviet Union disintegrated, intelligence's satellite, or overhead reconnaissance, infrastructure was impressive but appeared to have been deprived of its mission. That infrastructure was organized by information sources, in what intelligence officials call "stovepipes." Of those, the National Security Agency (NSA) was and is the most integrated; it is one-stop shopping for signals intelligence, or SIGINT — from designing requirements through breaking (and making) codes, to translating and interpreting signals, to publishing finished intelligence. The Central Imagery Office (CIO), created in 1992, and then the National Imagery and Mapping Agency (NIMA), founded in 1995, were successive efforts to mimic NSA for imagery, or IMINT. The National Reconnaissance Office (NRO), the biggest spender in the intelligence world, might be thought of as the base of the stovepipes, for it builds, launches, and operates satellites for both signals and imagery.

In 1997, the United States finally decided to make public the total figure for intelligence — $26.6 billion — thus confirming what public accounts long had indicated.[3] The individual agency numbers remain classified, but NRO spends about $6.2 billion (and employs about 1,000 people, a somewhat misleading number because most of its work is done by outside contractors), NSA spends about $3.7 billion (with 38,000 people), and the Joint Military Intelligence Program (JMIP), which groups the Defense Intelligence Agency (DIA) and the service intelligence arms, spends about $2 billion (and has 19,000 people).[4]

3   See *Washington Post,* October 17, 1997, p. A9.
4   See, for instance, *Washington Post,* June 12, 1994, p. A8, or *New York Times,* November 5, 1994, p. 54. In 1994, a congressional committee inadvertently confirmed the numbers, publishing by mistake a committee print without the usual deletions. The CIA requested $3.1 billion, the Pentagon agencies (NRO, NSA, CIO, and DIA) $13.2 billion, and TIARA

The Pentagon budget for the so-called TIARA is on the order of $12 billion.[5] For comparison, the total CIA budget is about $3.1 billion, and the CIA employs 17,000 people. The total all agencies spend for human intelligence, or HUMINT — mostly spying, but also monitoring foreign media and other open sources — is on the same order, about a tenth of intelligence's total.

At the Cold War's end, there was talk of big reductions. In 1991, for instance, intelligence officials were admitting that "the budget for big, expensive satellite systems will have to be cut back. The ones already aloft were sent up primarily to keep watch on the Soviet Union and, during the Gulf War, successfully refocused on Iraq. . . . [Now] there is no identifiable need for new ones."[6] In 1992, former DCI William E. Colby concurred that "the end of the Cold War had brought the chance for large cuts in the CIA, especially in its budget. . . . With the end of the threat that Soviet troops might suddenly invade Western Europe, the extremely expensive array of technology used to spot the preliminaries to an invasion is no longer needed."[7]

It didn't turn out that way. Just as the demise of the Soviet target was leaving overhead reconnaissance to search for new missions, advances in communications and data transfer technology were making the take from those satellites more useful than ever before to commanders on the battlefield.[8] New technology permitted old systems to find new purposes. If intelligence was shopping for a new mission, it had found itself a dandy.

(tactical intelligence and related activities) $10.4. See *New York Times*, November 5, 1994, p. 54. The Aspin-Brown commission also published a graph (*Preparing for the 21st Century*, Washington, D.C., March 1, 1996, pp. 131–132) that could be extrapolated to produce the numbers for individual agencies. See *Washington Post*, March 12, 1996, p. A11.

5   The TIARA budget numbers are somewhat arbitrary, hence changeable, because many tactical activities could be labeled either "operations" or "intelligence" and so are labeled according to fashion in budgetary support.

6   George Lardner, Jr., "In a Changing World, CIA Reorganizing to Do More with Less," *Washington Post*, July 5, 1991, p. A9.

7   Walter Pincus, "Ex-CIA Chief Backs Smaller Spy Agency; Gates Plan Would Transfer Some Intelligence and Paramilitary Operations to Pentagon," *Washington Post*, December 10, 1994, p. A4.

8   See Twentieth Century Fund report (*In From the Cold*, New York: Twentieth Century Fund Press, 1996), pp. 3–6.

The war against Iraq in 1991, Desert Storm, was only a dim hint of 2015's wars yet is nonetheless a convenient demarcation point in the shift from keeping tabs on the Soviet Union to supporting military operations.[9] It was not the first "information war," for it was mostly old-fashioned pounding. However, it did for the first time bring national intelligence systems to bear on tactical purposes, if not always too coherently. For instance, the Cold War's euphemistically named Defense Support Program (DSP) satellites are parked in geosynchronous orbits 24,000 miles above the earth. At that altitude, their orbit coincides with the earth's turning, so they appear to stare with infrared eyes at particular sectors of the globe. They were designed for one purpose — to provide immediate warning of Soviet nuclear missile launches by "seeing" the heat plumes of missiles during liftoff.

During Desert Storm, however, advances in software enabled the DSP satellites to be retargeted in order to see the launches of Iraqi Scud missiles. Images of a launch from two different DSP satellites enabled the location of the launch to be identified, all within 120 seconds.[10] Other Cold War systems also played an important role in Desert Storm. The Air Force's Talon Lance system allowed satellite information to be relayed into aircraft cockpits in under 10 minutes, versus the 90 minutes it had taken a few years earlier.[11]

During the Cold War, SIGINT satellites intercepted Soviet communications wholesale, and IMINT painstakingly compared photos to try to understand the Soviet military. In both cases, the process was for most of the Cold War too slow to be of much use to tactical commanders. First-generation reconnaissance satellites, for instance, ejected film canisters with parachutes, which were then snagged in the air by U.S. military aircraft. It was a matter of some hours, at least, before film could be recovered and developed.[12] According to former U.S. Air Force Chief of Staff Larry Welch: "Back in 1986, we never saw a [satellite] photo on the day it was produced. By 1989 [in contrast] there were

9   James A. Winnefeld, Preston Niblack, and Dana J. Johnson, *A League of Airmen: U.S. Air Power in the Gulf War,* Santa Monica, CA: RAND, 1994, especially pp. 181–221.
10   *Aviation Week and Space Technology,* April 8, 1991, p. 44.
11   *Aviation Week and Space Technology,* August 23, 1993, p. 71.
12   For a review of this history, see Jeffrey T. Richelson, "The Future of Space Reconnaissance," *Scientific American,* 264, l, January 1991, pp. 38–44.

over 400 photos every day that were produced by the system on that day."[13]

With digitized images and improved communication, "pictures" can now be flashed from satellites to ground stations to Washington and out to field commanders in small numbers of minutes. With some luck and advance preparation, communications of would-be enemy aircraft can be intercepted and returned to U.S. cockpits in time to provide detailed warning. The changes have meant that commanders in Bosnia in the late 1990s, for example, had virtually instantaneous access to NRO imagery using the Global Broadcast System developed by the CIA, the Defense Advanced Research Products Agency (DARPA), and the Defense Information Systems Agency.[14] These "national" intelligence agencies now can provide military commanders with near-real-time intelligence that would have been impossible ten years ago.[15]

Desert Storm also illustrated the technical obstacles. While the speed of retrieving images or signals from space had improved, the air war often outpaced retrieval times. The detection of Scud launches by DSP satellites was impressive, but the record of actually hitting, still more killing, Scud missiles was not.[16]   And on the ground, the U.S.-led coalition destroyed more Scud decoys than Scud launchers.

Intelligence's world beyond 2010 will continue to throw up very specific bad things or bad people. After Desert Storm, American military planners several times contemplated bombing strikes when Iraqi leader Saddam Hussein violated UN sanctions. The prime targets of interest were facilities associated with Iraqi weapons of mass destruction. But precisely locating those with traditional imagery or SIGINT was both imperative and difficult. If the United States killed many innocent civilians in an air strike, it risked ceding the moral high ground to Saddam, while if it missed the target with "precision" weapons, it would only embarrass itself.

13   Walter Pincus, "Military Espionage Cuts Eyed; Duplication Cited Among Pentagon Agencies," *Washington Post,* March 17, 1995, p. A1.

14   Pat Cooper, "NRO Opens Doors to U.S. Military," *Defense News,* August 19–25, 1996.

15   Twentieth Century Fund report, *In From the Cold,* New York: Twentieth Century Fund Press, 1996, pp. 35–37, 100–107.

16   See, for instance, General Accounting Office, *Operation Desert Storm: Evaluation of the Air Campaign,* Letter Report GAO/NSAID97-134, June 12, 1997.

The United States faced a similar dilemma in 1998 when it undertook cruise missile attacks in Sudan and Afghanistan after U.S. embassies had been bombed in Kenya and Tanzania. The target was alleged terrorist facilities associated with Osama bin Laden, but if the attacks killed many innocent people while the targets later appeared to be ambiguous, the United States ran the risk of seeming brutal or feckless or both. In 1999 when U.S. bombs mistakenly hit the Chinese embassy in Belgrade during NATO's campaign against Slobodan Milosevic over Kosovo, the diplomatic uproar risked distracting attention from Milosevic's ethnic cleansing.

Moreover, warriors trust pictures, not descriptions of pictures, which is hardly surprising. Yet getting pictures from national satellites to local commanders is no mean feat. It is expensive in the bandwidth of communication lines and so competes with a host of other communication needs. In particular, during Desert Storm there was not enough communications satellite capacity to serve all the users who wanted data.[17]

Intelligence's performance during the Gulf War was both praised and criticized. On the whole, military commanders praised satellite intelligence collection efforts but were dissatisfied with the intelligence analysis and dissemination. Former DCI Robert Gates conceded that "the 1991 Persian Gulf War exposed the huge processing and analytical problem that exists when the imagery product must be sent to where it's needed on a battlefield or for a policymaker."[18]

Moreover, on the battlefield the warriors didn't always understand and didn't trust what the "national" systems could do for them. General Norman Schwarzkopf, Desert Storm's commander, was eloquent, if perhaps overstated, on that score. He stopped short of open criticism of the intelligence collection systems but did roundly chastise the CIA's imagery analysis. During the conflict, Schwarzkopf charged that "battlefield damage assessments from national intelligence agencies during the Persian Gulf War were so hedged with qualifying remarks that they created serious confusion for commanders attempting to make wartime decisions."

Schwarzkopf, like other commanders, tended to trust the systems close at hand, ones he knew. He had more faith — misplaced, it turned

---

17   *Aviation Week and Space Technology*, April 22, 1991, p. 91.
18   Walter Pincus, "Another Intelligence Image Faces Change; CIA Chief Mulls Consolidating Analysis of Spy Satellite Pictures," *Washington Post*, October 15, 1995, p. A3.

out — in the damage assessments derived from pictures taken by *his* command's aircraft than in those derived from space satellites. After the war, testifying before the Senate Armed Services Committee in June 1991, he said that "based on some of the analysis that we were getting, we'd still be sitting over there waiting if we were dependent upon that [CIA] analysis." Battlefield damage assessment "was one of the major areas of confusion. . . . There were many people who felt that they were in a better position to judge battle damage assessment from photography and other sources, rather than allowing the theater commander, who is the person that really has to make the ultimate assessment, to apply good military judgment to what he is seeing." Moreover, intelligence was not relayed to senior officers on the ground in a timely, useful form. Schwarzkopf concluded that "the intelligence community should be asked to come up with a system that will, in fact, be capable of delivering a real-time product to a theater commander when he requests that."[19]

PLUS ÇA CHANGE, OR FORWARD TO THE PAST

In one sense, for intelligence to give primacy to supporting military operations is to march forward to the past. For most of history, when there has been intelligence, its purpose has been supporting war fighters. It was the stimulus of the turn from World War II toward the ensuing Cold War that challenged the military's monopoly over reconnaissance and led to the formation of the CIA. It is not so much that intelligence was demilitarized; rather it, and especially reconnaissance, became less tactical and more strategic, less strictly military and more national. That national purpose was, though, very much one of military security — keeping tabs on the Soviet Union and its military might.

The priority to the tactical has been markedly true of the shorter history of "aerial reconnaissance," as it was called prior to the development of satellites. Before satellites, the United States did that reconnaissance first using hot air and hydrogen-filled balloons and then with

19   Molly Moore, "Schwarzkopf: War Intelligence Flawed; General Reports to Congress on Desert Storm," *Washington Post,* June 13, 1991, p. A1. For the congressional report on intelligence during the war, see *Intelligence Successes and Failures in Operation Desert Shield/Storm,* Report of the Oversight and Investigation Subcommittee of the House Armed Services Committee, 103 Cong., 1 sess., 1993.

reconnaissance airplanes. Reconnaissance was strictly owned by the military and was used exclusively to support tactical military operations. There was no such thing as "strategic" aerial reconnaissance because the technology to accomplish it did not exist — no satellites or long-range, high-flying aircraft. It was only with the advent of intelligence gained from satellites that the more comprehensive label of "overhead reconnaissance" came into parlance.

Aerial reconnaissance in support of military operations, however, can be traced back to the Civil War. Union Army generals were the first commanders to put observers in balloons to spot the movements of Confederate forces and direct artillery fire.[20] Although the idea of taking photographs from the balloons was considered, it apparently never happened, and the balloon corps was disbanded shortly after the war. Given their attributes, airplanes soon supplanted other platforms for taking photos aloft, and the first airplane reconnaissance began as early as 1909. Within a few years after the Wright brothers flew their first plane at Kitty Hawk, military leaders on the battlefields of Europe during World War I were flying observers over enemy lines to obtain a tactical advantage. By the end of World War I, Britain was distributing as many as a million aerial photographs a month, and interpreting those photos was becoming a specialized military business.

With the end of World War I, the practice of aerial reconnaissance lapsed until the world next fell into war, World War II. It came of age during that war.[21] Germany began at the forefront, taking 4,000 photographs a day during one two-month period. All the major belligerents used aerial reconnaissance, but Japan used it mostly for mapping — a limitation the country later came to regret. As fighter aircraft improved, reconnaissance planes were forced higher, straining the resolution of lenses and exposing film to low temperatures — problems that prefigured those of the satellite era. In a war in which all the belligerents engaged in reconnaissance, what distinguished the more successful from the less was, in the words of one historian's assessment, not just "the ways they solved common technical problems [but also] the de-

20   See Amrom H. Katz, *Some Notes on the History of Aerial Reconnaissance*, P-3310, Santa Monica, CA: RAND, April 1966. He has a fascinating collection of references.

21   For a good, illustrated history, see Roy M. Stanley II, *World War II Photo Intelligence*, New York: Charles Scribner's Sons, 1981.

grees to which the resultant intelligence was integrated into their systems of military operations."[22]

If U.S. tactical intelligence was a great success in World War II, American strategic intelligence has to be counted a dismal failure. The Japanese attack on Pearl Harbor goes down as the greatest intelligence failure in American history — a failure that cast a long shadow over postwar intelligence arrangements. U.S. Army SIGINT had cracked the Purple Code, Japan's top diplomatic code. But cooperation between intelligence officers and military operators was ragged in both the Army and the Navy, and that between the services was more ragged still. The chief of naval operations didn't share information with Navy intelligence, and the U.S. ambassador in Tokyo didn't see MAGIC, as the decoded Japanese take was called, at all. MAGIC was brought to a small circle of officials and analysts but not left in their possession, so discerning patterns by noting changes in wording over time was more difficult.

The lack of sharing was compounded by the powerful biases carried in the heads of Americans, analysts and operators alike.[23] For instance, the Army saw the threat in sabotage terms, while others thought an attack was a very remote possibility. After all, Hawaii was a difficult target for Japan, and many of the signs of attack pointed southeast, not southwest toward Hawaii. Most important, virtually all official Americans shared a deep disdain for the Japanese and their military capabilities.

As often in the history of intelligence, mind-sets and convenience were mutually reinforcing: Japan wouldn't attack because it couldn't attack; perceptions of Japan's capabilities made an attack unrespectable. In the instance of India's nuclear tests in the late 1990s, the syllogism ran that India wouldn't test because it shouldn't test. Convenience was reinforced by a mind-set born of mirror imaging: What would we do if we were Indians? Perceptions of India's stakes made testing unwise,

22   Ibid., pp. 11–12.
23   The now classic source is Roberta Wohlstetter, *Pearl Harbor: Warning and Decision,* Stanford: Stanford University Press, 1962. See also Harold P. Ford, *Estimative Intelligence: The Purposes and Problems of National Intelligence Estimating,* Lanham, MD: University Press of America, 1993, pp. 9–18; and Monro MacCloskey, *The American Intelligence Community,* New York: Richards Rosen Press, 1967, pp. 42–47, 70–72.

just as perceptions of Japan's weakness had made an attack on Hawaii militarily unrespectable.

The end of World War II and the onset of the Cold War brought unprecedented changes in American intelligence. Pearl Harbor was still a fresh memory in Americans' minds, and preventing another surprise attack topped the agenda. The emergence of the Soviet Union as a rival superpower only reinforced the need for strategic warning as item number one on that agenda for intelligence. Military intelligence had been discredited by its failure at Pearl Harbor, a failure that led to a growing consensus that intelligence should not be solely the province of the uniformed military. When President Truman signed into law the National Security Act of 1947, creating the CIA, that action, in the words of a recent blue-ribbon panel, reflected "above all, his desire to avoid another Pearl Harbor."[24]

Given that the CIA's creation arose from Pearl Harbor and the failure of military intelligence, some rivalry between the new CIA and the military services was almost guaranteed. For the first time in America's history, intelligence was managed by a civilian agency, not a military one. Intelligence's prime consumers were civilian policy-makers, not just military leaders. Its mission was strategic warning first and support to military operations only second. While the present CIA is dominated by its clandestine service, with its analysts a distant second, in the early days the CIA was at the forefront of technical collection. Its early budgets were dominated by "metal bending" for technical collectors — the U-2 spy plane, the first reconnaissance satellites (code-named CORONA), and the SR-71 aircraft, in the form of its precursor, OXCART. It was only as technical collectors became big businesses in their own right that the CIA mostly ceded that mission to the stovepipes, though it retains a Directorate for Science and Technology (DS&T) and CIA officers continue to populate the NRO.

The president that presided over this Cold War transformation of intelligence was a military hero, Dwight D. Eisenhower, who captured the new attitude toward intelligence in drawing a distinction between the intelligence needs of a country at war and one at peace:

> In war nothing is more important to a commander than the facts concerning the strength, dispositions, and intentions of his opponent, and the proper interpretation of those facts. In peacetime, however, the necessary

24   See Aspin-Brown commission, *Preparing for the 21st Century,* Washington, D.C., March 1, 1996, appendix, pp. A–8 to A–10.

facts are of a different nature. They deal with conditions, resources, requirements, and attitudes prevailing in the world. They are essential to the development of policy to further our long-term national security and best interests.[25]

COLD WAR RECONNAISSANCE: WHO CONTROLS?

It was in this atmosphere that intelligence satellites were born. The Cold War was on, the memory of surprise attack was still vivid, and fears of the preeminent enemy were paramount. All this ensured that, despite fighting in Korea, overhead reconnaissance during the Cold War would not be controlled by the uniformed military. The question of control, though, was first posed not by satellites but by the U-2 spy plane.

In the early 1950s, the Air Force sought bids from aircraft designers for a reconnaissance jet that had long range and could fly high enough to avoid enemy surface-to-air missiles (SAMs). Lockheed's famed "Skunk Works" (formally, the Advanced Development Projects Group), though not officially asked, submitted a bid based on the F-104 fighter with radically lengthened wings and a modified undercarriage. The Air Force rejected the proposal in favor of two competing designs, but the CIA gave Lockheed $22 million to build the first prototype. Only eight months later, the first U-2 spy plane took its maiden test flight.[26] Its first mission was in August 1955.

At a cost of less than $1 million each, the U-2 was able to fly over the entire Soviet Union with impunity. By contrast, the Air Force's best reconnaissance plane, the RB-47, could only safely penetrate a few hundred miles into Soviet airspace. After the first trials of the U-2 demonstrated its ability to complete its mission, the U-2 operation was given to the CIA over the objections of the Air Force, which desperately wanted control of the plane and its mission.[27] Not even General Curtis

25   Quoted in Monro MacCloskey, *The American Intelligence Community*, New York: Richards Rosen Press, 1967, p. 7.
26   Curtis Peebles, *Guardians: Strategic Reconnaissance Satellites*, Novato, CA: Presidio Press, 1987, pp. 16–19.
27   David Wise and Thomas B. Ross, *The U-2 Affair*, New York: Random House, 1962, pp. 47–48.

LeMay, a wartime legend and dominant figure in Washington, could rescue the U-2 for the Air Force.[28]

But the U-2's days as a strategic reconnaissance platform were numbered as soon as it rolled out. With the development of the Soviet high-altitude SA-2 SAM, even the high-flying U-2 was becoming vulnerable to Soviet missiles — a fact tragically driven home by the shooting down of Francis Gary Powers's U-2 over Russia in May 1960. The U-2 had served its purpose — indeed, a single mission would have justified the program, and the U-2s flew 24 missions[29] — but what happened to the Powers flight underscored the urgent need for reconnaissance satellites that could conduct surveillance of the Soviet Union without risk of being shot down.

Satellites had been first considered for reconnaissance in a report entitled *Preliminary Design of an Experimental World-Circling Spaceship,* which the Army received in 1946 from a spin-off of Douglas Aircraft that eventually became The RAND Corporation. The report suggested that satellites could perform the overhead surveillance mission; they would be invulnerable to SAMs or fighter jets because of their high altitude and tremendous speed.[30] In 1955, a presidential technological capabilities panel headed by James R. Killian, Jr., submitted a report to Eisenhower entitled *Meeting the Threat of a Surprise Attack.* The report was a strong brief for developing reconnaissance aircraft and satellites:

> If intelligence can uncover a new military threat, we may take steps to meet it. If intelligence can reveal an opponent's specific weakness, we may prepare to exploit it. With good intelligence we can avoid wasting

28   William Burrows quotes Richard Bissel from a direct interview in "Satellite Reconnaissance and the Establishment of a National Technical Intelligence Apparatus," *The Intelligence Revolution: A Historical Perspective,* Proceedings of the Thirteenth U.S. Air Force Academy Military History Symposium, Washington, D.C.: Office of Air Force History, 1991, p. 235.

29   See Paul Lashmar, *Spy Flights of the Cold War,* Annapolis, MD: Naval Institute Press, 1996, p. 154.

30   William Burrows quotes Richard Bissel from a direct interview in "Satellite Reconnaissance and the Establishment of a National Technical Intelligence Apparatus," *The Intelligence Revolution: A Historical Perspective,* Proceedings of the Thirteenth U.S. Air Force Academy Military History Symposium, Washington, D.C.: Office of Air Force History, 1991, p. 234.

our resources by arming for the wrong danger at the wrong time. Beyond this, in the broadest sense intelligence underlies our estimate of the enemy and thus helps to guide our political strategy.[31]

While the strategic argument for reconnaissance satellites was plain enough, American scientists and engineers suffered a frustrating series of failures in their efforts to launch a successful photographic satellite, a failure made all the more frustrating when Russia launched Sputnik in October 1957. It was not until August 1960 that the first American reconnaissance satellite, Discoverer 13, was launched as part of the CIA program code-named CORONA. The first image was a Soviet airfield, and the program lasted a dozen years, until 1972.[32]

There was no real debate in the 1960s over how intelligence satellites should be used. All agreed that imagery should primarily be used to provide intelligence on strategic targets, especially Soviet military ones, to better understand the nature of the threat and work toward providing adequate warning of any Soviet attack. There was debate, however, on whether the CIA or the Air Force should manage the new satellite systems. At the time CORONA was launched, the Air Force was fiercely competing with the CIA to develop its own system, known as the Satellite and Missile Observation System, or SAMOS.[33] Indeed, the bureaucratic battle over who would control satellite reconnaissance made the conflict between the Air Force and the CIA over the U-2 look pretty tame.

For the Air Force, fending off CIA attempts to control overhead reconnaissance was no mere question of turf. It seemed a matter of doing the Air Force's job. The Air Force reasoned that it was the responsibility of the Strategic Air Command (SAC), not the CIA, to destroy enemy targets, and therefore it should be SAC that had the responsibility to locate those targets and determine what the Air Force would need to attack them. The Air Force, and its predecessor, the Army Air Corps, had

31   William Burrows in "Satellite Reconnaissance and the Establishment of a National Technical Intelligence Apparatus," *The Intelligence Revolution: A Historical Perspective,* Proceedings of the Thirteenth U.S. Air Force Academy Military History Symposium, Washington, D.C.: Office of Air Force History, 1991, pp. 234–235.

32   For the declassified history of CORONA, see History Staff, *CORONA: America's First Satellite Program,* Washington, D.C.: Central Intelligence Agency, 1995.

33   Curtis Peebles, *Guardians: Strategic Reconnaissance Satellites,* Novato, CA: Presidio Press, 1987, p. 86.

always controlled the aerial reconnaissance and photo-interpretation missions; it was steadfast in its belief that the CIA could not duplicate its expertise, developed over years of practice in war fighting. The Air Force was bound to see the CIA's attempts to control satellite reconnaissance as, in the words of General George Keegan, one-time head of Air Force Intelligence, "dangerous, politically motivated . . . incursions that went back to the agency's founding in 1947."[34] In Keegan's words again:

> The Air Force strategic reconnaissance requirement in the 1950s and the 1960s was driven by the needs of its own targeters, as well as those officers on the air staff who were responsible for assessing the intentions of their opposite numbers in the Warsaw Pact, and specifically as those intentions related to the numbers of Soviet military aircraft and their capabilities."[35]

Since analysis of photos from the new satellites would bulk so large in determining America's Cold War military requirements, the Air Force was determined that it, and not the CIA, should control the analysis and thus shape the requirements. Keegan said as much in an interview: "The Air Staff was convinced that its photo interpreters, not those in another service, and certainly not in the CIA, were best suited to analyze other air forces."[36]

The stakes were high. The ultimate purpose of intelligence is to shape the way policy-makers see the world. For many issues, intelligence would have competition from State Department political reporters or foreign correspondents, or the policy-makers' own experiences. Not so, though, for Soviet missiles and military might. Intelligence would assess threats in terms both of numbers and capabilities, and so play a crucial role in how the United States responded to those threats, all without ever trespassing on the domain of "policy." Intelligence thus went to the heart of military preparedness.

34 General George Keegan, former head of Air Force intelligence and the Air Intelligence Agency, in an interview with William Burrows in "Satellite Reconnaissance and the Establishment of a National Technical Intelligence Apparatus," *The Intelligence Revolution: A Historical Perspective,* Proceedings of the Thirteenth U.S. Air Force Academy Military History Symposium, Washington, D.C.: Office of Air Force History, 1991, p. 235.
35 Ibid., p. 236.
36 Ibid., pp. 234–235.

To resolve the contention between the Air Force and the CIA, in August 1960 Eisenhower approved a National Security Council (NSC) plan to have space surveillance managed jointly by the Department of Defense and CIA under a new organization known as the National Reconnaissance Office (NRO), whose existence remained an official secret until 1992. The system relied on shared control, with the Pentagon and the CIA contributing personnel. The NRO was lodged in the Pentagon, under an assistant secretary of the Air Force, but the shared control prevented the Air Force from controlling space reconnaissance and surveillance, which was precisely the idea.[37]

Eisenhower sided with the CIA in this battle, just as he had earlier given it the CORONA program, mostly because he knew the Air Force well enough not to trust it. He is said to have "wanted to make damn sure" that the Air Force did not control NRO.[38] By the time of his famous farewell speech, he was warning the nation against the military-industrial complex — the military services plus the U.S. defense industry becoming self-serving to the point of concern in their judgments of threats and their framing of hardware requirements.

Eisenhower's immediate mistrust was understandable, for as president he had already been through one gap, the famous "bomber gap" in the Soviet favor that had turned out not to exist. Once burned, he was all the more wary of the Air Force tailoring estimates of the Soviet Union to suit the service's interests in new systems. His second term ended with Democratic charges of "missile gap." That gap also turned out not to exist, but the time lapse between the shooting down of Powers and the first photographs from the CORONA program meant that it was not until the Kennedy administration that satellite imagery confirmed American superiority. Eisenhower, though, knew enough to beware of giving the Air Force control over determining the extent of the strategic threat.[39]

37   Ibid., pp. 236–237.
38   Jeffrey T. Richelson, *America's Secret Eyes in Space: The U.S. Keyhole Spy Satellite Program,* New York: Harper and Row, 1990, pp. 46–47.
39   William Burrows in "Satellite Reconnaissance and the Establishment of a National Technical Intelligence Apparatus," *The Intelligence Revolution: A Historical Perspective,* Proceedings of the Thirteenth U.S. Air Force Academy Military History Symposium, Washington, D.C.: Office of Air Force History, 1991, pp. 236–237.

Yet despite the shared control, Eisenhower's decisions and the creation of the NRO left the satellites themselves belonging to the Pentagon, paid for out of the Defense Department budget. The civilian intelligence community, the CIA in particular, had a role, particularly in the tasking of what the satellites would photograph. Yet as long as the Pentagon "owned" the satellite infrastructure, control of overhead reconnaissance could shift back to the pre–World War II state of affairs, with tactical and operational purposes dominating.

NATIONAL AND TACTICAL: NEW MISSIONS FOR OLD SYSTEMS

It took the end of the Cold War to produce that shift. The enormous satellite system remained, but its mission, keeping tabs on the Soviet Union, had ended. The Cold War's end gave new missions to old intelligence systems acquired for other reasons. Supporting military operations was one obvious area in which puzzles remained and will continue to exist. Enemy units do not send announcements of their positions. Americans and their allies who venture into harm's way will depend on puzzle solving where secrets matter.

The major action of R. James Woolsey's tenure as director of central intelligence (DCI), from 1993 to 1995, was reshaping intelligence's satellite architecture.[40] One aim was to cut costs and reduce the duplication that had been produced by the desire of every service — not just the Air Force and the CIA, but the Navy as well — not to be left out of space. Thus, the total number of satellites was to be cut, and the number of ground stations cut still further.

The specifics of the debate, however, were ultimately driven by the requirement of precise geolocation for American warriors. The particular issues were how many SIGINT satellites and in which kind of orbit, highly elliptical (HEO) or geosynchronous. Geosynchronous satellites, fixed over particular points on the earth's surface, have the advantage of being able to dwell on particular points. Civilian analysts preoccupied with "national" purposes wanted to listen to the content of particular communications, COMINT, and for that purpose, having fewer satellites in geosynchronous orbits was good enough, provided they had access to the communication lines in question.

40   See John D. Morrocco, "CIA Slashing Satellite Network," *Aviation Week and Space Technology*, 142, 3, January 16, 1995, p. 64.

For the war-fighters, by contrast, what was more important is called electronics intelligence, or ELINT — not the content of conversations but signals identifying technical characteristics of units or weapons *and* their location. For that purpose, having more satellites is better, just as earlier ocean navigators could learn more about their location by triangulating from several stars. HEO satellites have some additional technical advantages. In the end, the war fighters triumphed over the budget cutters, and the architecture comprised more satellites, including HEO ones.

In parallel, the intelligence debate after Desert Storm had piqued congressional interest in the overlap of strategic and tactical and of civilian and military intelligence. Shortly after Schwarzkopf's testimony, David Boren (D-Oklahoma), the chairman of the Senate Select Committee on Intelligence (SSCI) asserted that

> Two separate empires have been built up over the years — civilian intelligence and military intelligence . . . with a lot of duplication and overlap. We just can't afford it any more [and] we've got to force them together for budgetary reasons. . . . [Therefore,] civilian intelligence will be called on increasingly to collect more of the kind of information the military needs and put it in a form that a military commander can use if he has to act on it in a hurry. . . . We've really got to blend these two cultures in a much more effective way. . . . Each side has some reason for distrusting the other, but we've got to bring them more closely together.[41]

The cultural divide between intelligence and the military was, however, both deep and of long standing. For many intelligence professionals, a merger of military and civilian functions would be a shotgun marriage. For their parts, many of the military were like Schwarzkopf but more so, distrustful of the civilian agencies. They wouldn't ask them to do anything. They wouldn't really know what they were capable of doing.[42] In 1991, a Senate committee had noted the gap between tactical and strategic reconnaissance. Its report concluded that because of the mistrust between the military and the intelligence community, "the tactical and national intelligence communities appeared to be ex-

---

41   George Lardner, Jr., "Intelligence Overhaul Urged; Agencies Could Be Compelled to Cooperate," *Washington Post*, February 6, 1992, p. A1.

42   George Lardner, Jr., "In A Changing World, CIA Reorganizing to Do More with Less," *Washington Post*, July 5, 1991, p. A9.

cessively isolated from one another, leaving each free to pursue self-sufficiency in their particular realms."[43]

NIMA: CREATING AN IMAGERY STOVEPIPE

At the same time, and also spurred by Desert Storm, official Washington began talking in earnest about another idea that was not new — creating a counterpart to NSA for imagery by consolidating the various intelligence imagery efforts into one agency. The idea was controversial from the start. Most intelligence professionals, such as then DCI Gates, recognized the weaknesses in the existing photo-reconnaissance system. The lack of reliable coordination between NRO satellite builders and IMINT producers resulted in cost overruns, and weak connections between those producers and imagery users at times left the military in the dark about what kind of intelligence was available. Gates convened a panel of intelligence officials that strongly recommended creating a single agency to build and operate the satellites *and* process the results. This would have created a stovepipe more consolidated than NSA by giving NRO's responsibility for building and operating IMINT "birds" to the new agency.

Gates conceded the shortcomings that had elicited Schwarzkopf's criticism during the Persian Gulf War, but for him those criticisms had to do with delivery of tactical reconnaissance to the military and not with the community's imagery program in general.[44] He was wary of too much control of imagery by the military and thus wanted the CIA — which then ran Washington's premier imagery analysts, the National Photographic Interpretation Center (NPIC) — to retain both analysts and access to coverage for "national" purposes. For him, "combining tactical and national reconnaissance programs in a single agency . . . might result in contagion in the wrong direction . . . [so] it would be best to wait for the Defense Department to strengthen the tactical program first."[45]

In the end, Gates settled for the Central Imagery Office (CIO), a much smaller organization and one part of the Defense Department but located at CIA headquarters. In practice, the CIO did little more than

43   Ibid.
44   George Lardner, Jr., "Gates Rejects Overhaul of Spy Agencies; CIA Head to Install 'Evolutionary' Plan," *Washington Post*, April 2, 1992, p. A4.
45   Ibid.

try to solve one of Desert Storm's imagery shortcomings by serving as a focal point for tasking the various IMINT collectors. The CIA's NPIC retained the community's largest cadre of imagery analysts, and other agencies, especially in the military, also had their own IMINT analysts. It was Gates's successor, John Deutch, moving from deputy secretary of defense to DCI, who proposed at his confirmation in May 1995 "to consolidate the nation's disparate spy satellite efforts into a single National Imagery Agency."[46]

Again there was opposition and again for the same reasons. For instance, Senator Bob Kerrey (D-Nebraska), vice chairman of the Senate Intelligence Committee, believed "the proposed merger would be a big mistake" if it led to less political and diplomatic coverage. Furthermore, a senior congressional intelligence expert asserted that "members of the House and Senate did not oppose the idea of the combined imagery agency but had 'concerns' that by being controlled more by [the] Pentagon, it would support military operations and that national intelligence support to policy-makers would be taking a back bench." Legislators were worried, despite reassurances from Deutch, that the agency "would not serve national interests."[47]

CIA officers, in particular, echoed related concerns that if the CIA lost its photo interpreters to a defense agency, it would also lose its ability to task and interpret imagery for nonmilitary purposes. As one was reported to have put it:

> A consolidation could reduce the close controls [the CIA has] exercised over satellite coverage. . . . During Cold War days, for example, the CIA would order detailed satellite photos of Moscow to plot out drops where agents could pick up secret messages. Or when the communists were thought to be infiltrating guerrillas into East African countries, CIA officers could make a "critical" request to send a bird over Ethiopia to see what was going on. We got the raw film, processed it and our analysts read it with enormous skill.[48]

46   R. Jeffery Smith, "Deutch Is Confirmed Without Senate Dissent: New CIA Chief to Move on Shake Up," *Washington Post, May 10, 1995,* p. A6.

47   Walter Pincus, "The Federal Page — CIA, Pentagon Back NIMA Concept, "Combining Spy Satellite Photo Units," *Washington Post,* November 29, 1995, p. A23.

48   Walter Pincus, "Another Intelligence Image Faces Change; CIA Chief Mulls Consolidating Analysis of Spy Satellite Pictures," *Washington Post,* October 15, 1995, p. A3.

There was no question about where Deutch stood. As deputy secretary of defense, he had controlled the Pentagon's spy satellite operations and viewed support for war fighters as imagery's primary mission. Deutch's goal was "to provide the military commander so much information so quickly that U.S. forces will have a unique dominant battlefield awareness."[49] He believed that

> the Gulf War made clear the tremendous potential of technical intelligence in support of military operations. . . . The critical user [of imagery] is the Defense Department because technical intelligence is so important to support military operations. When we buy a new satellite system . . . it usually is to meet a predominant military need. Defense is not [however] the sole user of satellite capabilities. The department of State, the National Security Council, and the CIA are also important customers. Thus while military needs drive NRO systems, the particular needs of other users must be accommodated as well.[50]

Deutch and then Secretary of Defense William Perry sought to address concerns about the new organization, adjusting the plans for NIMA. In November 1995, Perry proposed a joint space management board designed to allow "one-stop shopping" for adjudicating the disputes over imagery that the previous fractionated structure (the Defense Department, NRO, and intelligence agencies) had been unable to resolve.[51] When NIMA formally came into being, in October 1996, it had a customer advisory board cochaired by the vice chair of the National Intelligence Council (NIC) and the deputy director for operations (DDO) of the joint staff (J-38). Perry's management board had become a senior steering group co-chaired by the undersecretary of defense for acquisitions, the vice chair of the joint chiefs of staff, and the deputy director of central intelligence (DDCI). NIMA's creation left untouched NRO's role as satellite acquirer and operator.[52]

49　Walter Pincus, "Another Intelligence Image Faces Change; CIA Chief Mulls Consolidating Analysis of Spy Satellite Pictures," *Washington Post*, October 15, 1995, p. A3.

50　DCI John Deutch, "The Future of the NRO," speech at ARPATech 96 18th S&T Symposium, Atlanta, May 22, 1996.

51　Joseph Anselmo, "Pentagon Approval of Space Board Nears," *Aviation Week and Space Technology*, November 27, 1995. The fourth member of the board was originally to be Keith Hall, who at the time was executive director for the intelligence community staff.

52　Jeffrey Richelson, "Spook World Unveils New Imagery Agency," *Defense Week*, December 4, 1995.

NIMA did consolidate elements from the eleven military and civilian agencies that did their own imagery analysis. A Pentagon agency, it gathered more than 10,000 people, most prominently including the entire Defense Mapping Agency and the CIA's NPIC. It also included the analytic department of the CIO plus the imagery departments from the Defense Intelligence Agency (DIA), the Defense Airborne Reconnaissance Office (which controls unmanned vehicles used to take battlefield photos), the imagery analysts maintained by the separate services and the joint staff, and similar elements based in worldwide military commands.[53]

Notwithstanding the reassurances from Deutch and Perry, NIMA's creation did signal the transition to SMO as the principal intelligence mission. Eisenhower's approach of three decades earlier was being reversed. Instead of civilian, "national" purposes retaining primacy, they would become secondary to supporting military operations. Instead of control over satellite reconnaissance being shared between military and civilian intelligence agencies, military concerns would dominate. The shift raises a host of issues. These include which systems and at what cost, but the preeminent one is mission: What is intelligence for?

WHICH SYSTEMS, AT WHAT COST?

At a minimum, the militarization of intelligence will raise questions of trade-offs and hence of cost. The existing satellite constellation, designed for the Soviet target, has proven adaptable but is hardly ideal for the new SMO purposes. Ideally, technology supporting info-warriors should be able to loiter over targets and transmit images of the battlefield in real time. Satellites, however, whiz by targets at thousands of miles an hour, spending only minutes watching any given point of interest to the warriors. In addition, since satellites are many miles above their targets, their cameras must trade area for resolution; that is, they can "look" roughly at larger areas or sharply at smaller ones, but not both.

This trade-off between resolution and search area also forces a trade-off between missions. Military planners usually want a view over large

53   Walter Pincus, "Another Intelligence Image Faces Change; CIA Chief Mulls Consolidating Analysis of Spy Satellite Pictures," *Washington Post*, October 15, 1995, p. A3.

areas in order to locate major weaponry or enemy formations, while national analysts verifying arms control or hunting for nefarious weapons in the hands of rogue states often are interested in getting a close look at a particular object, for instance a North Korean No Dong missile. However, the two purposes — called wide-area and high-resolution imagery, respectively — are incompatible because they require different technology, both for taking images and for transmitting them back to ground stations.

For many SMO purposes, unmanned drones, or unmanned aerial vehicles (UAVs), and small satellites will do better than expensive satellites.[54] UAVs can loiter over targets for 24 hours or even more. How low they fly is determined mostly by how much risk the United States is willing to take that they will be destroyed by enemy fire from the ground. In any event, their altitudes are measured in thousands of feet, not the tens of thousands or miles needed for satellites, so the trade-off between area search and resolution is less sharp for them than for satellites. UAVs cost a fraction of the $1 billion-plus bill for a satellite.

However, UAVs are also vulnerable in a way satellites are not. Few nations can do anything about satellites flying many miles above their territory, so over time this lack of alternatives has turned into reluctant acquiescence, which has softened into tacit acceptance. Now hardly anyone complains about satellites as an infringement of national sovereignty. Drones, however, operate inside a nation's airspace, and airspace is plainly a different matter, if only because nations can do something about it. In shooting wars, international law would count for little, and the concern that UAVs might create ill will would be replaced with worry that they might be shot at and hit. So drones are likely to be most useful in ambiguous situations that might or might not turn into wars. And it would be precisely at such times that diplomatic sensitivities would be the sharpest — imagine the argument inside Washington if, in the late summer and early fall of 1990, intelligence had proposed sending up drones to keep tabs on Saddam Hussein's military exercises.

Small satellites are another possibility. These "cheap sats" could combine some of the advantages of drones and of satellites without en-

---

54 For a nice, now slightly dated summary of possible UAV roles in intelligence, see Richard A. Best, Jr., "Intelligence Technology in the Post-Cold War Era: The Role of Unmanned Aerial Vehicles (UAVs)," Congressional Research Service, July 26, 1993.

tailing the enormous costs of today's satellites. In the early days of satellites, launching them was a significant fraction of the cost. As a result, today's models, dubbed "Battlestar Galactica" by insider wags, are hugely expensive platforms playing host to many different sensor systems. But the cost of putting payloads in orbit has been declining. Thus, the United States might build and stockpile satellites to be launched when circumstances dictated. These new satellites could be built for a specific purpose, then launched into an orbit chosen to match that purpose. Costs will go up as the small sats get larger, with more sensors, but they still could be inexpensive by comparison to today's models.

Drones and cheap sats could serve what have been regarded as "national" purposes, such as supplying information on a rogue state's missile test facilities or even a terrorist training camp. But these purposes would also be of interest to warriors if, for instance, cruise missile targeteers wanted to hit the test facilities, and the most probable uses of UAVs and small satellites would be to support warriors directly by locating artillery or enemy columns on the battlefield.

The militarization of intelligence is, in principle, open-ended: It will always be possible to provide more precise and useful information to American warriors. The availability of precise information is in fact key to certain military decisions. For instance, the lack of specific intelligence is a principal reason why U.S. special operations forces, such as the Delta force, have so seldom been used against terrorists despite having been created for that purpose. Special operators would like to know, in the words of one intelligence official, not just where the entrance to the terrorist headquarters is but which side the knob is on. Lacking that detail, the United States usually decides not to risk sending U.S. soldiers into harm's way; instead it employs what another official called "TLAM therapy" — cruise missile attacks.

Given this open-ended potential for intelligence in supporting warriors, the question is, At what point does the cost become too high? During the Cold War when the Soviet Union was the overriding threat, it was hard to settle for less than the best, but the quest to learn as much as possible about the Soviet Union provided spillover capability that could be used for other purposes. Without such an overarching threat, should the United States settle at a point short of what is technically possible? Existing systems represent impressive technical achievements, and replacing them will be expensive, even with more use of UAVs or cheap sats. A number of DCIs and NSA directors have complained about how much satellites cost. While neither of the NRO's troubles with Congress during the 1990s (over a $350 million headquarters and a several billion dollar contingency fund) was very important in and of itself, both reflected the legacy of operating during the Cold War, when cost was only a secondary consideration.[55]

Over the longer term, the continuing assistance, if not the existence, of both IMINT and SIGINT will come into question. In the case of IMINT, the question will be competition. Within a decade, sophisticated imagery technology will be widely available on the open market. Would-be foes or targets of the United States will be able to buy images if not systems of their own. They will be able to see what they look like from satellites or the sky and take measures to conceal the activities they want to keep secret or deceive the United States about what is going on. Recall that U.S. intelligence failed to warn of the 1998 Indian nuclear tests in part because India had earlier been shown U.S. imagery and so had some idea what to hide. As a result, India kept the level of activity at the test site high for weeks before the tests so that U.S. imagery analysts would not be able to note any change in the immediate prelude to the tests.

Already, commercial firms offer imagery that is nearly as good as that provided by U.S. intelligence. One measure of quality is resolution — that is, how small can something be and still be seen and generally identified? In a 1-meter image of the U.S. Congress, cars in the parking lots would be clearly identifiable, but their specific makes could not be detected.[56] People could be seen, usually because of their shadows, but not identified. One-meter resolution has been a kind of watershed for U.S. intelligence; by contrast, 3-meter resolution technology had been

55 On the headquarters affair, see *Washington Post,* October 6, 1994, p. A29.

56 A bridge, for instance, can be detected by an image of 6-meter resolution, identified generally by 4- to 5-meter resolution, precisely identified at 1 to 2, described at 1, and analyzed in detail only at 0.3. For an aircraft, comparable numbers might be 4 to 5, 1 to 2, 1, 0.2, and 0.05. See Vipin Gupta, "New Satellite Images for Sale," *International Security,* 20, 1, Summer 1995, p. 109.

licensed for commercial sale by the U.S. Commerce Department as early as the mid-1990s.[57]

Still, the virtues of 1-meter imagery or less should not be oversold, nor should the advantages of access to it be dramatized. Potential buyers who would use the information for military purposes will seek control; they will want to receive images secretly and use them with confidentiality. However, the first transfers will come with restrictions attached — for instance, government regulators of sellers will try to reserve "shutter control," giving those governments the right to cut off buyers in a crisis. But buyers will push for coproduction, then technology transfer, and the conditions imposed on both will become harder and harder to enforce. The United States could continue to have advantages over other nations through its ability to rapidly retarget and integrate imagery into tactical battle plans, but those advantages will be of a different sort than in the past.

SIGINT faces even sharper challenges, from digitizing, packet switching, fiber optics, and encryption. Digitizing makes it possible to send huge amounts of information over a single channel and thus vastly compounds the challenge of sorting out particular communications of interest. Packet switching means that the routing of a message may be changed in the middle of a communication and that the addressee of a message can be sent in a different packet from the message itself. With the improvement in cable transmission made possible through fiber optics, many fewer messages are sent into the open air, where satellites or ground stations can intercept them. If SIGINT is to be useful in the future, it will have to get physically close to the communications channels it seeks to intercept.

With privately developed, inexpensive encryption software, it will soon be possible for anyone to buy essentially unbreakable coding systems at the local Radio Shack. Less sophisticated nations will make mistakes, and the pressures of war will lure opponents into shortcuts that let their messages be read. But encryption will more and more limit SIGINT to what is called "traffic analysis" — keeping track of when and where messages are being sent — useful intelligence to be sure, but not as useful as knowing the content of the messages. Moreover, sheer

57   Russia sold images with 2- to 3-meter resolution and was prepared to sell still better imagery. See James R. Asker, "High Resolution Imagery Seen as a Threat, Opportunity," *Aviation Week and Space Technology*, May 23, 1994, p. 51.

volume and packet switching also make traffic analysis much harder. In a 1999 report on the budget, the House intelligence committee declared that "NSA is in serious trouble. . . . Money and priority alone will not revive NSA, nor the overall [SIGINT] system."[58]

Already, the mismatch between where SIGINT puts it resources and where its intelligence is produced is enormous. The exact percentages are classified, but satellite collectors consume the majority of the resources, while ground stations, most of them clandestine, produce the bulk of the intelligence. In war, urgent need will tempt opponents to use simpler communications, easier to intercept and decode, and so increase the output from resources used by satellite collectors. But this gain will be offset by the fact that American info-warriors will need ever quicker answers. "It was *there* five minutes ago" may have been good enough for those warriors in Desert Storm when they confronted an Iraqi tank column; it will not be nearly good enough for their counterparts in 2015 facing threats from fifth-generation Scud missiles.

OWNED BY WHOM?

There is a certain irony to the current state of affairs, in which SMO dominates technical collection, but battlefield commanders, like General Schwarzkopf, do not feel they own the collectors. In a sense, the Defense Department always has owned those systems. The budgets for them reside in the defense budget. More than four-fifths of the nation's intelligence budget is executed by agencies such as NSA, most of them in the Pentagon, that are not controlled by the DCI, who has no line authority over personnel other than the CIA's.[59] In the 1970s, the White House proposed to give control of the big technical collectors to the DCI. Then Secretary of Defense Donald Rumsfeld replied, in effect if not in fact: "If they're in my budget, I'll run them."[60] Over time, DCIs have been given a broader mandate to "coordinate" all the intelligence

---

58 See Vernon Loeb, "Back Channels: The Intelligence Community to the Woodshed," *Washington Post,* July 17, 1999, p. A17. For a somewhat overheated but largely accurate account of the challenges confronting NSA, see Seymour M. Hersh, "The Intelligence Gap: How the Digital Age Left Our Spies Out in the Cold," *The New Yorker,* December 6, 1999, pp. 58–76.

59 Aspin-Brown commission, *Preparing for the 21st Century,* Washington, D.C., March 1, 1996, p. xix.

60 Quoted in *Washington Post,* March 17, 1995, p. A1.

agencies but without getting much more real authority to run them or even much capacity to conduct independent analysis.

The irony has been compounded because it has seldom been easy to figure out who is in charge. The United States has had, and continues to have, a director of military intelligence — in effect, the secretary of defense, given his control of the major technical collectors. Taking the DCI's perspective, I always assumed that DCIs had trouble exercising influence over those collectors because secretaries of defense would not concede it. However, recent interviews with Pentagon budgeters have suggested they held the obverse view: They felt they were frozen out because the DCI was in control. Thus, managers of the collection stovepipes may have carved out considerable autonomy for themselves, while DCIs and the Pentagon each thought the other was paying attention.

The confusion runs all the way up through both Pentagon and intelligence organizations. Those, for instance, who design spy satellites and those who design precision-guided weapons work in separate compartments, isolated by walls of ignorance and classification. Given the current arrangements, it is virtually impossible to conceive of the task from sensor to weapon on target.[61] Thus, it is only a happy accident if weapons' capacity to hit targets matches intelligence's ability to find them. Because there is too little cross-communication, critical trade-offs are never posed, much less made. Weapons, such as the Tomahawk cruise missile or the F-117 Stealth fighter, often emerge from the military's operational experience without enough attention to what intelligence will be needed for their effective use. Weapons designers are tempted to assume that the intelligence their designs require will be there; thus, weapons frequently need costly fixes when that turns out not to be the case. Or designers assume a standard intelligence package and design accordingly, only to discover later that spending a little more

61   On these issues, see a clutch of RAND publications: Myron Hura and Gary McLeod, *Ensuring Adequate Intelligence Support for the Acquisition of New Weapon Systems*, DB-125-CMS, 1995, and *Intelligence Support and Mission Planning for Autonomous Precision-Guided Weapons: Implications for Intelligence Support Plan Development*, MR-230-AF, 1993; John Birkler et al., *A Framework for Precision Conventional Strike in Post–Cold War Military Strategy*, MR-743-CRMAF, 1996.

to create better intelligence could have saved big money in the design of the weapons themselves.

National intelligence needs a focal point. Thus, it may be time to recognize the Pentagon's control over the big technical collection systems. Better to ensure that *someone* is in control than to leave things as they are now. If the big national systems are to support warriors, they should be managed by and for the Pentagon. The logic of having the Pentagon control intelligence for the info-warriors would be to overturn the efforts to give DCIs more control over the national collection agencies — efforts that include the recent commission reports on intelligence, all of which repeat the ritual calls for more power for the DCI. In any case, technology is blurring the distinction between "national" and "tactical," so it makes little sense to separate the national budget, which is overseen if not really controlled by the DCI, from the TIARA budget, which remains the province of the secretary of defense.[62]

The change would recognize intelligence's preeminent mission in the world beyond the Cold War and would put someone in charge of it. Tactical commanders would come to better understand what they could and could not expect from the national collection systems, an understanding that will become more important as technology permits them to see the battlefield afar. With luck, the shift might impel intelligence architects and weapons designers to work together, making trade-offs between what sensors can see and shooters can hit.

SERVING INTELLIGENCE'S NATIONAL PURPOSES

The shortcoming of this defense-secretary-run structure is that it would turn DCIs into special pleaders for national missions. Deprived of any handle on the big collectors, they would surely lose. Yet, DCIs cannot run those collectors; the shift toward SMO does not make it logical, and the Pentagon's ownership of the collectors' infrastructure would not permit it in any case. There is no practical alternative to some form of joint suzerainty of the DCI and the defense secretary over the collection barons as the intelligence confederation becomes still looser.

---

62 See John Hollister Hedley, *Checklist for the Future of Intelligence*, Occasional Paper, Georgetown University Institute for the Study of Diplomacy, 1995, p. 12.

In the future as in the past, much will depend on how well those suzerains work together. The Cold War's implicit balance between them was upset by the disappearance of the great national target and the reemergence of SMO. Then, the DCI's chairing of the interagency committees for tasking the collectors, such as the SIGINT committee, provided a kind of counterweight to the Pentagon's ownership of the hardware. It was the secretary's toys but the DCI's game. Their shared rule continues to suffer from weak instruments for evaluating collection programs and connecting those to what consumers need. Providing more such capacity is imperative; it is a subject of chapter 7.

Consolidating imagery in NIMA, an end-to-end organization, should permit better choices among satellite and aircraft reconnaissance capabilities, as well as making it clearer to users, especially military users, exactly where and how to get their needs into the system. The downside is that consolidation will also create yet another durable stovepipe; making choices within IMINT will be made easier at the price of making trade-offs between IMINT and the other collectors harder.

For the near future, the shift to SMO is one of sunk costs: The systems already exist. The systems themselves are flexible enough that "national" purposes, such as tracking would-be proliferators, can continue to be served, but they become the spillovers, reversing the Cold War's order. Over the longer term, however, the militarization of intelligence will raise issues of *which purposes* are to be served. Already, there is competition for, say, satellite images during crises, when satellites are diverted from customary routines. Now, satellites take many more images than can be processed. But if systems were fewer and more specialized, the competition would be sharper.

The risks of the shift to SMO are that the concentration on the military will drive out important "national" purposes and that the focus on the tactical will drive out attention to the strategic. As one of my former colleagues (ironically, one who works in the world of open sources) put it: "We all work for the Pentagon now." Nothing wrong with that. It is a mission that sells. But it is not intelligence's only mission. Nor, in the long run, is it intelligence's main mission.

4

＊━━━━━━━━━━━━━━━━━━━━━━━━━━━━━━━━＊

Designated readers: the open source revolution

On December 20, 1994, the government of the newly elected Mexican president, Ernesto Zedillo, announced an effective 15 percent devaluation of the peso. He thus publicly acknowledged what the government had earlier tried to hide: The country's financial reserves were
being exhausted. Global financial markets responded by stepping up
speculative attacks on the peso, Mexican reserves dropped sharply, and
two days later the government was forced to let the peso float freely.
Further capital flight ensued, and the peso plummeted to levels below
those of the 1982 debt crisis. Mexico's inflation rate soared to 40 percent, and the country fell into a recession from which it took painful
years to emerge.[1]

What befell Mexico was the scenario that played out in other countries in later years — in Asia, and in Russia and in Brazil. It also had
predecessors, most notably in the Latin American debt crises of the
1980s. No two of these crises were identical — the ratio of public debt
to private varied, as did the exposure of U.S.-based banks — but the
broad outline was the same. In all cases, too much outside capital was
seeking too large returns too quickly, based on too rosy assumptions

---

[1] For good accounts of the crisis, see Philip Zelikow's "American Intelligence
and the World Economy," in *In From the Cold,* Report of the Twentieth
Century Fund Task Force on the Future of U.S. Intelligence, New York:
Twentieth Century Fund Press, 1996, pp. 207–214; and *Lessons of the
Mexican Peso Crisis,* Report of an Independent Task Force, New York:
Council on Foreign Relations, 1996. For an assessment of the Mexico
crisis, its roots and implications, see Moisés Naím, "Latin America, the
Morning After," *Foreign Affairs,* 74, 4, July/August 1995, pp. 45–61.

either that nations never defaulted on their debts or that international patrons never let them.

The U.S. government responded to the immediate crisis with unprecedented financial actions. It authorized up to $20 billion from Treasury's Exchange Stabilization Fund (ESF), and it twisted the arm of the International Monetary Fund (IMF) to provide an $18 billion loan. The ESF funding, done without congressional authorization, was twenty times larger than any previous use of the fund, and the IMF loan, seven times Mexico's IMF quota, was the largest in the institution's 50-year history. Caught by surprise, the Clinton administration responded heroically, though its heroism earned it criticism from those in Congress and elsewhere who accused it of using taxpayers' money to bail out rich investors. (In fact, the loans worked as intended, restoring confidence that let Mexico weather the immediate crisis, and Mexico repaid the U.S. Treasury.)

As the storm clouds gathered around Mexico's finances during 1994, intelligence had begun paying more attention. Intelligence's warnings of crisis never were very sharply etched and so were dismissed by Treasury and other officials in charge of the issue. But the NIC's national intelligence officer (NIO) for Warning produced cautions about Mexico's finances that depended neither on secret sources nor on fancy analytic techniques. She monitored the publicly available reports of Mexico's foreign exchange reserves, which were being spent rapidly in an effort to prop up the peso. They dropped to $17 billion in October 1994 and to $6 billion the day before the devaluation. The simple mathematics of decrease suggested that Mexican policy would fail and that sooner rather than later Mexico would have to devalue the peso.

She was also in direct contact with some Wall Street analysts, a minority at the time, who were bearish about Mexico. They turned out to be right, though different Mexican policies might have proven them wrong. In any event, they had a useful warning to convey, and the NIO's strength was that she reached out to them; she broke out of the isolation that was — and is — all too characteristic of American intelligence.

For a time, the ostensible experts mostly dismissed her. The optimists told complicated stories about how the expensive peso was the natural product of the austerity measures Mexico had needed. The loss of confidence that was putting the peso under pressure was only temporary; if Mexico stayed the course, investor confidence would return, interest rates could come down, and economic growth would resume. The pessimists, at the Federal Reserve both in New York and Washington, argued that the peso had been overvalued for some time, perhaps by as much as a quarter. As a result, domestic producers were uncompetitive, the current account deficit was huge, and Mexico's finances were dangerously dependent on a bubble of speculative foreign investment, the so-called *tesobonos*.[2]

The U.S. Treasury, in control of the issue, mostly came down on the side of the optimists. In May 1994, the secretary's senior officials for international issues told him: "In our view, Mexico's current exchange rate policy is sustainable."[3] The documents do not reveal much of the evidence for that conclusion, except for occasional references to what Wall Street was saying. There were only a few cautions about Mexico's growing reliance on the *tesobonos* to sustain the inflow of foreign capital. These *tesobonos* protected investors from devaluation by being denominated in dollars (though redeemable in pesos); they offered high, short-term returns. As a result, while they attracted foreign capital (and induced Mexican capital to stay at home), they sharply increased the government's exposure in the event of a devaluation.

In a critical sense, the debate, such as it was, turned less on economics than on politics. Treasury, like most of Wall Street, believed or assumed that the Mexican government had both enough technical competence and enough political security to take the steps necessary to defend the peso. In those beliefs, especially the latter, it was wrong. Intelligence analyses, by the NIC's NIO and the CIA, seem to have cap-

2   For a summary of the pessimists' argument, see a memorandum from Rudiger Dornbusch to the Federal Reserve Board of New York, "Stabilization, Reform, and Non-Growth," May 1994, released in declassified form by the Senate Banking Committee and cited in Philip Zelikow, "American Intelligence and the World Economy," in *In From the Cold*, Report of the Twentieth Century Fund Task Force on the Future of U.S. Intelligence, New York: Twentieth Century Fund Press, 1996, p. 208.

3   See, for instance, the memo from the office of the assistant secretary for international affairs (OASIA), "Background and Talking Points: Macroeconomic Developments," May 1, 1994; Summers to Bentsen, "Briefing for Your Meeting with U.S. Ambassador to Mexico James Jones," May 2, 1994; or Shafer to Summers, "Dinner with Mexican Finance Officials," May 6, 1994, all cited in Zelikow's "American Intelligence and the World Economy," in *In From the Cold*, Report of the Twentieth Century Fund Task Force on the Future of U.S. Intelligence, New York: Twentieth Century Fund Press, 1996, p. 208.

tured the political dilemma confronting Mexico but did not marshal compelling evidence or argument to press those political pressures on Treasury and other parts of the U.S. government. Intelligence said the right things but not very clearly, or very loudly.

As Senators Arlen Specter and J. Robert Kerrey reported of the retrospective staff analysis done for the Senate Intelligence Committee:

> CIA analyses made clear that a large, delayed devaluation of the peso would have significant ramifications for Mexico's economy and political situation. In particular, there was the difficult dilemma that Mexican policymakers faced in deciding whether to take painful economic steps before an election, when such actions might affect the very outcome of that election, or to delay those steps and accept the risk that the economic situation might get out of hand as a result.[4]

Throughout 1994, Mexico suffered the jitters of foreign investors occasioned by the uprising in Chiapas at the beginning of the year. That, and then the assassination of the ruling party's first presidential candidate, Luis Donaldo Colosio, in March 1994, hung over Mexico's own deliberations about whether to devalue. The fact that inflation was coming down argued that devaluation might be acceptable; moreover, devaluations before presidential elections had become almost routine in Mexico.

Yet the other side of this Mexican argument was also weighty. The 1994 Mexican election was unusual because the ruling party, the Institutional Revolutionary Party (PRI), while not about to lose the election, was in disarray, so a preelection devaluation that increased prices in Mexico was unattractive. Moreover, the U.S. Congress was still debating the North American Free Trade Agreement (NAFTA), so any sign of Mexican profligacy was certain to become another argument for U.S. opponents of NAFTA. Finally, the outgoing president, Carlos Salinas de Gortari, later discredited in scandal, still harbored hopes of becoming head of the new World Trade Organization (WTO), and this was yet another reason for probity in Mexican economic policy.

These more political arguments that Mexico might not do the economically "right" things seem to have glanced off Treasury's handling of the issue, which was dominated by short-term influences on the peso. Treasury was also in its familiar posture, a defensive crouch, fearing

---

4   Letter to Senators Alfonse D'Amato (R-New York) and Paul Sarbanes (D-Maryland), Senate Banking Committee, SSCI Number 95-1327, March 29, 1995.

that to talk of possible devaluation was to make it a self-fulfilling prophecy. So while U.S. Federal Reserve analysts in October advised their boss, Alan Greenspan, to warn his Mexican counterparts about the costs of tying themselves to an unsustainable rate for the peso, a month later, after the sharp attacks on the peso had begun, the Treasury undersecretary, Lawrence Summers, was negotiating with his Mexican counterpart over the reassuring public language that Treasury Secretary Bentsen might use in commending Mexico's economic fundamentals.

What was striking, though, was that neither the NIO's arguments nor those of her critics depended on secrets. The information was there. The art lay in interpreting and projecting it. It turned out that secrets could have mattered because the Mexicans stopped publishing their reserve numbers. In fact, reserves seem to have stabilized for a few months after April, but the market's eventual reaction was sharper because investors felt tricked.[5] Had the United States, not to mention the financial markets, had access to secrets, the argument might have been sharper, but it would not have changed in character. It still would have been an argument over whether Mexico's adjustments and the market's responses to them would produce a crisis or avert one. So, too, while more knowledge of the Mexican government's own internal debate over devaluation in the summer of 1994 might have been helpful, the lines of the argument were well known in Washington.

Mexico's finances were a mystery, not a puzzle. Mind-sets mattered more than secrets. Interestingly, Wall Street did no better than the government. It, too, was dominated by the mind-set that the Mexican government would do the right thing. That view was convenient, just as Washington's view of India's BJP nuclear policy five years later was convenient. In this case, the private sector also accepted the Mexican government's argument that the current account deficits were the result of a buoyant private sector that was financing plant and equipment investment through open credit markets.

Indeed, because the short-terms offerings, *tesobonos* in particular, were so attractive, there are questions about just how objective the research done by Wall Street and the rest of the private sector actually was.[6] Everyone wanted to have a piece of the Mexican market. In that rush, financial analysts were under pressure to be "on the team," a

5 *Lessons of the Mexican Peso Crisis,* cited above, p. 11.
6 For a sharp critique, see Henry Kaufman, "Why Alarms Didn't Ring Over Mexico," *Wall Street Journal,* January 26, 1995.

pressure familiar to government intelligence analysts. The distinction between research and marketing became blurred — for the private sector, something similar to intelligence "getting on the team" or being "politicized" in the government.

AMERICA'S COLD WAR INTELLIGENCE

If the Soviet Union's passing left the United States with a network of technical collectors that is pretty impressive at supporting military operations abroad, its demise also was in part a product of the most dramatic change confronting intelligence. The instance of Mexico underscores just how dramatic. The age of information has multiplied sources, most of which are not secret but are instead what intelligence calls "open source." American intelligence as it emerged from the Cold War defined its business as secrets where *collection,* primarily with regard to the Soviet Union, was the supreme task. In the world looking to 2010 and beyond, its business will be information defined as a high-quality understanding of the world using all sources, where secrets matter much less and where *selection* is the critical challenge.

With the shooting war over, President Truman had ordered America's wartime intelligence service, the Office of Strategic Services (OSS) to terminate operations in late 1945.[7] Its constituent pieces dispersed. The research and analysis (R&A) branch, about a thousand officers, went to the State Department, where it became part of the Interim Research and Intelligence Service. The War Department took the secret intelligence branch, responsible for espionage, and X-2, the counterespionage branch, combining the two in the Strategic Services Unit (SSU). Truman hoped that State would take the lead in coordinating intelligence, whatever that was to mean. Indeed, his executive order was accompanied by a letter that conferred on the secretary of state the responsibility to "take the lead in developing a comprehensive and co-

7   There are many sources on this history. The first, and still basic, history was done by Anne Karalekas for the Senate's Church Committee in 1975. See Senate Select Committee to Study Governmental Operations with Respect to Intelligence Activities, *Final Report, Book IV: Detailed Staff Reports on Foreign and Military Intelligence — History of the CIA,* 94 Cong., 1 sess., 1976 (hereafter cited as "Karalekas history"). For one terse, readable account, see Mark M. Lowenthal, *U.S. Intelligence: Evolution and Anatomy,* Westport, CT: Praeger, 1992.

ordinated foreign intelligence program for all Federal agencies concerned with that type of activity."[8]

To be sure, the legacy of the war suggested more central coordination for the military services themselves and, with the Pearl Harbor lesson vivid in Americans' memories, for intelligence as well. The question that remained, though, was, How centralized and coordinated by whom? In early 1946, Truman created a National Intelligence Authority (NIA), composed of the secretaries of state, war, and navy, and his own special representative, Admiral William D. Leahy. The NIA was to oversee the new Central Intelligence Group (CIG), headed by a director of central intelligence (DCI). All in all, the arrangement was not much different from a plan the military joint chiefs of staff had offered in 1944 in response to OSS leader William Donovan's proposal for a central agency.

The newly created CIG, however, at first had neither people nor money. Absent both, its "coordination" did not amount to much, and it did little more than publish daily and weekly bulletins that were fashioned to contain little analysis and so step on no departmental toes, particularly those at the State Department. This rather weak CIG evolved toward a much weightier CIA as much by default as for any other reason.

Much of the default was that of the State Department, which remained stony terrain for a serious intelligence operation. Dean Acheson, who returned to government as undersecretary, wanted a strong central intelligence staff in the department, but he was opposed by the operating desks. Those operating desks, organized by region of the world, traditionally had dominated the department. They did not want a central intelligence staff as competition (and they were not above murmuring about the loyalty to State of the transferred R&A officers). Faced with congressional pressure over budgets, Secretary James Byrnes acquiesced in dispersing the old OSS R&A officers, now in an Office of Research and Intelligence, to State's operating desks.

When State ceded the field, the CIG formed its own Office of Research and Evaluation (ORE), and the espionage function reverted to CIG from the War Department. Thus, even before the National Security Act of 1947, the CIG had moved from coordinating intelligence to both collecting and producing it.

8   Cited in *Evolution of the Intelligence Establishment, 1945-50*, Foreign Relations of the United States, Washington, D.C., 1996, p. 182.

In these circumstances, the National Security Act moved forward the creation of a CIA that was more than a coordinator. Interestingly, though, while there were debates about whether the new CIA should have a military or civilian leader, and how to prevent it from becoming a threat to Americans' liberties, the prevailing expectation remained that it would coordinate and evaluate intelligence, not become a major collector or producer. Then DCI General Hoyt S. Vandenberg — a nephew of the influential Republican senator, Arthur Vandenberg — played down the covert collection role of the new agency, taking pains to emphasize that most of what it collected would be overt and that it would be careful to avoid duplication and would not supplant the other agencies.

The centralization of intelligence was probably inevitable given the trauma of Pearl Harbor's lesson, and the Soviet Union's secretiveness ratified the primacy of secrets, but the emphasis on puzzle solving was less foreordained. In part, Pearl Harbor had turned warning into a puzzle: Have they decided to launch an attack? All those Soviet nuclear weapons seemed to do the same for Cold War warning: The first necessity was recognizing with certainty that an attack had been launched. Precisely because the missiles existed and were so fearsome, it almost didn't seem to matter whether Moscow ever really intended to launch them or not. Besides, understanding intentions was hard and inconclusive; by contrast, America's technical wizardry shortly would provide impressive solutions to many of the puzzles.

The early CIA was not so dominated by tactical considerations as it later became. At the time, it couldn't provide much tactical help, because sources of information that were most relevant to solving puzzles were in short supply. Spy networks in Eastern Europe and the Soviet Union were just being assembled, and the big technical collectors were still in the future. While insiders seem always to have bemoaned the crowding-out of longer-term thinking by current intelligence, the first national intelligence estimate (though it was not then called that) in September 1947, was not tactical; it was a pithy assessment of the world situation.[9] It sharply identified the Soviet Union as the main threat, but it also was direct about Soviet military shortcomings, and it answered the day's overarching mystery — would Moscow attack Eu-

9   Central Intelligence Agency, *Review of the World Situation As It Relates to the Security of the United States*, CIA 1, December 26, 1947, declassified November 18, 1977.

rope? — by laying out the arguments why it would not. It also did not stop short of drawing the policy conclusions of its analysis. Preventing the collapse of Western Europe had to be America's top priority, then the Middle East, including Greece, with the Far East only a third priority, and Latin America lower still.

The original national estimates process, the Board and Office of National Estimates (ONE), then part of the CIA, had a stature in its early years that it could not sustain later. First headed by Harvard professor and wartime OSS veteran William L. Langer, the board attracted some of the country's best minds. Many of the officers who staffed it, a group of 25 to 30 at any given time, went on to distinguished careers inside and outside government.[10] From the beginning, interestingly, ONE reached out to the academic world, and in the circumstances of the 1950s, the reaching was easy. Academics had been very much part of the war effort a few short years earlier, and the family feuds within universities, over Vietnam in particular, that made "intelligence" a dirty word were still in the future. ONE convened the outsiders in Princeton, New Jersey, to work over draft estimates sent out in advance. The groups were a "who's who" of U.S. thinkers, primarily but not exclusively about the Soviet Union; according to participants, their give-and-take, on the implications of Stalin's death, for instance, was of high intellectual quality.

By the 1970s, however, the process had aged into a kind of stodginess, and its products seemed too academic to be very helpful. The nature of policy-making also had changed. The Kennedy and Johnson administrations operated in much less formal ways than had the Eisenhower administration, and so the highly structured estimates process, which had fit well with Eisenhower's military-style staff procedures, was more awkward for the new administrations. Moreover, by the early 1960s the senior policy officials who had known the board members were gone, replaced by people who were on the whole more knowledgeable about foreign affairs and who were inclined to be their own analysts for many issues.

DCI James Schlesinger, who had made a study of intelligence for President Richard Nixon, intended to reshape the estimates process, and

10 On this history and on estimating more generally, the best source is Harold P. Ford, *Estimative Intelligence: The Purposes and Problems of National Intelligence Estimating*, Lanham, MD: University Press of America, 1993.

his successor, William Colby, actually accomplished the task. Influenced by his experience with a senior special assistant for Vietnamese affairs, Colby replaced ONE with NIOs, experts themselves who would also be able to gather the best analysis from anywhere in the government. They would provide "one-stop shopping" across their areas of expertise, for the benefit of DCIs and of policy officials alike.

ONE had outlived its usefulness, but its demise also reflected the increasing priority of the tactical. NIOs as one-stop shopping centers could be as helpful in providing tactical support as strategic advice. To be sure, not all national intelligence estimates (NIEs), earlier or later, dealt with mysteries, nor were they all strategic. Indeed, the Cold War's best-known NIEs, the 11/3 series about Soviet nuclear capabilities, was mostly a continuous puzzle-solving exercise, with updated versions produced every year: How accurate are Soviet missiles? Do they have multiple warheads?[11] These puzzles were strategic ones, not tactical.

INTELLIGENCE FOR AN AGE OF INFORMATION

The world ahead is a far cry from the one to which intelligence has been accustomed. Intelligence formerly could be preoccupied with solving puzzles about the Soviet Union. Now, though, the critical questions facing American foreign policy are diverse and mostly mysteries, not puzzles. Whether Mexico would devalue in 1994 was a mystery, and so was whether Thailand would follow suit in 1997. Whether India would test a nuclear device in 1998 was also a mystery; it became a puzzle only at the very end, once the Indians were determined to test.

For mysteries, information collected secretly may be helpful, but that information seldom is as critical as it was for Cold War puzzles. Then, information was scarce; now it is overwhelming. Then, hints of Kremlin politics had to be guessed from pieces of previous puzzles that had been solved. It was not hard to see what secrets contributed to framing mysteries; if the value added was often small, the ignorance to which it added something frequently was large. Now, Russia's politicians talk as freely as any others.

11   The CIA has declassified and published a selection of these estimates. See Donald P. Steury, ed., *Estimates on Soviet Military Power: A Selection,* Washington, D.C.: Central Intelligence Agency, 1994.

The House of Representatives' IC21 study reported the findings of an analysis done of the intelligence sources used in the preparation of the classified *National Intelligence Daily* (NID), for January 1993:

> Not surprisingly, open source and Department of State reporting were the most frequently cited sources of information. They were followed by . . . : DO reporting, SIGINT, imagery, and Defense Attaché reporting. By issue, the DO was the most important intelligence source in the areas of weapons proliferation, economic security, Europe, Africa, Latin America, terrorism, counternarcotics, and Somalia.[12]

Cold War intelligence regarded its world as one of small amounts of information deemed, if sometimes mistakenly, reliable — primarily satellite photos, signal intercepts, and spy reports. Now, intelligence confronts vast amounts of unreliable information. Much of the world used to be "denied areas," closed to Americans. Now, only North Korea and a few similar states are truly closed. Intelligence's problem is coping with a world of openness. Simply observing, which might be called "eyeball INT," can replace IMINT.

The age of information means that policy-makers will be more, not less, reliant on information brokers. Policy-makers will not surf the Net themselves, or at least will do so only infrequently, because they won't have time. Quite the contrary, as access to information multiplies, their need for processing, if not analysis, will go up. If collection is easier, *selection* will be harder. Technology will let policy officials be in direct touch with information sources, both those that are publicly available and those that are unique to the government. They will choose to be in touch from time to time. But mostly they will be overwhelmed with information and will be more and more dependent on the people who process it for them.

There will also be more information brokers and more competition among them. Intelligence analysts will be one sort of broker. CNN anchors (or their producers), journalists, academics, and a burgeoning industry of for-fee processors will be others. Amidst such competition, policy-makers will prefer "pulling" information, rather than having it

---

12 See House Intelligence Committee, *IC21: The Intelligence Community in the 21st Century*, Washington, D.C., March 4, 1996, pp. 186–187. The study added: "Although this is, of itself, a good reflection of the value of the DO's product, it does not capture it all, since the NID does not typically reference much of the DO's best reporting that is disseminated only within highly restrictive 'blue border' compartments."

"pushed" on them. Instead of receiving a rush of separate bits of information, they will want to pull up puzzle answers or frames of reference if and when they need them.

During the Cold War, collectors could be separated from analysts, since what to look for was not a problem: Almost anything about the Soviet Union would do. Now, openness is blurring the distinction between collection and analysis. The best looker is not a spymaster, much less an impersonal satellite, but rather someone trained in the substance of the subject — an analyst. The Web is rich in sources but short on reliability. Over time, search engines will improve and help provide first-cut assessments of reliability. Still, the best Net surfers are experts who can make sense of the Net's stew of fact, fancy, and mistake. Finally, intelligence used to restrict its communications with the outside world lest secrets leak out. Now, communications need to be opened in a thousand directions lest critical information not seep in.

DISTRIBUTED INTELLIGENCE?

Intelligence traditionally has been thought of as a cycle, as shown in a very stylized form in Figure 1. That cycle goes from information needs to tasking and then to collection, analysis, and dissemination.[13] The idea of a cycle is deeply ingrained; it runs through all the blue-ribbon panel pronouncements on intelligence.

In this overly simple representation of what occurs, policy officials would articulate their information requirements — or "needs," depending on your taste in intelligence jargon — perhaps through a relatively formal process led by the National Security Council (NSC). The sense of priorities for information that came out of the process would, in turn, be translated into a more detailed assignment, or "tasking" — that is, someone or some technical collector would be asked to do something.

If, for instance, the requirements process gave priority to understanding whether Saddam Hussein was preparing to invade Kuwait again, that would generate a number of taskings. Open source analysts would be asked if they could detect any change in the tenor of Saddam's public statements, CIA spymasters would be charged with relaying what their

13   See Bruce D. Berkowitz, "Information Technology and Intelligence Reform," *Orbis*, Winter 1997, pp. 107–118.

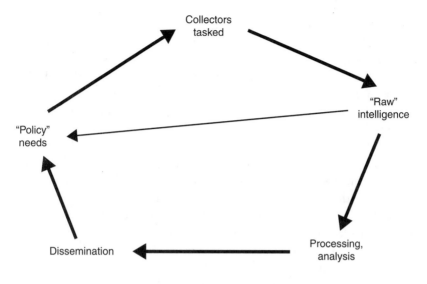

Figure 1. Stylized Intelligence "Cycle"

spies could learn about Iraq's internal deliberations, imagery satellites would be targeted to see if Iraqi troops had moved forward, SIGINT birds would be focused on communications lines that might indicate an increase in Iraqi military readiness, and so on.

The information would then be collected, processed or analyzed, and disseminated to the consumer. For instance, a SIGINT satellite's intercepts would go to the National Security Agency (NSA) to be analyzed, and NSA might then produce a summary of recent SIGINT findings. Imagery analysts would do the same for imagery, and, eventually, all-source analysts at the CIA, the Defense Intelligence Agency (DIA), or State's Bureau of Intelligence and Research (INR) would try to put the pieces together. If there were time and especially if there were serious disagreements among the agencies, the National Intelligence Council (NIC) might try to "publish" an NIE or other communitywide analysis of whether Saddam would invade Kuwait again.

To be sure, even this stylized version of the cycle takes into account the fact that the formal process is often interrupted. If, for instance, the CIA received input from an Iraqi spy reporting a conversation with Saddam's son-in-law, that piece of "raw" — that is, unassessed — intelligence would be passed directly to policy officials (represented by the arrow through the center of Figure 1). In this case, given the importance of Iraq, the raw report, along with some additional commentary about other recent intelligence that tended to confirm or contradict it, probably would be printed in the President's Daily Brief (PDB), the special CIA document done each day for the president and a handful of other senior officials.

In fact, the real cycle looks more like Figure 2.[14] This representation recognizes that policy officials seldom have the time or patience to articulate their information requirements precisely. Nor do most of them know enough to task intelligence operators effectively should they find the time to try. "More on Iran" or "better stuff on Saddam Hussein's intentions": This is the level at which most policy officials express their intelligence needs. Thus, the intelligence cycle is more likely to be impelled by what intelligence can collect and what it can infer about the needs of policy. The cycle is driven by intelligence "pushing," not policy "pulling."

By organizing the process in this way, each bit of intelligence stands by itself as a discrete commodity. Each bit can be updated, but the up-

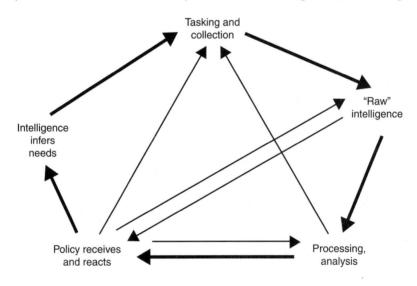

Figure 2. "Real" Intelligence Cycle

14   See Michael Herman, *Intelligence Power in Peace and War,* Cambridge: Cambridge University Press, 1996, p. 295.

dating, too, comes in discrete chunks. The cycle creates the perception that the product of intelligence is "products," most often pieces of paper (or symbols on a computer screen). In fact, by contrast, those pieces of paper are only inputs. The output of intelligence is better understandings in the heads of people who must act or decide. Building those understandings is a continuous process, not a series of discrete cycles.

The PDB is an intriguing example of the traditional intelligence process. It is the signature CIA publication, on which time and attention is lavished. A special staff produces it through the night to be ready for the president and a select circle of senior officials in the morning. It is produced in whatever form a particular president finds useful, but whatever its form, it contains the best secret tidbits, photos or SIGINT or spy reports, that intelligence has gathered recently. Presidents have also varied in how they want to receive the document: Some DCIs have tried to deliver the document in person, as a way to ensure they got some face-to-face time with the president, and more than one national security advisor has done the same, for the same reason.

What struck me, though, during the Clinton administration, was that while the PDB was an interesting set of discrete facts, it was not much more than that. It seemed less than helpful in building an understanding of any issue, because it didn't convey much sense of what was more important than what, of how today's information fit with yesterday's or last week's, or of how what the PDB reported was different from what the president had read in his morning *Washington Post.*

This traditional view of intelligence dates from the postwar and Cold War eras and presumes obsolete notions about consumers and their needs, as well as static standoffishness in relations between intelligence and policy. In the intelligence world of today, and still more tomorrow, would-be consumers will not throw their requests over the transom, then wait for their answer to be delivered the same way. And intelligence will not be used to support discrete "decisions" taken by "the government." Rather, it will provide a stream of information to a variety of coalition partners, actual and potential.

Those attributes — intelligence as discrete products, standoffish relations between intelligence and policy officials, and the fact that the initiative begins within intelligence — may have been appropriate, or at least unavoidable, in the 1940s and 1950s, but they make little sense for the future. Then, information was scarce, the response times of the technical collectors long, and communications slow, so thinking of intelligence as discrete products and leaving the initiative with intelligence to decide where its limited information would add value may have been the best that could be done. Not so today or tomorrow: Information is available in torrents, the response time of collectors is becoming shorter and shorter, and communication now permits intercepted signals to be relayed to U.S. pilots' cockpits as the mission takes off — or permits Washington-based policy-makers or analysts to be in direct contact, continuous if they choose, with collectors of information abroad.

The new technical possibilities open the way to a revolution in intelligence.[15] Intelligence can be decentralized, not centralized, and it can be connected to both consumers and colleagues, not kept behind walls either of secrecy and compartmentation or of doctrine about separating intelligence from policy. The directions are clear, but the implications for existing organizations and structure are radical.

OPEN SOURCES AND SECRETS

The odd term *open source* reflects the culture of Cold War intelligence. There is one other source besides intelligence's specialized INTs: everything else. That "everything else" equals open source. At the NIC, we used to quip that if academics sometimes did better than intelligence analysts, it was because the former weren't denied access to open sources! Senator Moynihan's remark in the wake of the Indian tests had a barb but a similar point: It didn't take spies or spymasters simply to read what India's leaders said and to take it seriously.

Computer networks have compounded intelligence's preoccupation with secret sources. All the analysts, whether at the CIA or elsewhere, work from a single set of sources, virtually all of them secret, over a small set of networks. For many of those analysts, if it isn't in the collection of classified files of SIGINT or HUMINT on their computer screens, it doesn't exist. For instance, CIA analysts can do competent assessments of particular industrial sectors in given foreign countries. Yet, alas, they usually do so in ignorance of what Wall Street or other private sector analysts are doing, sometimes better.

15   This discussion both parallels and has been enriched by Bruce Berkowitz's work. See his "Information Technology and Intelligence Reform," *Orbis*, Winter 1997, pp. 107–118.

In contrast, the virtue of the NIO for economics before the Mexican crisis was that she paid attention to what was available openly. Economic issues are an example of possible roles for intelligence in a more open world. Imagine the range of situations in which the United States might want to gather economic information, or intelligence. Those can be represented as a matrix of purposes for the information or analysis:[16]

- *Tactical* (intended to be used in taking one action or making one decision) or *strategic* (intended to improve a pattern of policy over time);

- *Offensive* (intended to protect American interests) or *defensive* (intended to advance American interests against a foe or negotiating partner [admittedly, the distinction is subjective]); and

- *Governmental* (intended to help the state) or *private* (intended to help American citizens or companies, even if those private Americans never know of the assistance).

The result is the eight cells shown in Figure 3, not all of which are interesting, though none is empty.

If a government agency such as the CIA took advantage of an opportunity to collect information about a foreign company and used the information for the benefit of American companies, it would be engaging in tactical-offensive-private intelligence. The government might, for instance, seek ways to make available to interested private companies information that it collects incidentally in the process of learning about foreign industries for the purposes of government policy. Information does get collected this way and is, on occasion, passed to private industry.[17] Whether doing so is wise is an issue for the next chapter. In

16   This matrix is based on one developed by Randall Fort within the CIA. I adopted and adapted it while I was on the NIC. For a related set of categories, see Loch K. Johnson, *Secret Agencies: U.S. Intelligence in a Hostile World,* New Haven: Yale University Press, 1996, pp. 147–150. Johnson distinguishes between "microeconomic intelligence" for the benefit of business and "macroeconomic" for the government. See, also, *Worldwide Intelligence Review,* Hearings before the U.S. Senate Select Committee on Intelligence, 104 Cong., 1 sess., 1995, p. 126.

17   See Loch K. Johnson, *Secret Agencies: U.S. Intelligence in a Hostile World,* New Haven: Yale University Press, 1996, pp. 152–153, 161, 168; and Maurice Ernst, "Economic Intelligence in CIA," in H. Bradford

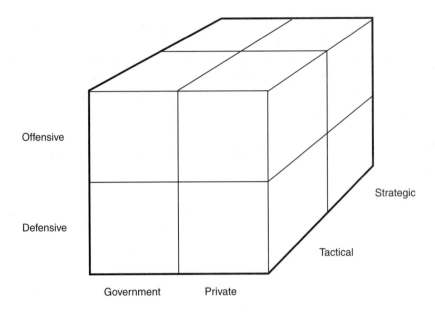

Figure 3. Economic Intelligence Matrix

theory, the government could go one step further: It could work with private companies to task secret collectors to produce information of interest, in which case the spying or eavesdropping might be thought of as strategic-offensive-private.

The defensive-private cells would contain intelligence helping American companies deal with potential threats from foreign intelligence services or, conceivably, the spying of competitors. A number of recent steps demonstrate the government's move in that direction. The Economic Espionage Act of 1996 and the creation of the National Counterintelligence Center (NACIC), like the earlier National Industrial Security Program designed to better protect classified information used by defense and other national security contractors, have both broadened the government's assistance to private companies. If that help were incidental, proffered only when intelligence came across threats to U.S. companies in the course of other work, it would be tactical. If intelli-

Westerfield, ed., *Inside the CIA's Private World: Declassified Articles from the Agency's Internal Journal, 1955–1992,* New Haven: Yale University Press, 1995, p. 328.

gence worked in cooperation with companies from the outset to identify threats and ways to counter them, it would be strategic.

One of intelligence's new or newly salient economic tasks, and a growth area, is "leveling the playing field" for American companies by learning of special inducements foreign companies or their governments offer in competing for contracts with other foreign governments. Leveling the playing field falls under tactical-defensive-private on the matrix. The area is secrets-rich, for just as nations seldom advertise their nefarious weapons programs, neither do they advertise the bribes or side payments they make in pursuit of international contracts. In effect, the United States seeks to enforce its own Foreign Corrupt Practices Act internationally through such intelligence.

Leveling the playing field is tactical almost by definition because it depends on tips, sometimes from the companies concerned. The cases intelligence builds are ones to be acted on by the U.S. government; sometimes the American company that benefits remains unaware of the government action on its behalf. The CIA says that in 1994 it uncovered 51 such cases involving contracts worth $28 billion.[18] In a 1993 case, the CIA found that France had bribed Brazil to land a $1.4 billion radar contract. The CIA then told the State Department, which complained to Brazil. In the end, Raytheon got the contract (though its Brazilian venture ended unhappily). In 1994, U.S. firms snatched away from France a clutch of arms and aircraft sales to Saudi Arabia, partly as a result of such intelligence.[19]

Leveling the playing field is classic intelligence puzzle solving, and it often requires contributions from several INTs. A human source might provide the initial tip. In a 1980s case, which went beyond a tilted playing field, Japanese and Norwegian firms circumvented agreements prohibiting the transfer of sensitive technology to the Soviet Union. A disaffected Japanese employee provided the initial tip.[20] He first wrote the international group for controlling exports, the Coordination Committee for Multilateral Export Controls, or COCOM, in 1985, alleging that a Toshiba subsidiary had sold Moscow machinery that would make Soviet submarines quieter. COCOM passed the allegation

18   Amy Borrus, "The New CIA: I Spy — for Business," *Business Week,* September 17, 1994, p. 23.
19   Reported in *The New Republic,* March 27, 1995, p. 10.
20   See "Taking Toshiba Public," in my *Making American Foreign Policy,* Englewood Cliffs, NJ: Prentice-Hall, 1994.

to the Japanese government, which dismissed it as unfounded. The employee then took documents supporting his charges to the American embassy in Tokyo. From then on, information pieced together from a variety of sources corroborated the charges and strengthened the case.

Several other cells of the matrix are also secrets-rich. Spying or eavesdropping on friends for the benefit of U.S. economic negotiators — say, in trade talks — seeks tactical advantage through the use of secrets and would fall into the tactical-offensive-government cell. For reasons set out in the next chapter, this practice is as unwise as it is popular with policy officials.

Strategic-offensive-government operations might be called "counter-economics" — understanding the critical nodes in the economies of foes well enough to destroy them. This area also is relatively secrets-rich, since many potential U.S. enemies will be secretive. Yet the picture of Baghdad's electricity grid that let American bombers destroy it during Desert Storm depended more on "gray" (i.e., not secret but not entirely open either) information than on secrets, more on information from foreign contractors and domestic utility operators than on documents classified by the Iraqi state. On the first day of the air war, January 17, 1991, a still-secret weapon dropped thousands of metallic filaments onto the Iraqi electrical network at key points to create huge short circuits and blackouts.[21]

While many of the matrix's cells are secrets-rich, those that are not are even more noteworthy. For instance, Cold War analyses of the Soviet economy might be labeled strategic-defensive-government since their purpose was not in the first instance knowing what to target; it was understanding output to calibrate Soviet military power. These analyses became an enormous CIA undertaking. In the first years, the 1950s, the analyses did not depend much on secrets, for satellite photography did not yet exist and such spies as America had were fully occupied with topics more important than factories. They relied instead on a painstaking combing of what literature the Soviets published and on interviews with anyone who might be able to add a puzzle piece.

Yet that economic task became by the 1960s an important target for U.S. space sensors. NSA, in particular, gobbled up signals wholesale from the Soviet Union, hoping to glean tidbits about the state of the economy from conversations among Soviet managers. Now, though,

21   See *New York Times*, June 3, 1991, p. A1.

Russia is like Mexico. Virtually all the information is openly available. It may not be good information, but it is not as though Russians have any that is better. They may distrust their statistics as much as we do. The problem is assessing a mystery, not solving a puzzle.

The same is even truer for the other nations, most of them friends and some of them allies, whose economies are of interest to policy. If the U.S. government needs models of their economies, it can buy them. It is nice to be able to manipulate those models in secret, but that is not imperative. More generally, the wherewithal for understanding those economies, their key industrial sectors, and how economic factors are entangled with politics is at hand. As the Aspin-Brown commission put it:

> In some areas, such as economic analysis, it is estimated that as much as 95 percent of the information utilized now comes from open sources . . . [but] an adequate infrastructure to tie intelligence analysts into open source information does not appear to exist.[22]

More information could be had by looking, not spying, one of the next chapter's subjects. But the most important information resides not in the world of secrets but in the world at large. It can be found through making connections to Wall Street, to the international financial institutions and the academy, and to people engaged in business or in charitable causes in countries that have not earlier been priorities for, and so are unfamiliar to, the U.S. government.

LEARNING TO READ: USING OPEN SOURCES

Conceiving of intelligence as information, not just secrets, would begin to provide arguments for new priorities and for reshaped institutions. Sadly, intelligence has been moving in exactly the opposite direction. For instance, the intelligence community created the Community Open Source Program Office (COSPO) as a focal point for innovation in using open sources, but by the late 1990s, COSPO was to be wound down as intelligence returned to a preoccupation with secrets.

The Cold War culture of intelligence also dominated in 1996 when the CIA proposed to cut its premier open source collector, the Foreign Broadcast Information Service (FBIS), by 25 percent. In an unusual

22 Aspin-Brown commission, *Preparing for the 21st Century*, Washington, D.C., March 1, 1996, p. 88.

coalition, outside scholars joined inside analysts in opposing the cuts, and the CIA backed down.[23]   FBIS began operating in 1941, and throughout World War II and into the Cold War, it was useful to diplomats and policy and military staffs that needed up-to-date and reliable accounts of what foreign governments and officials were saying. In an odd partnering between U.S. intelligence and British media, FBIS and the British Broadcasting Company (BBC) split up the globe, monitoring different regions and pooling their information. FBIS's high point was perhaps the Cuban missile crisis of 1962, when its monitoring of Radio Moscow let it be the first to give President John F. Kennedy news of the Soviet decision to withdraw missiles from Cuba.

However, in reality FBIS needed to be not merely saved but also reshaped, for as always in Washington's budget wars, the white hats and black hats were not so cleanly distributed as public accounts implied. While former U.S. ambassador to Moscow Jack Matlock referred to the cuts as "not only penny wise and pound foolish . . . [but] just plain dumb," the case for reshaping, if not cutting, FBIS was a strong one. It had been hard-pressed to keep up with advancing technology. The World Wide Web was mushrooming its sources of information, for instance, and machine translating was revolutionizing the ways it could do business. Through the years, too, it had acquired its own clientele, outside government as well as inside, and much of its output could be seen, fairly, as catering to the narrow interests of that clientele.

In addition, much of what FBIS had monitored could now be bought directly by the U.S. government, so FBIS needed to concentrate on what was not so readily available. That indicated priority to closed countries and, among those, to the ones that, unlike China, are not of interest to the commercial world. It would mean less monitoring and more collecting, especially of gray sources — for instance, the semiofficial and unofficial pamphlets that circulate in closed countries. A reshaped FBIS

23   See *Washington Post*, February 6, 1997, p. A21. FBIS would continue to monitor, translate, and publish accounts from about 3,500 foreign broadcast and press outlets in 55 languages and newspapers. The CIA refused to comment on any aspect of FBIS operations except to say that it would be "virtually 100 percent" spared the budget ax. FBIS quit publishing its foreign broadcast and press translations in paperback volumes in 1996 and now carries its reports on the World News Connection (wnc.fedworld.gov), an electronic site on the Web. Nongovernment subscribers pay about $50 a month to read the foreign media translations.

would do less wholesale translating and more archiving of materials, to be looked at when and if they became relevant.

Technology is making it possible for individual users to tailor their own systems and maintain their own dedicated data systems, in addition to being connected to central information systems. Information technology, especially software, is cheap enough to permit such tailoring. COSPO's plan for analysts had been "one screen and two boxes": A workstation would have, in effect, two computer hard drives, one for classified information and the other for open. Analysts could, using Windows or equivalent software, shift from one to the other, but in moving information, the membrane would be permeable in one direction only. Material could be pulled from open into classified but not vice versa.

The world of intelligence is opening to the Web but very, very slowly. By contrast, the private sector first replaced mainframes with personal computers, then began reconnecting those personal computers into large-area networks. Neither the intent nor the effect of those new networks, however, was to recentralize information systems, for the networks are distributed ones. They permit users to share data and processing but only so far as is efficient. And, unlike mainframes, they are adaptable, easily changing with relationships among users.

Various parts of the intelligence community have begun to experiment with open source databases. The DCI's Non-Proliferation Center (NPC) has been the most aggressive, and, perhaps surprisingly, it has found real value. Proliferation would appear to be a secrets-rich area, but careful combing of databases and the foreign press provides hints, tip-offs, and partial confirmations. Or, since nefarious programs may depend on aggregations of apparently innocent imports, open sources can reveal who is buying what. In monitoring a comprehensive ban on nuclear testing, dramatic changes in technology, along with real-time data communication in a much more open world, have made possible a prototype international monitoring and verification system based on data from an *open* global network of geophysical sensors. This might not substitute entirely for a U.S. national system but surely could complement it.[24]

24   See Charles Meade, "Monitoring Nuclear Tests," *Science*, 281, September 25, 1998, pp. 1967–1968.

As the monitoring of nuclear tests suggests, the possibilities for openness may be the greatest where they might seem to be the least. Another case in point is intelligence support for military operations. America's military interventions looking beyond 2010 will be as hard to predict as they were in the 1990s; in the future as in the past, many of them will be in places unfamiliar to most Americans, including those in intelligence. They will come about for reasons ranging from real humanitarian need, to the CNN effect, to the necessity of helping allies. Intelligence cannot hope to sustain expertise on all these places, any more than it could on Somalia or Rwanda.

The first instinct of the intelligence agencies is to find internal ways to build a surge capacity — by creating a reserve corps of intelligence analysts, for instance. It is true that some kinds of analytic talent — military analysts, for instance — are not developed anywhere but in intelligence, and so it is necessary to build some surge capacity in-house. But most of the expertise on local conditions in far-flung nations is to be found outside intelligence and outside government, not inside. It resides in the private relief agencies and other NGOs that have had people on the ground and in a few venturesome academics with specialties such as anthropology, history, or politics.

In its contingency planning, the United States Pacific Command (PACOM) found it useful to distinguish between the information requirements of major wars, on the one hand, and peace or humanitarian operations, on the other. For the former, such as a war in Korea, secrets would be very important. By contrast, it is very hard to foresee where peace or humanitarian operations will occur or what they will look like when they do. They are not likely to happen in places that have been priority targets for traditional intelligence. PACOM discovered that the NGOs, with years of experience in the countries concerned, have unique insights not just into the local politics and people, but also into infrastructure and other local assets that might be brought to bear in a conflict.

In Somalia in the early 1990s, for instance, the United States made mistakes through failing to understand aspects of the local culture that could have been discovered.[25] The Somali "warlords" — the term itself

25   On the Somalia case, see John L. Hirsch and Robert B. Oakley, *Somalia and Operation Restore Hope*, Washington, D.C.: U.S. Institute of Peace, 1995; Terrence Lyons and Ahmed I. Samatar, *Somalia: State Collapse, Multilateral Intervention, and Strategies for Political Reconstruction*,

contributed to the misunderstanding — had been struggling for power their entire adult lives. Having braved the prisons of colonial powers and local autocrats, they were not going to be easily cowed by a small international force, even one that included Americans. Or take the fact that the UN secretary-general, Boutros Boutros Ghali, was an Egyptian. For Americans, that was unimportant; he was, after all, an international civil servant. But Somalis saw his role through the lens of Egypt's past as the dominant power in the region. For this reason, mediation by some organization other than the UN — the Organization of African Unity, for instance, or even the United States on its own — would have been preferable.

These insights were not easily at hand but could have been learned. What was required was relevant expertise, in particular, people who knew something of Somali history and the region's culture. Intelligence did turn to Washington taxi-drivers who were Somali nationals for language expertise, but it needed to be organized to make use of networks of NGO and other private citizens. Most of that helping could have been done "virtually" via the Internet. All that was required was some organizing in advance, most of which could have been done on the cheap. As my NIC experience suggests, most NGO and academic experts would have been prepared to cooperate, and all the more so if the facilitating organization were a federally funded research and development center (FFRDC) or other institution that was private in form, and thus untainted by the word "intelligence," but well connected to both intelligence and the government.

Existing intelligence organizations were not at the forefront of efforts to develop these open sources, as PACOM came to realize. Instead, the command came to the idea of a "virtual information center" through its own gaming and workshops. Such a center would draw upon and bring together a wide variety of information from inside and outside the government; it might use low-earth orbiting satellites and mobile communications that would enable it to operate even during natural disasters. And, perhaps most important, these peace and humanitarian operations inevitably are coalition operations. While the U.S. military is a nec-

Washington, D.C.: Brookings Occasional Paper, 1995; and United Nations, *The United Nations and Somalia, 1992–95*, New York, 1995, the documents in particular.

essary partner, it is only one among many. As a PACOM paper puts it, for these operations, C3 is not "command, control and communications" but "collaboration, cooperation and coordination."[26]

The more open world and the world of coalitions are indeed breaking down the distinction between collection and analysis. During the Mexico crisis, the NIC's NIO for Warning, in personal touch with Wall Street, was both. If analysts pull information off the Web or use what they know from a secret source to validate what they read on a Web site, is that collection or analysis? With easy communications, the right intelligence person to debrief an American businessman who has returned from Sinkiang is not an all-purpose debriefer but rather the expert, an analyst. Going further, in a world of much more distributed collection, analysts might be in direct contact with, say, sensors from which they seek information.

Connections between processors or analysts and policy officials will be even more transformed. At first, Intelink, a major innovation and the intelligence community's classified version of the Internet, was a better way of communicating secret information within intelligence, but not of opening it to the outside world.[27] But it could be. After all, it was the Pentagon that first created the Internet. Intelink is based on the same freely available software as the Internet. Different components of the community have their own home pages and decide which of their documents to put onto the system. At first, the system was limited to no more than Top Secret material, thus excluding compartmented intelligence. But next steps will include codes to identify authorized users, permitting the originating agencies to maintain a second check on who has access to their documents.

Initially, the system was experimental and was mostly a convenient means of sharing finished intelligence. Depending on how well prepared the documents entered into the system are, users can click on key words to find additional biographical information or to move to related

26   See David G. Haut, Sean Conners, and Michael G. Sovereign, *An Update on Humanitarian Assistance and Disaster Relief (HA/DR) for the Next Century,* and Stephan P. Kane, *PAC CHEST Final Report,* PACOM, both available at www.dodccrp/Proceedings/DOCS/wcd0001/wcd00102.htm. Also see Michael G. Sovereign, *Humanitarian Assistance and Disaster Relief in the Next Century: Workshop Report,* Washington, D.C.: Department of Defense, C4ISR Cooperative Research Program, 74, October 28–30, 1997.

27   See *Washington Post,* December 28, 1994, p. A4.

intelligence. Logically, though, the system would permit communications among analysts and, eventually, question asking and answering between consumers and analysts. Again, though, it will not be senior policy-makers who browse either the Net or the Link. It will be their staffers or their experts.

PROCESSING INFORMATION, NOT SECRETS

On some reflection, there is little denying the need for more *processing* and for more information intermediaries.[28] Yet if the secrets content of the data flows being processed is low, why should intelligence do the processing? The first answer, that "no one else does it," is not compelling. At the NIC, that was often the answer to questions about why we were starting an NIE about peacekeeping, or humanitarian issues, or the AIDS pandemic, or other issues of plain interest to policy-makers but not of such plain comparative advantage to the intelligence community. For me then, that answer was good enough. It isn't, though, for the government more broadly.

In principle, if the senior levels of the government need more information processing, more analysis, then why not create something akin to the Congressional Research Service for the government as a whole? That service could be the government's designated surfer of the Internet and other open sources. Intelligence could then add "the secret bits" as appropriate for relevant consumers.

The second answer to why intelligence does the processing is that it has to do it in any event because assessing the value of secrets requires knowing what is already available publicly. The CIA's clandestine service, the Directorate of Operations (DO), sustains a career structure of reports officers whose mission is to provide context for and validate the reports that spies send in. (At the NIC, I kept my list of howlers received from spies — recitations of the obvious obtained through circuitous means. "The French dislike GATT" might be an example. The spymaster who recorded that insight thought it was correct and important. It was; it just wasn't news.) However, in principle this validating function could be performed by connecting the validators inside intelligence to the surfers of the Net, who could be outside intelligence.

28   For a strong case along these lines, see "Business and the Internet," a special section of *The Economist*, June 26, 1999, p. 5ff.

A third answer is that however little policy-makers trust intelligence to do the processing, they trust anyone else less. It is true that, overall, intelligence strives hard — too hard, in my view, a point for later — to be a teller of truth, free of biases and preconceptions. It does have its biases, but those derive from professional values, matters of temperament, and operating style, usually not from views on substance.

The processors could, though, be dispersed to the various policy-makers. If Treasury needs information mediators, why not have them at Treasury rather than in the intelligence community? Indeed, it is not obvious now why Treasury should have a person or two working on the German economy while the CIA has twice that capability. It might be convenient for the processors to have a role with respect to secret intelligence as well; those who surf the Net need to be experts and so do those who judge the value of the secret bits.

There is a more telling, though seldom stated, reason for having the intelligence agencies do information processing or analysis even when the secrets content is low. That reason is that other agencies would not do it, or at any rate not much of it. Treasury or Commerce could have analysts if they chose, but they just haven't spent their money that way. The fate of the State Department's INR is instructive. It does some very good work but remains a bureaucratic stepchild. Foreign service officers shun assignments there.

So, bureaucratically as opposed to logically, the analytic or information processing capability might not easily be transferred from the intelligence agencies to their policy counterparts. It might simply go away, to be replaced by passport stampers or tax collectors. That would be a comment of sorts on the perceived value of analysis. But we might not share that comment. Intelligence has been a public good, virtually free to policy officials.

ORGANIZING FOR TACTICAL SUPPORT

Intelligence has been moving in a tactical direction, somewhat paradoxically so given that the Cold War's end has thrown up so many mysteries. In large part, the turning of national systems to the purpose of supporting tactical warriors is responsible. Yet beyond the war-fighters, policy officials are most appreciative when intelligence tells them something they didn't know before. Solving a tactical puzzle is elegant and visibly helpful; putting some shape to a strategic mystery is much less so.

Tactical or strategic, and puzzle or mystery are two related but separate dimensions. Puzzles, such as how big and how accurate Soviet missiles were, can be strategic, and mysteries can be tactical — how will Milosevic respond to tomorrow's bombing of Serbian Kosovo? Secret or open is a third dimension, one that is also related to the other two because most puzzles require secret pieces. So the striking trend now is best stated as tactical support, mostly puzzle solving (including some strategic puzzles, especially military) with a high secrets content.

Congress has encouraged this trend by legislating in ways that convert intelligence findings, often ones that are solutions to puzzles, into policy decisions. Congress is especially tempted to do so when government is divided, with one party in control of the presidency and the other a majority in Congress, and so the congressional majority is wary of giving discretion to the president. Given that wariness, congressional enthusiasm for doing something about missile proliferation or arms sales or other evils takes the form of legislation requiring that the executive branch automatically respond if foreign nations are discovered in particular acts.

For intelligence, such legislation is uncomfortable in the extreme. If the law requires, for instance, that the executive branch impose sanctions on both countries if China has sold M-11 missiles to Pakistan, and if intelligence uncovers evidence that amounts to a pretty good case that China has done so, what, then, does intelligence do? It faces the choice of either fudging its case, opening itself to criticism from Congress when it finds out, or compelling its executive branch masters to take an action they may want to avoid. In principle, the case intelligence can make about whether China has sold the M-11 missile is information. It does not settle the policy question about China, because policy must balance nonproliferation against other U.S. interests in China.

Organizations have reflected this pride of place to puzzle solving and to tactical support to policy. Other than the creation of the Central Imagery Office (CIO) and then the National Imagery and Mapping Agency (NIMA), most of the organizational change that occurred after the fall of the Berlin wall was tinkering within organizations, and most of that was designed to do better at tactical support. Both the CIA and DIA are examples. In the decade of the 1990s, DIA went through if not permanent revolution, then a carousel of reorganization, one driven by the primacy of tactical support. It first broke away from an organization by world regions to an almost completely functional organization.

The change was entirely motivated by the goal of better supporting military operations. Its logic was that in a world of unpredictable conflict arising, perhaps, in little known places such as Somalia, DIA couldn't afford cadres of dedicated regional specialists. It was bound to guess wrong. Instead, what it needed was more versatile analysts composing a surge capacity. Thus, it reorganized by major battle functions — ground, sea, and air. When conflicts arose, DIA would then be able to bring lots of analytic talent to bear on the place or problem in question.

The logic was appealing, but the practice was awkward. DIA's regional analysts became orphans. More fundamentally, during the Cold War, Soviet military potential could be assessed without much regard for internal politics or economics. Now, however, that is no longer true for Russia, and it is still less true for other potential U.S. foes such as Iraq, Iran, and North Korea, and the DIA organization aroused concerns about just how good military analysis could be if were separated from regional expertise. The functional organization was cumbersome and, to boot, seemed to cut against the Pentagon's insistence on real jointness among the ground, sea, and air services. Finally, even if DIA's organization had been ideal, the rest of the government remained organized by region, so DIA was the odd agency out, including the Pentagon's own dominant regional commands. In 1995, it reversed the functional organization.

In 1994, the CIA at last decided to do what it had not done for nearly a half century — make the Directorate of Intelligence (DI) and DO if not partners, then cohabitators, through "colocating them," in the CIA phrase. The logic was to put DI analysts close enough to the collecting of secrets to influence what was asked for. The vision was a CIA focused on tactical puzzles with a high secrets content. (This move also demonstrated how far the CIA had come. In the early days of CIA's Langley headquarters, armed guards had controlled access to the entrances of the DO wings of the building, including the access of CIA officers from other directorates.)

Colocation reflected, in its way, the merging of collection and analysis: Why should the DO have its own cadre of reports officers to guide and grade field reporting when it had real customers in-house as guiders and graders — DI analysts? In fact, insiders had grumbled about the reports officers for years. Despite some stellar exceptions, they were mostly treated as second-class citizens. That most of them were women made the way they were treated all the worse; it seemed a relic of the old days, when the DO boys sallied forth in the world carrying their shields while the girls kept the home fires burning.

Yet did colocation come 40 years too late, when puzzle solving is less pressing, if no less popular, than during the Cold War? The answer depends on how the CIA's mission is defined. Colocation makes sense if that mission is primarily tactical; it would then let the DI guide the espionage that the DO conducts. The risk in colocation for the DI is that it will wind up not guiding the much larger DO but rather becoming its tail. Still, the DO is in such dire need of direction that putting tactical analysts close at hand to drive collection could make a difference. Not only might it make for a shorter list of clandestinely collected howlers, like those I assembled when I was at the NIC, it also might help both the clandestine service and the tactical analysts stay focused on the small set of issues for which secrets matter most.

THE TACTICAL FRANCHISE

How tactical should the mission of intelligence become? This is, in many respects, the overarching question for the future of intelligence. It can't be conclusively decided, but the broad choice of direction has enormous implications. Moving toward the tactical, which is intelligence's current choice, gives pride of place to secrets. Moving in the other direction, toward the strategic, would define intelligence as information, not secrets. Because consumers tend to be most appreciative of intelligence when it tells them something that they didn't know before, being responsive to those consumers will almost surely reinforce the move toward the tactical. So the broad choice can be seen as how much to follow consumer preferences and how much to lean against them.

In the world ahead, the tactical and strategic purposes of intelligence will be distinct enough to call for separate organizations. The two purposes do overlap and so will the products of the respective analysts. The purposes overlap just enough to confuse us into thinking they should be done by one set of processors or analysts. But they should not be.

For both purposes, given the mushrooming of information, intelligence agencies will need to conceive of themselves as part of a chain of processing. Most basic processing will be done outside governments and will be either acquired by the government for free or bought from the processing services that will continue to proliferate. As processing moves closer to government policy-makers, the arrangements for accomplishing it might range from contracting with special processors, to creating new institutions akin to the current FFRDCs with one leg in the academy and one leg inside government.

As processing moves still closer to the ultimate consumers, intelligence could add two elements. It could shape the information and the processing to the agendas of particular policy agencies or officials. This tailoring is why the issue of "duplication" in analysis, which is always decried by congressional overseers, is so hoary and ultimately so phony: What looks to the outside observer like duplication seems to the inside user like tailoring to his or her specific purposes. At some point, too, information from secret sources would be added to the processing. Analysis would become "all source."

On the tactical and military side, the franchise is secret information. That has been the stock-in-trade of intelligence throughout the Cold War. It retains value now, even if that value is diminished. For analysts, it means close attention to the value of their "special" information. They need some sense for what is available openly in order to know what their secrets add. But for many of the issues on their agenda — from Iraq's order of battle to North Korea's nuclear program — the basic building blocks of information will still come from secret sources, and open information will provide hints to pursue or confirmation of what secrets suggest.

In these circumstances, asking analysts to know and help direct secret collectors *and* remain close to the agendas of their customers *and* stay in touch with the world of analysis and information outside the government is simply asking too much. Intelligence should make it easier for them to interact with fellow specialists outside government, but their issues and their sources will, much more than is true for the rest of intelligence, remain the province of the government. For them, the world beyond the Cold War will not look all that much different from the world of the Cold War.

They will continue to benefit, too, from a relatively welcome reception for their information. Many policy-makers think they understand European politics, and some consider themselves experts on Wall Street, but few of them, even of those in uniform, come to their jobs as experts on China's exports of missiles to other countries. They quickly understand the role secret intelligence can play. Indeed, in my experience, they sometimes welcome secret tidbits when they shouldn't. While on the strategic side, intelligence is often unwelcome because it is too inconclusive, on the tactical side, it is often *too* welcome. It substitutes for thought or decides policy, or it seems to.

The tactical analysts will need to remain close to their special sources because the secrets that those sources provide are the core of the tactical franchise. Ideally, they would be close to all of their special sources — imagery, signals, and spy reports. One of the arguments against the CIA's colocation of the DO and the DI was that DI analysts needed comparable proximity to collectors other than HUMINT. Similarly, integrating SIGINT into analysis has always been a problem. And while many of the other agencies' arguments against NIMA were parochial, it was fair to worry that creating an imagery stovepipe would undo what has been a success: The dispersion of imagery analysts throughout the community, to DIA and CIA in particular, has meant that imagery *is* well integrated in all-source analysis. If colocating the DO and DI is a second-best in the short run, the long-term goal should be creating teams that bring together tactical analysts with experts from all the special collection disciplines.

AND THE STRATEGIC FRANCHISE

For strategic analysis in the transformed international system beyond the Cold War, secrets don't provide much of a franchise, and comparative advantage is harder to demonstrate. Analysts on this side need to be oriented outward, not inward. Their franchise will be the judgment they can bring with them, not the facts that they can call forth from collectors. Their challenge will be to demonstrate to consumers that they add value, and they will do so, if they do, by assembling the best judgments not just inside the Washington Beltway but outside as well, and by adding their own wisdom tailored to the problem that policy confronts.

The task indicates that they be both close to outsiders and close to consumers. For the more strategic issues, especially, the message is inseparable from the messenger. Senior consumers will want to know of and to be able to calibrate the analysts. At senior levels, this suggests bringing distinguished outsiders inside, as well as giving careerists the outside experience they need to be recognized as at the top of their profession.

Moreover, all the pressures in American political life shorten time horizons, and, at least below the very top of government, the more senior the official, the shorter the horizon; the tenure of assistant secretaries is not much more than a year, on average. As intelligence moves toward tactical support, it is all the more important to construct the capacity to lean against that wind, to stretch time horizons and to see issues in their time stream. Part of the mandate for the strategic franchise should be the intelligence side of policy planning.

My experience at the NIC convinced me that if the government is to do any serious foreign policy planning, intelligence must initiate the process. While intelligence alone can't do the planning, it does have both the luxury of some time and a focus on the right starting point for the process, which is the reality "over there" in the foreign places America seeks to influence. In contrast, given time pressures, policy agencies, including those with planning titles and mandates, either won't do serious thinking beyond current events or will do so primarily in terms of the impacts at home, especially in domestic politics.

At the NIC we tried an experiment in policy planning, one that is suggestive of what is conceivable but also instructive about what is possible. Then National Security Advisor W. Anthony Lake convened the deputies of the major national security departments in his office informally for lunch. For each meeting, he would have chosen an issue for discussion, and, in advance, we at the NIC would have collaborated with State's policy planners to produce two two-page papers — ours outlining scenarios and critical factors over the next decade or so, and theirs focusing on U.S. interests and desired goals.

The NIC's chair, Joseph Nye, directed the conversation, first pushing it out to possible results a decade or more hence and to critical drivers of those results, then walking back through intermediate outcomes to still more immediate policy choices. It was precisely an effort to *plan*, to see near-term choices in the shadow of more enduring interests and realities. The motto for these meetings was one I've made my own for planning more generally: If long-term planning doesn't affect what you do today, it's just entertainment.[29]   The meetings we held, on Korea and Asia and on Cuba, were good ones, and the conversations were

29   I owe this maxim to my RAND colleague Jim Dewar.

thought provoking for all concerned. Yet the planning sessions couldn't compete with the press of regular business. We kept scheduling future sessions, only to have them bumped off the calendar. Eventually, the initiative ran down.

ADDRESSING MYSTERIES: NATIONAL INTELLIGENCE ESTIMATES

In a world of more openness but also more mysteries, the analytic challenge for the strategic franchise is demonstrating that it can help policy officials think about a future that is profoundly uncertain. For the Soviet Union, information was a problem, but, with information at hand, there was little mystery, and even without much information, predictions of continuity usually came true. Now, information is less of a problem, but Russia's future is a far cry from the seemingly glacial immobility of the Soviet Union. Predictions of continuity thus are bound to be wrong. But predictions of discontinuity are surely not bound to be right.[30]

Trying to provide some shape to mysteries is the primary task of the NIC, whose watchwords are "estimative" and "community." The NIC's formal products, most notably NIEs, reflect both. As estimative, they deal with the unknown and, especially, with the not yet knowable — what might happen in the future. Thus, while NIEs sometimes do estimate the present, in assessing the military capacity of possible enemies, for instance, they usually aim toward the future. As community, they are products of the entire intelligence community, for better or worse. They draw on the information and analyses of the CIA, DIA, NSA, the State Department's INR, and the other analytic components of the community.

Estimates get produced through a painstaking process in which every sentence is scrutinized by representatives of the various intelligence agencies — an arduous interagency process known, with some irony, as "coordination." The driving philosophy is not to produce a "least common denominator" result. Rather, the intent is the opposite — to hope that out of the clash of hypotheses and the testing of evidence, a

---

30   The best source on intelligence estimating in general, and its history in particular, was written by Harold Ford, one of my predecessors as vice chair of the NIC. See his *Estimative Intelligence: The Purposes and Problems of National Intelligence Estimating*, Lanham, MD: University Press of America, 1993.

better and more useful product will result. However, estimates often have been criticized, fairly, for glossing over differences through the use of ambiguous or tepid wording.

Particularly, once the Board of National Estimates was abolished, the coordination process became a quasi-judicial one, dominated by assuring procedural fairness for all agencies concerned. *Who* held a view became as important as the view itself. Little wonder that NIEs often decayed into lowest-common-denominator compromises replete with woolly wordings that dulled issues rather than sharpened them. (Once during the arguing about a draft NIE, in one of those "coordination" sessions, a versatile editor and writer who worked for me at the NIC was arguing a point. He was confronted by someone from one of the agencies: "Why are *you* here? Who do *you* represent?" My colleague, a wonderfully difficult square peg who never fit easily into the uniform round holes of the CIA personnel system, stiffened. "I represent the English language," he replied. And so he did.)

In my time at the NIC, we tried hard to make coordination sharpen differences when they were important to policy and, critically, to lay out the reasons for those differences. I came away thinking that we had only half succeeded. I was more and more depressed by the inherent conflict between the due process of coordination and the desire for sharp, timely advice. There is a need for the analytic community occasionally to butt heads or build collegiality or demonstrate due process — the process can be described differently depending on one's point of view. But the current practice is the enemy of interesting analysis. That butting of analytic heads does not necessarily require estimates. Estimates should be thought of as something to be done only rarely, for important subjects when there is real danger that the perspectives of the various departments are diverging dangerously or misleadingly.

During the Clinton administration, North Korea was a case in point. As an issue, both its military might and its nuclear ambitions made it important enough to merit continuous attention, and views about it did divide along agency lines. Not surprisingly, the State Department was the most "dovish" about North Korea's intentions (not that it was all that dovish), and it was also the agency most inclined to believe that negotiating with North Korea could be fruitful. A colleague, an NSC staffer, not an intelligence analyst, caricatured the State Department view with the image of several Americans standing at the bottom of a deep bomb crater. The officer from State was saying: "I think North Korea is sending us a subtle and nuanced message."

It turned out, though, that the deep differences among the intelligence agencies were more apparent than real, and there was more to be said for State's position than I first thought. It was as though the agencies had been defending trenches of argument long after anyone could remember why the trenches had been dug where they were. The agreed products that resulted from this particular butting of heads were not as insightful as we would have liked, particularly about the ultimate question of North Korea's intentions, but they were useful nonetheless. They played a part in leading to the agreement with North Korea in 1995 that gave the United States and the international community some leverage over North Korea's nuclear program.

In addition to due process, the other traditional function of estimates is probably less important now. That purpose was to give working level consumers, especially in the military, some sense for what "the government" thought. The 11/3 series on Soviet strategic weapons had this character. For the senior working levels of government, these NIEs were a kind of document of record, setting forth what the intelligence community thought about a foreign situation or issue. That audience, particularly its military members, was best served by data-rich, detailed estimates. The need for these estimates-for-the-record is less now that the Soviet threat is gone, but a reference point is probably still useful for some enduring puzzles, such as Iraq's military capabilities or Russia's nuclear doctrine and arsenal.

DOING WELL AT ADDRESSING MYSTERIES

Shaping mysteries is hard, whether it is done by a single analyst or a committee. It requires moving beyond the evidence into terrain where many analysts are uncomfortable. It is necessary to delineate clearly the trail from evidence to more-speculative, estimative judgments. That is what distinguishes estimates from hunches.

In my experience, NIEs and other assessments of mysteries often went awry at the beginning, with the question to be assessed. Framing questions well at the beginning is imperative. Too often the question that the intelligence community wanted to ask was broad and vague: Whither Poland? But the questions on policy-makers' minds are more specific, ones that have some operational consequences, such as, Will

Poland be interested in the Partnership for Peace program? Given their interests, a "whither-Poland" estimate will seem, perhaps, interesting but not useful; it will glance off their interests. The estimate will get put in the stack to read "when there is time," but there will never be time. If the process worked well, NIOs would be in touch with their policy counterparts as they started estimates to make sure that the key questions to be addressed were those that were on the minds of their counterparts. If they were, there would be less chance that we would have to redirect a project later on, and the resulting NIEs actually might help policy-makers do their jobs.

We also tried to be transparent about evidence. Why does intelligence think or judge something? If I could have, I would have made the word processors at the NIC refuse to accept phrases such as "we estimate" or "we judge." If the truth were told, our policy colleagues did not care what we thought. What they wanted was a discussion of the issues, argued with evidence and reasoning, not just a conclusion. In shorter pieces, there was no space to lay out all the evidence, but, even there, some indication of sources and chains of reasoning made the estimate more credible. Laying out the evidence allowed readers to judge for themselves how much credence to give to the judgments based on it. It was especially important to indicate where the evidence ended and where inference or speculation began.

We sought, too, to be candid about how confident we were in the judgment and to craft language that reflected that relative confidence. If, on a scale of one to ten, the confidence was only three, then the language should not sound as though it were eight. By the same token, we tried to be careful in dealing with probabilities. Different people hear very different messages from the same words, especially in expressing probabilities. For one person, a "small but significant" chance is one in a hundred; for another it may be one in five. Such language is not precise enough for estimates, and we opted instead for bettors' odds, saying whether the judgment was one in five or one in a hundred. Bettors' odds were hardly ideal, but they were preferable to percentages because the latter can convey a sense of too much precision. Bettors' odds were also less likely than percentages to be regarded as somehow scientifically derived.

Conveying a consensus view in an estimate rarely is of much help to policy-makers, because they are already likely to share it. Expressing differences of view can convey important new information, provided the reasons for those differences are spelled out. To assert only that "some analysts think this, while others think that," will confuse, not enlighten policy-makers. The difference becomes meaningful only when the roots of that difference are exposed. Is the difference based on alternative patterns into which the available evidence can fit, or on an alternative train of logic, or on a different interpretation of how the foreign government works, or on something else?

Laying bare the sources of differences is easier said than done precisely because estimating often begins where the evidence ends. As a result, differences seldom result from different facts; they are more likely to stem from differing interpretations of the facts. In the instance of North Korea, there was much less information than we would have liked and the least on the questions for which policy-makers most wanted answers: What are North Korea's negotiating aims? Differences of opinion on that issue were based less on indications from evidence than on deductions from differing broad principles or theories: How do totalitarian states, or Asian states, or failing totalitarians behave?

We also tried to be creative in constructing "excursions." Intelligence owes policy its best judgment about the future. Even if those policy officials are likely to share that judgment, it still is a useful baseline. If the judgment is conventional wisdom, at least the estimate serves a validating function. Yet, to use a business analogy, best judgments are like the market price. They are useful, but no one ever got rich by betting on the market price. Making money requires being contrarian. So, too, estimates can be most helpful when they express different views about an uncertain future. To do that, estimates should examine several excursions from the best judgment. Ideally, the excursions should focus not on the most likely alternatives, but on those that would have the biggest impact on policy.

For instance, the best judgment of South Africa's nuclear program in 1980 might have suggested that the country would have a dozen or more nuclear weapons by 2000. In fact, the actual number turned out to be zero. South African politics was discontinuous; the white government ended the nuclear program in anticipation of the transition to majority rule. A useful excursion in a 1980 estimate might have addressed such a possibility. It might have asked what it would take to produce a South African future of zero nuclear weapons, as well, perhaps, as one of a hundred nuclear weapons or more. The point would not have been to predict the future but to compel thought about what would have to happen to make the excursion come true, along with signposts that might indicate that the excursion was becoming more likely.

Excursions are preferable to scenarios because, used badly, scenarios merely confuse. There is a temptation to build broad scenarios that, in effect, cover all the possible futures (as well as the analysts' backsides). Once, at the NIC, an analysis of an election in a foreign country got to the top of my reading pile only after the election had occurred. Thankfully, the analysis was not a NIC product, for it had so carefully hedged its bets and covered all possibilities that, even knowing the election outcome, I still couldn't make up my mind whether the analysis was right or wrong!

Once a best bet about a particular future is identified, constructing several improbable-but-high-impact excursions not only can stretch the thinking of policy and intelligence alike, but also can identify which factors would have to change to make those excursions come true. In the South African case in 1980, the excursion to zero nuclear weapons might have directed attention, first, to a rapid change in government; but it also might, on some reflection, have sparked interest in how the white government might prepare for a longer transition. Examining the changes may sharpen analysts' bets about exactly how likely the excursions are; it almost certainly will be a test of whether previous analysis has correctly identified the key variables.

Describing the task does not make it easy. Not only do experts typically find it hard to conceive of dramatic departures from present trends, but analysts and policy-makers typically use very different forms of logic. Analysts think analytically, applying logic to the available evidence. By contrast, senior policy officials, especially politicians or non-career civil servants who work for them, frame alternatives and judgments intuitively, sometimes hopefully. Thus, it is of little surprise that intelligence and policy often do not connect; that gap is the subject of chapter 6.

BRINGING OUTSIDERS INSIDE

Rigorous analytic techniques can help make analysis better, and perhaps even more useful to policy-makers, but it would require breathtaking hubris for intelligence to presume that it had a monopoly on either the information or the wisdom to address these mysteries. Thus, drawing on experts in academia and the private sector is imperative. At the NIC, we tried a number of experiments to extend or test openness, since most of our estimate work dealt with mysteries, not puzzles.[31] These experiments hardly exhausted the range of the possible.

We brainstormed almost every major estimate with outside experts in meetings that were seldom classified. On an important new subject, humanitarian crises, we began an estimate with a conference at which major NGOs, such as CARE, presented brief papers — an unusual and happy collaboration for both intelligence and its newfound partners outside government. Those papers constituted, in effect, the first draft of the NIE.

In another experiment, we commissioned think tanks to write what were, in effect, "parallel estimates" to those being done in the usual way within the intelligence community. These parallel estimates dealt with longer-term mysteries for which the comparative advantage of secrets was small, such as the future of Russia or of the European Union. We sought both to illuminate the substance at hand and, as important, to see what we could learn from outsiders about the process of producing estimates. Our purpose was not to grade who did better — for better or worse, estimative judgments about mysteries usually cannot be graded for years — but to see what we might learn about the process of framing those mysteries.

This experiment superficially resembled a similar one two decades earlier, the so-called Team A/Team B competition. A team of outsiders critiqued intelligence's estimates of Soviet strategic nuclear capacity. However, that exercise was undertaken on a very politically sensitive subject in an intensely political climate, which was not the case for our parallel estimates.[32] It was instructive, though, that when the outsiders had completed the Europe paper we had commissioned, our colleagues inside intelligence declined to do their own estimate. They argued that they were too short of manpower to do it, but they also admitted that

---

31   These innovations, most of them not really new, are described in more detail in my "Estimating Beyond the Cold War," *Defense Intelligence Journal*, 3, 2, Fall 1994, pp. 5–20.

32   See U.S. Senate Select Committee on Intelligence, *Report: The National Intelligence Estimates A-B Team Episode Concerning Soviet Strategic Capability and Objectives*, Washington, D.C., 1978.

they didn't think they had much to add to what the outsiders had produced.

The next steps in involving outsiders would be to bring them directly into the writing of estimates or other papers, not just into parallel projects. We experimented by asking outsiders to answer the key questions of estimates, and then we appended their answers to the "official" estimates. But intelligence might turn to outsiders to draft estimates, perhaps in conjunction with a conference to consider ideas or drafts. Depending on institutional arrangements, think tanks or other outside institutions might convene insiders and outsiders; the convener outside government might bring to the table better contacts with academia and NGOs than intelligence will have.

For their part, the insiders could bring special sources or perspectives to bear, as appropriate. For instance, for an estimate we did on the implications of the AIDS epidemic, virtually all the basic data were openly available. Yet the focus of our analysis ultimately became the implications of the epidemic for foreign militaries and leadership groups. That subject was scarcely treated in analysis outside government, and for it, special intelligence sources were helpful, if not decisive.

Insiders also bring a sharper sense for the questions at issue within Washington policy-making. For instance, the general purpose of the estimate on humanitarian emergencies was to foresee imminent needs, but the specific objective was to help the U.S. Air Force Transportation Command (TRANSCOM) plan its deployments over the next year. TRANSCOM knew it would be involved ferrying relief and had come to the sensible conclusion that it was better to think ahead than be entirely surprised. Insiders kept the specific concerns of that government consumer in mind throughout the drafting.

ESTIMATING AS PROCESS

Agencies that produce intelligence analysis traditionally lavish most of their resources on their written products, just as the NIC gives pride of place to its NIEs. In more than one sense, that is appropriate. NIEs force NIOs to do their homework and keep them in touch with "their" community of analysts. In another sense, though, the emphasis on written products is misplaced. The policy culture is very much an oral one and, given how fast policy deliberations move, written products often arrive too late or out of focus.

That is true in spades of NIEs, given the cumbersome process by which they are produced. The more we could learn about the state of the policy discussion and its timing, the greater the chance that an NIE or other analysis would make a difference. We searched for points in the policy process that might be particular targets of opportunity for NIEs. For instance, in the run-up to a visit by a visiting head of state, an NIE done two months before might find its way into the paper mill of interagency preparation for the visit. We might get one done the week before the visit into the president's reading pile. However, an estimate that was finished three weeks before the visit probably would be too late for the interagency process but too early for the president's last-minute reading.

We also tried to keep in mind that the NIC's main audience, assistant secretaries and above in the policy agencies, had neither the time nor the inclination to wade through a long estimate. To try to reach them, we created a President's Summary of each estimate. These summaries were no more than four pages long, so they could be browsed in several minutes. They were fully consistent with the longer estimate but were not merely a summary of it. Instead, we organized the summaries to highlight the points that were, as near as we could tell, those in which senior policy-makers were interested. The President's Summary was then hand-delivered to the president and to cabinet-level recipients of the PDB. We hoped that if the president did not always read something called the President's Summary, at least assistant secretaries would feel compelled to!

5

―――――――――――――――――――――――――――――――――

Spying, looking, and catching criminals

As a young Senate staffer I was once briefed by Ted Shackley, then the head of the East Asia division of the Directorate of Operations (DO) and later deputy director for operations (and still later under suspicion for questionable arms dealings once he'd retired from the CIA). It was 1976, and we were sitting in a room at CIA headquarters in Langley with a combination lock on the door. Shackley began by saying: "I'm in the business of producing spies. If I wanted to produce widgets, I'd be in private industry." At the time I was mightily impressed. I had studied at a school of management, and most of my reading about and experience of foreign affairs had left me with the impression that its practitioners didn't think they produced anything. In contrast, Shackley did. He knew what he produced.

It was only later that I realized I was wrong and so was Shackley. He didn't produce spies. He didn't even produce information. What he really produced, or sought to, was useful insights in the heads of policy-makers who needed to act. Spies were only a way station to those in-sights. So was information. Yet the culture of the DO treats producing spies as the goal, not the way station.

It is not easy for outsiders to write about spying. But if war is too important to be left to the generals, espionage is too sensitive to be left to the spymasters. All of America's foreign policy institutions had their worlds upended by the end of the Cold War, but the change was sharpest for America's clandestine service, the CIA's DO. It is now shambling about without a mission, many of its best young officers leaving and its morale reeling from the aftershocks of discovering

136

traitors in its midst, Aldrich Ames and Harold Nicholson. It needs to be entirely reshaped.

THE RANGE OF CLANDESTINE OPERATIONS

The starting point for change is distinguishing among DO operations that, while kindred, are separable — liaison, espionage, covert action, and counterespionage. Liaison activity involves sharing information and working with foreign intelligence and police services. The CIA maintains liaison with 400 different foreign intelligence, security, and police services around the world. Those connections involve varying mixes of cooperation and competition. As former Deputy DCI (DDCI) William Studeman put it: "We are all each other's partners, and we are all each other's targets."[1] In the CIA's relations with traditional counterparts where the relationship is of long standing, the equation is weighted toward cooperation: no spying on each other, though nothing requires that each partner tell the other the whole truth; crown jewels remain national secrets. Other liaisons, though, are less durable "marriages of convenience" rife with "infidelity." The CIA uses such arrangements to get access to a foreign service and its operatives, while the foreign service seeks something from the CIA as well, usually help or information. Liaison functions carry risk (the extent depending on the country) because they associate the CIA with the actions of those foreign services and the foreigners who staff them.

Even though there is a degree of risk inherent in liaison activities, they can be usefully distinguished from espionage — persuading foreigners with money, ideology, or other inducements to provide information secretly on their politics and institutions. Common usage labels CIA officers as "spies," but they are not. The spying is done by foreigners whom those CIA officers recruit. The CIA spymasters, known as "case officers," then manage (or "run") their "assets," or "cases" — the foreigners who do the spying.

Covert action is the obverse of espionage. Both depend on secret links to foreigners. But espionage involves extracting information and usually requires CIA case officers to be patient, passive, and quiet as they wait for the information to flow from the foreign spy to them. To be sure, the case officer will ask questions and provide guidance: Can

---

1   Quoted in Tim Weiner, "The CIA's Most Important Mission: Itself," *New York Times Magazine,* December 10, 1995, p. 80.

you find out about this or that negotiating position? But, for safety's sake, much of the initiative is left to the spy, and all the paraphernalia of spying — "dead drops," disguises, coded messages, and the like — are employed to protect the spy and his or her connection to the American government and the CIA.

The aim of covert action, by contrast, is to influence events in the short run in foreign countries. The case officer asks the foreign connection to act and to do so in a specified time frame. With timely action, the risk that the secret connection to the CIA and to the United States will be revealed goes up. These differences — action versus passivity, short-run versus long-range goals — lead to organizational cultures for spying and covert action. At the CIA's beginning, the United States had for a time two clandestine services, one for spying and one for covert action. That proved unwise, for the two services found themselves competing for agents, but the tension between the two clandestine tasks is inherent.

Finally, most spy novels, such as those written by John Le Carré, are not about either espionage or covert action but about counterespionage; not about seeking information or influencing events but about detecting when one's own service has been penetrated by a "mole" or double agent, pretending, like Aldrich Ames, to be a loyal officer but in fact working for an enemy service.

SHAPING AMERICA'S CLANDESTINE SERVICE

The lessons of Pearl Harbor and World War II pointed, as chapter 3 outlined, to a centralization of intelligence. However, just as those lessons did not foreordain that the central agency would not just coordinate intelligence but would also collect, analyze, and produce it, they did not make inevitable that the same agency would also dominate all three clandestine functions — espionage, covert action, and counterespionage. The grand debate about reshaping the U.S. government became more intense as the nation's challenge shifted from learning the lessons of the last war to preparing to fight the next one, which became the Cold War. The debate encompassed both Congress and the executive branch, and as the debate within the latter crystallized, the reshaping began. The National Security Act of 1947 — which created the National Security Council (NSC) and the CIA and made the Air Force a department separate from the Army — ratified the results of the debate until then and set the terms for the next round.

On the espionage side, the transfer of the Office of Strategic Services (OSS) functions to the War Department in 1946, like that of the analysts to State, had been no more than an interim holding action. At the War Department, the OSS espionage and counterespionage officers had been combined in the Strategic Services Union (SSU). Once the Central Intelligence Group (CIG) was created, it and the SSU were partly merged while the process of selecting who and what would be permanently transferred to the CIG went on. As early as July 1946, National Intelligence Authority (NIA) Directive 5 gave the Director of Central Intelligence (DCI) the mandate to conduct "all organized Federal espionage and counter-espionage operations outside the United States and its possessions for the collection of foreign intelligence information required for the national security."[2] Espionage became the province of the CIG's Office of Special Operations (OSO).

The CIG's monopoly, however, was not uncontested. The Army insisted that it be allowed to conduct clandestine intelligence operations, an insistence that prefigured later military operations. That argument dragged on for a year, into the debate over the National Security Act. The FBI, which had conducted wartime espionage and counterespionage in Latin America, also asserted its claim. In December 1944, FBI Director J. Edgar Hoover had proposed a worldwide intelligence operation run by the bureau on the lines of its Latin American operations.

Hoover's plan had some support, in particular from within the State Department. President Truman, however, thought the FBI should be confined to the United States. He was also concerned that giving an intelligence mandate to the FBI would create a "gestapo organization" and that the image such an agency would have might undermine good neighborly relations in the hemisphere.[3] Given Truman's view and the CIG's creation, Hoover stopped pushing his own plan and wound down FBI operations in Latin America by the end of 1946.

The National Security Act formalized the CIG as the Central Intelligence Agency. The CIA was authorized to conduct "such other functions and duties" as the NSC might direct, but, surprisingly in light of

2 Cited in *Evolution of the Intelligence Establishment, 1945–50*, Foreign Relations of the United States, Washington, D.C., p. 233.
3 Cited in Mark M. Lowenthal, *U.S. Intelligence: Evolution and Anatomy*, Westport, CT: Praeger, 1992, p. 4.

what had gone on before and came soon after, the debate turned on espionage, not covert action. The War Department's inheritance from the OSS had included "special operations" — the range of psychological and propaganda operations and direct support to partisans behind enemy lines during World War II. While SSU's War Department overseers worked hard to sustain a capacity for espionage until a national decision could be made about a successor, they took no similar pains to sustain covert action operations, and the capacity dwindled even before the OSS was wound down.

Events of 1947, as the Cold War seemed to verge on becoming hot, reawakened interest in covert action. Communist governments took power in Poland, Hungary, and Romania, and the communist coup in Czechoslovakia in February 1948 sent particular shock waves through Washington, for the country had been a democracy before the war. Given the near-hysteria over Soviet gains in Europe, the debate centered on *how* to conduct covert actions rather than on *whether* to conduct them. In one sense, it was logical for the State Department to take on these operations as a secret adjunct to its open information work. Yet then Secretary of State George Marshall would have none of it; he feared that any exposure would undercut the department's overt diplomacy.

Washington's internal debate then split into two streams, one dealing with foreign information programs managed by State and the other dealing with covert action. State's attitude toward covert action remained an uneasy mix of fastidiousness about forming too close an association and worry about what the CIA might do on its own. The result of these pullings and haulings was NSC Directive 10/2, approved by the NSC in June 1948, which fashioned an Office of Special Projects within the CIA. The office would have considerable autonomy under a head who would be nominated by the secretary of state but would be acceptable to the DCI and would retain special ties to State and Defense as well as the NSC.[4]

The compromise was unworkable almost from the start. In Washington, it was awkward for the CIA and galling to the DCI to have covert operators who were in but not entirely of the CIA. In the field, the problem was one of cultures within cultures; the apparent similarity

4   The document is reprinted in *Evolution of the Intelligence Establishment, 1945–50*, Foreign Relations of the United States, Washington, D.C., p. 713.

between espionage and covert action is misleading, and it confused operations. They are misleadingly similar because they both depend on clandestine networks of foreigners, so giving the action role to the CIA seemed natural. The confusion results from the contradictory purposes of the networks. The espionage network is quiet, with an emphasis on secrecy and protecting the foreign assets, and the role of Americans is limited to asking questions.

For covert action, by contrast, the Americans' role is driving, and the purpose is doing something to affect the politics of a foreign country. Thus, the risk that the secret network will be "blown" is much greater. To OSO's spymasters, the covert actions specialists, in what was named in purposeful obfuscation the Office of Policy Coordination (OPC), sometimes looked like a band of dangerous cowboys. By contrast, to OPC operators, the OSO's spymasters could easily look too leisurely and too passive in combatting the Soviet threat. Relations between the two in the field were uneasy to the point that they actually competed for agents.[5]

As a result, it became plain that despite the difference in culture, if the United States was to have a clandestine service, it should have at most one (though the military services, the Army in particular, from time to time sought and received permission to run its own secret intelligence operations). After 1950, OSO and OPC were gradually integrated within the CIA's Directorate of Plans (artful obfuscation again), later Operations. The two-cultures problem, however, is built in, and it persisted in the DO.

FRAMING AN ASSESSMENT

How effective has the CIA been at spying? Toting up the balance of gains and risks for espionage is made difficult by the secrecy of the enterprise, yet the evidence that can be assembled is damning. The CIA's efforts through its DO to gather secret information about other countries with spies and paid informants can yield important, useful information. When bungled, though, these clandestine activities have proven to be costly, not only in financial and human terms, but also to the nation's public image. The Ames debacle is the most damaging in a long string of foreign policy embarrassments attributable to clandestine ac-

5   Karalekas history, p. 385.

tivities. Fundamental changes are in order, or else the costs of spying will continue to outweigh the value of the information obtained.

The DO's entire Iran operation, put together after the hostage crisis of 1978, was rolled up by Iran in 1988.[6] A long-time insider reports that there was not a single significant Soviet recruitment; all of the best Soviet sources were walk-ins during his Cold War tenure. A senior CIA analyst judges that in his twenty years of working on the Soviet military, he received help from HUMINT only once — from Oleg Penkovsky, a walk-in.[7] The CIA learned that all of its East German and Cuban spies were in fact double agents.[8]

Young DO officers say they are laboring under the tyranny of numbers; they need to notch "scalps" — that is, recruit spies — without regard to their value. This results in many sources but few that have much value. These young officers also report that they feel under pressure to convert their contacts into sources — to turn open conversations in which they pose as something other than CIA officers into clandestine relationships, with all the trappings of espionage. The relationships then become secret and indirect, and the sources are often asked to take a lie detector test to verify their authenticity.

When asked what differentiated the targetings they received in their cover jobs from those they were given by their CIA superiors, often the answer is "not much." Indeed, in many places it is an open secret that genuine American diplomats can be distinguished from CIA officers posing as such by the quality of the lunch the Americans host. The CIA is much better funded than the State Department, so if the lunch is generous, the host must be a CIA officer in fact, regardless of what his or her business card indicates.

6   See Stephen Engelberg and Bernard E. Trainor, "Iran Broke C.I.A. Spy Ring, U.S. Says," *New York Times*, August 8, 1989, p. A6.

7   See Jerrold L. Schechter and Peter Deriabin, *The Spy Who Saved the World: How a Soviet Colonel Changed the Course of the Cold War*, New York: Scribner's, 1992. Penkovsky's take was so rich that in disseminating it within government, the CIA attributed it to a number of different spies to protect his identity. His information on the Soviet missile program was instrumental in shaping the U.S. response to the Cuban missile crisis. Penkovsky, a risk taker who was fond of a picture of himself in his American colonel's uniform, was eventually caught and executed by Moscow.

8   For a sharp indictment of the clandestine service, see an account by a former officer, Edward G. Shirley, "Can't Anybody Play This Game?" *The Atlantic Monthly*, February 1998, pp. 45–61.

The numbers-driven incentive structure runs through the DO, where senior officers have grown up in the system and therefore are not likely to overturn it. It will require dramatic changes to arrive at a system that provides incentives for quality recruitments against hard targets, rather than quantity recruitments against relatively easy ones. As it is, most DO officers recruit most of their spies in their first two tours of duty.

The tyranny of numbers, as well as the issue of risk versus gain, is illustrated by several recent episodes. In 1995, France and the United States tangled over spying on each other.[9] Two years earlier, a female U.S. officer, operating under nonofficial cover — that is, posing as engaged in business or some other private pursuit — had approached a French official. She purported to represent a Texas foundation and asked the Frenchman to write reports on French economic issues. The official, reputedly Henri Plagnol, was an economic advisor to French Prime Minister Edouard Balladur. He met five times with CIA officers in Paris hotels and took money from them. However, when French counterintelligence confronted him with the CIA connection, he agreed to cooperate in building the case against the U.S. official.

France expelled the officer and four CIA colleagues, whose names were leaked to the French paper *Le Monde*, in February 1995. The affair became a public row mostly because of French domestic politics, particularly the feuding between Balladur and his interior minister, Charles Pasqua, who probably was responsible for the leaks. Pasqua and the U.S. ambassador to France, Pamela Harriman, traded public statements over who was responsible for the open dispute over matters usually handled discreetly, at least between friends.

The episode raises questions about having CIA spymasters operate under nonofficial cover, but it also suggests larger issues about the value of the information in relation to the risks taken in obtaining it. The spymaster's quest for information had intensified in December 1993, as the Uruguay Round of the global trade negotiations was nearing a conclusion. France's position and its leverage within the European Union were critical on a number of issues — agriculture and telecommunications, in particular — so there was a basis for the urgency Washington

---

9   This account is based on interviews and on published accounts. See *Washington Post*, January 12, 1995, p. A18; February 22, 1995, p. A19; February 23, 1995, p. A1; February 24, 1995, p. A15; March 7, 1995, p. A10.

felt.   Whether Plagnol's information was decisive or trivial is hard to determine; however, he argued later, as was plainly in his self-interest, that he provided information that was available to any attentive reader of French newspapers.   One of his written reports to the U.S. officer was titled "France's Relations with NATO" — not exactly an unknown subject.[10]

The CIA's involvement in Guatemala raises the issue of balancing the gain versus the risks from espionage in even sharper terms.   In this case the risk was not just embarrassment for the United States, but the involvement of Guatemalans who were on the U.S. payroll in acts that violated U.S. or international law and prevailing moral, ethical, and human rights standards.[11]   From 1984 until the early 1990s, the CIA had on its payroll a Guatemalan military officer, Col. Julio Roberto Alpirez. A number of Guatemalans implicated Alpirez in the 1990 murder of a U.S. citizen and the 1992 death of a guerrilla fighter married to American lawyer Jennifer Harbury.   Congress was not told until 1994 that Alpirez was a CIA asset, even though the CIA had informed the Justice Department in 1991.   Indeed, the State Department did not know of the connection for some time either and thus misled Congress about the nature of U.S. contacts with Alpirez in good faith.

In January 1996, the president's own Intelligence Oversight Board (IOB) reported on its investigation of the case.[12]   It found that the CIA had employed many informants in the Guatemalan government and military forces over the previous decade whom agency officials knew were involved in assassinations, torture, kidnappings, and murders in that country.   The IOB also concluded that CIA officials wrongfully kept information about these crimes and other human rights abuses committed by their paid Guatemalan informants from Congress, thus continuing to violate U.S. law until late 1994. The specific law at issue was the 1980 requirement that the House and Senate intelligence oversight committees be kept "fully and currently informed . . . of any significant intelligence activity and any significant intelligence failure."

10   See *Washington Post*, March 7, 1995, p. A10.
11   This case is based on interviews and on published sources. See, especially, *Washington Post*, January 29, 1996, p. A1, and October 3, 1995, p. A14.
12   "Report on the Guatemala Review," June 28, 1996, available at www.us.net/cip/iob.htm.

One unnamed informant "was the subject of allegations that in multiple instances he ordered and planned assassinations of political opponents and extra judicial killings of criminals," the report said. Another was alleged to have "planned or to have had prior knowledge of multiple separate assassinations or assassination attempts." A third was accused of involvement in killings and kidnappings, while "a few" others were accused of "acts of intimidation."

In addition to finding that the CIA's station in Guatemala failed to investigate reports about questionable activities by some of its informants, the board confirmed a long-standing suspicion in Washington that the CIA's officers in Guatemala became too close to their Guatemalan assets — a common risk in spying — which led to not asking enough questions about what their spies were doing. In an instance documented by the CIA inspector general in 1994 but publicly described in detail for the first time by the IOB, the CIA station chief "delayed, diluted, and suppressed some reports because he feared they would hurt the reputation of the Guatemalan military services and his ability to work with them."

Whatever the tangle of who knew what when, the essential point is that during this period the CIA became involved with the Guatemalan military for one purpose — countering leftist movements in Central America. Richard Kerr, then the CIA's deputy director, said the CIA was at that time doing "hard things with tough people" such as the Guatemalans.[13] It was getting on with that job, and it was not pausing to consider with whom it should or should not work. The potential for such abuses is built into secret relationships. The CIA may establish links for one purpose, but it cannot escape association with other acts by those it is aiding or from whom it is seeking information. In this case, finding out about unsavory characters meant associating with those characters and then becoming associated with them once the connection was disclosed publicly.

THE CULTURE OF SPYING

The dilemma of spying is that the culture it has spawned in the DO is powerful, but one that is fundamentally at odds with accountability in

13   Quoted in *Washington Post*, October 3, 1995, p. A14.

the U.S. government, however one judges the results of espionage. Just as intelligence often is equated with spying, the DO *is* the CIA. Picture badges worn by officials in other foreign affairs agencies also carry the bearer's name. That is not the case for all CIA badges, because it would be awkward to append names to the badges of those DO officers under cover. Using pseudonyms would be silly and confusing to co-workers, but using real names would mean that the badges would have to be left inside the building, thus negating their main purpose — controlling entry to and exit from the building. The reason my daily schedule at the NIC was classified Secret, I later understood, was because I might have a meeting with a DO officer under cover. I occasionally did have such a meeting, but it was instructive that the building's starting practice was not to delete names (or surnames) on those rare occasions, but rather to classify my entire schedule all the time.

A deputy director for intelligence (DDI) once said to me, poignantly, that the organization chart made it appear that all four CIA deputy directors were equal. That's hardly true, he said, for the deputy director for operations (DDO) is clearly something more than first among equals. Indeed, as a practical matter, he, as DDI, had to get clearance from at least several of the DO's senior subordinates — the chief of the CE division, the old Soviet division, for instance — if his plans intruded on their areas. The DO is about three times the size of the DI, and its budget is at least that much larger. The difference in status, though, runs deeper than money or people. Spying is intelligence but analysis is not quite. In any case, spying is uniquely an intelligence function; it is where intelligence began. By contrast, many people around official Washington do analysis; intelligence analysts are only one such set of analysts among many. Robert Gates was the first, and so far the only, DI officer ever to become DCI; in contrast, several of his predecessors had come from the DO.

The essential dilemma of the clandestine service is that those attributes that have enabled the DO on occasion to be effective and creative are precisely the opposite of accountability in the American system of governance. The dilemma runs through all of government but is painfully sharp for the DO. When the clandestine service has been effective, it has been so because junior officers were cut a wide swath of discretion and encouraged to react quickly to changing circumstances. They are rewarded for acting, for solving problems, not referring them to superiors, and their dedication to duty is legendary. The action is abroad, in the DO's stations, not in Washington; station chiefs abroad often effectively outrank their Washington division chief "bosses."

However, these attributes of discretion and autonomy run directly against the principles of accountability in the American government, which, for better or worse, seeks to narrow discretion downward while it pushes authority upward. The DO is a more disciplined and bureaucratic structure than it was when I first encountered it seriously two decades ago. It is probably also less dynamic. Yet its very effectiveness has depended on traits that are the opposite of accountability. The same attributes that produced a Bob Ames, the DO's legendary Middle East hand and penetrator of the Palestine Liberation Organization (PLO), also made possible an Aldridge Ames.

Aldridge Ames's career is a kind of caricature of the attributes of the clandestine service. He had begun working for Moscow in 1985 but was not arrested until 1994. By then, the information he had provided had helped the Soviets roll up the entire U.S. spy network in the Soviet Union, including the execution of ten spies. His actions also led to serious concerns that, knowing who was spying for the United States, Moscow had fed disinformation back to the CIA, false information later disseminated throughout the top of U.S. officialdom.[14]

Ames had been spotted by FBI agents watching the Soviet embassy and tracking Soviet officials in Washington soon after he started working for Moscow in 1985, but the FBI did not follow up. For its part, the CIA failed to offer explanations for the meetings even though Ames had not reported most of them to his superiors, which was a direct violation of CIA rules. In effect, Ames disappeared into the legendary black hole of competition and mistrust between the CIA and the FBI. Interest in the case picked up in early 1986 because two Soviet double agents then reporting to the FBI while working in Washington were recalled to Moscow and executed (the CIA is not allowed to run spies in the United States, so agents are handed off to the FBI if they are posted to this country).[15]

At first, attention focused on Edward Lee Howard, a failed junior CIA officer who had been cashiered in 1983 and subsequently managed

14   See James Adams, *Sell Out: Aldrich Ames and the Corruption of the CIA*, New York: Viking, 1995.
15   See, for instance, *New York Times*, January 27, 1995, p. A18, and January 30, 1995, p. A16.

to defect to the Soviet Union. But the investigators could not make Howard fit: He had not been in a position to identify both the double agents for Soviet intelligence. There had to be a mole in U.S. intelligence other than Howard. A December 1990 memorandum, written by Ames's supervisor but apparently not shared with the FBI, pointed to Ames, then one of a score of officers under suspicion, as a man who had recently spent more than $600,000 from unknown sources.[16]

Yet the mole hunt waxed and waned in intensity over the years after 1986, and it was not until 1991 that the CIA and FBI really began to work together on the case. From then on, the noose slowly tightened around Ames's neck, but only as exhaustive reconstructions of the movements and meetings of Soviet officials in the mid-1980s kept showing Aldrich Ames as part of the picture.[17]

In one sense, his DO colleagues treated Ames no differently from the way most people treat their colleagues or subordinates. When things went badly for him, they cut him slack, hoping the trouble would blow over. No superior wants to come down hard on a subordinate who is having problems, so Ames's erratic behavior was attributed to his drinking, not a rarity among his clandestine service fellows, or his messy divorce.

Yet Ames worked for no ordinary organization, and the culture of that organization interacted with the all-too human foibles of his supervisors to produce disaster. By custom, the CIA administered the polygraph in a severe manner to would-be entrants. Indeed, I had two former colleagues in government who had risen to senior positions, both of assistant secretary rank, in other foreign policy agencies after having failed the CIA polygraph as young people. Ironically, both had access to the same documents they would have been cleared to see had they become CIA careerists.

Compounding the irony, the CIA tended to administer the polygraph much more leniently to officers with tenure in the agency. It did so with Ames, just at the point when midlife disappointments over money, love, and career made him vulnerable to turning, or being turned, to the other side. Ames had, officials said, given deceptive answers in 1991

16   Reported in *New York Times*, August 2, 1994, p. A1.
17   See *New York Times*, November 24, 1994, p. A15, and December 1, 1994, p. A29.

during a lie detector test when asked, in effect, whether he was a spy.[18] The CIA polygrapher regarded the test as routine and, instead of following up the deception, rephrased the question to help Ames through the test.

Ames was, in broad government terms, a middle ranking officer, not a senior one. His career had not been successful, but neither had he been a complete flop. He continued to have assignments that put him into contact with some of the CIA's most sensitive secrets, the names of some Soviet agents whose lives depended on the secrecy of their connection to the United States. He had responsibility that did not seem commensurate with his middling status. In that responsibility, though, while he was unusual in the government, he was not unusual within the DO. In the DO, middle officers are given considerable discretion.

This dilemma — that success at espionage rubs against accountability in the American government — cannot be wished away. It can only be limited. Spying may be the world's second oldest profession (or even the oldest), so the argument that it cannot be made to go away has some merit. In the world of the 21st century, the United States will, as chapter 2 noted, face dangers to its security. The dangers will not be mortal, but some of them will be lethal and secretive — terrorists and remaining rogue states, and the weapons of mass destruction produced even by states that are not enemies. They will not advertise their bombs or their plans for taking hostages.

Beginning to build a basis for reshaping the clandestine service would be advanced by a searching review, one that was constructed to be credible outside the DO and outside government as well as inside, of just how well the DO has done at espionage. Counterespionage failures, such as Ames, get investigated in painstaking detail, but espionage is evaluated only in the context of failures such as the Indian tests. The Ames affair was the subject of a number of investigations, and those results, together with cases such as Guatemala and France, provide some calibration of the risks of conducting espionage. What is lacking is a sense of "compared with what gain?" With the passing of the Soviet Union, there is both a need and an opportunity to conduct such a review. The congressional intelligence committees might take the lead, or, better, they might work with an administration in creating an Aspin-Brown-like panel but more sharply focused. Not all of such a review

---

18   See *New York Times*, March 8, 1994, p. A1.

could be made public, but, given the passing of the major Cold War espionage targets, much of it could.

TO SPY OR NOT

Not to prejudge such a review, but at first blush, the record of American espionage seems unimpressive. Its signal successes are relatively few, and its failures are embarrassing. Against that record and in the context of a more open world, why not forswear espionage? The question is less easily dismissed out of hand than it is in the public debate. So much more information is available openly. Not all of that information is there for the asking — some of it takes careful looking — and what is there for the asking requires meticulous culling of useful tidbits from the Web's indiscriminate stew.

Whether espionage could be ended depends on which objectives the United States wants to achieve. When I was running the national intelligence estimates (NIE) process, I was preoccupied with mysteries. At this distance, I cannot recall a single spy report that shaped or affected my view of a particular mystery. Indeed, in those closed countries that were moving toward more open politics, such as Russia, spies often reported what was later available in the *Financial Times*. And sometimes the *Times* scooped the spies!

The reasons why spying added so little to understanding those mysteries are not hard to fathom. For the Soviet Union and other closed societies, basic data, the building blocks for unravelling mysteries, were secret and so had to be ferreted out by spies or secret technical collectors. Now, while specific documents or deliberations may be secret, basic data are less and less so. Not that the data are easy to assemble: Russia's own economic managers may be hard-pressed to calculate this month's domestic output. Yet the point is that their uncertainty is real. It is not that those managers could tell us the number if only they would, or that a well-placed spy could steal it from them.

By the same token, while a well-placed spy might have helped the U.S. government understand how long Boris Yeltsin might live, by passing along detailed medical reports that were not released to the public, Yeltsin felt the pressure of democracies to make more and more information available about his health. He invited foreign doctors to witness his heart operation. Moreover, even if spies might have helped the CIA to assess Yeltsin's health more accurately, they could not have been of much help in understanding what would ensue after he passed from the political scene.

By contrast, during a succession crisis in the Soviet period, those spies might have provided basic leads about who was up and who down in the Politburo. It is not that unraveling the mystery of what might occur is easier now; indeed, it may be harder now than it was before, for there is so *much* information and so much of that is noise. It is just that spy reports aren't likely to be of much help in sorting through that noise. Those reports would mostly record the views of close-in observers, many of whom would report the same view openly, if discreetly, to official Americans. Reports from spies might be regarded as less tainted by the tendency of the Russians in open conversations to tell Americans what they thought those Americans wanted to or should hear. Yet spies themselves are not disinterested. They have their own reasons for exaggerating their own roles, knowledge, or influence.

I suffered from the effects of this tendency of spies to exaggerate once early in my own career. When I was a young NSC staffer, I had limited authority to talk with a representative of a country, a man who was formally a diplomat but in fact was an intelligence officer. My authority was limited to specific business we needed to conduct with his country. Yet I, although young, was a "White House" official and so was probably the most impressive contact this officer had. When my White House bosses learned of one of his reports, it turned out that he had attributed all he had learned about what was going on inside the U.S. government at the time, from Asia to the Camp David peace process, to me. It looked as if I had been talking out of school! I hadn't, but even my NSC colleagues found it hard not to give credence to a spy's report with all the aura of secrecy, so I still felt the sting of rebuke.

The secrets that spies can reveal are more useful with regard to puzzles, but their usefulness depends on the nature of the puzzle at hand. For very immediate operational puzzles, secrets can be decisive, and they are almost always reassuring. They can supply the missing puzzle piece. As Iraq began to move troops toward Kuwait in 1990, an Iraqi spy's report apparently added weight to the argument within official Washington that Iraqi troop movements were the preparation for an invasion, not just Saddam Hussein's bluster in pursuit of extorting money from Kuwait.

In other cases, spies' secrets can seem to reveal the puzzle's solution and so be especially reassuring. In my experience, if a spy could steal for us a foreigner's negotiating position, our negotiators were unvaryingly appreciative. In one sense, their enthusiasm always surprised me because it seemed to me that if they, as negotiators, weren't pretty confident what their foreign counterparts would propose, they weren't doing their job very well. Yet life *is* uncertain, negotiations are tense, and no negotiator wants to be surprised. So I came to think that knowing the other side's position was like the huge briefing books that legend has Henry Kissinger preparing for every encounter with a fellow foreign minister but never opening — a welcome security blanket.

However, spying for these tactical purposes is a target-of-opportunity enterprise. What spies may hear or steal today, or be able to communicate to their American case officers, they may not hear or see or be able to get out tomorrow. What is decisive today may be unobtainable tomorrow. Worse, the crisis moments when information from spies is most valuable to us may be precisely when they are most exposed, when to communicate with them is to run the greatest risk of disclosing their connection to us. To the extent that the foreign policy business at hand depends on repetition, the target-of-opportunity secrets that espionage produces are less valuable.

Secrets are more valuable with regard to enduring puzzles, ones that will still matter tomorrow if they are not solved today. A foreigner's negotiating position is a perishable secret; after today's round the U.S. negotiator will know it. By contrast, the order of battle for the Iraqi military is an enduring puzzle: Whatever we know today, another puzzle piece will always be welcome tomorrow. Similarly, some hints about the organization of the Hizbollah terrorist organization will be useful even if we fail to get tactical warning of today's terrorist operation. For these puzzles, spying will continue to be useful. Indeed, sometimes it will be the only way to obtain a missing puzzle piece.

RESHAPING THE CLANDESTINE SERVICE . . . IN SERVICE OF NSA?

The United States will not forgo espionage given the continuing threats, outlined in chapter 2, from terrorists, rogue states, and other secretive foes. Yet if it is to conduct espionage with less risk of costly errors and embarrassments, it needs a completely overhauled clandestine service, one that is small, tightly targeted, and mostly operates independent of American embassies abroad. Indeed, the task of reshaping the clandestine service is so sweeping as to make one nostalgic for 1946 when the wartime OSS was disbanded. When the United States again created a clandestine service in the CIA several years later, it could start over but begin with a cadre of experienced hands from whom it could pick and choose.

The required reshaping of the clandestine service goes well beyond what is imaginable in today's political climate, but the basic principles can be set out. First, espionage should be narrowed to focus on potential foes near U.S. troops deployed abroad, the governments of a small number of potentially destabilizing rogue states, and closed groups that threaten to engage in terrorist activities against the United States.[19] In the post–Cold War world, far-flung clandestine activities across the globe can no longer be justified. The cost in terms of risk of clandestine operations warrants their use only when the information obtained covertly would significantly enhance U.S. national security. A streamlined clandestine service would yield a greater payoff for the United States.

Second, this streamlining implies that the CIA would no longer have stations everywhere around the globe. There is merit to the counter-argument, that tomorrow's untidy world makes it impossible to predict where the United States will want to act, and so some infrastructure for spying should be sustained almost everywhere. The argument is particularly strong with regard to supporting military operations. When the United States intervened in Somalia in 1991, for instance, it had no existing network of local agents and so had to try to build one from scratch.

Yet recent experience suggests that *where* the United States dispatches troops abroad will be hard to predict with much advance warn-

---

19   The language of the Aspin-Brown commission is on the mark: "The Commission believes that CIA's recruiting efforts should focus on those 'hard' targets that cannot be adequately covered by other means. These would include the 'rogue states' whose activities threaten U.S. interests, states that deny access by the outside world to their territory, and transnational groups that threaten U.S. security. The CIA should be working against these targets, wherever and however they may present themselves, as its first priority. Collection against lesser targets which is more easily accomplished but is relatively unimportant to U.S. interests should be avoided. In the view of the Commission, it is preferable to try against the hard targets and fail, rather than to succeed against easier but unimportant targets." (*Preparing for the 21st Century*, Washington, D.C., March 1, 1996, p. 68.)

ing; yesterday it was Somalia and Haiti and Bosnia, but tomorrow it might be Burundi or Liberia or Peru. The only way to be prepared in advance to support American troops would be to sustain an infrastructure for spying virtually everywhere. On balance, the risk of such a far-flung presence outweighs the gain.[20] It is a matter of judgment, but in today's more open world to sustain CIA stations in countries that otherwise would not be priorities for espionage is to insure that there will be more Guatemalas and more Frances — more nasty flaps over spies and spymasters for too little gain.

Third, the narrowed targeting of the clandestine service means it should be tasked separately from, and more narrowly than, the rest of the intelligence community. It should focus only on those high-value secrets that cannot be collected another way. The value of those secrets can, to be sure, only be assessed in light of what is available openly. But the task for the clandestine service is obtaining the critical secrets.

Fourth, the reshaped clandestine service would have few stations abroad, and those would mostly be limited to liaison activities. Instead, it would operate from the United States and through case officers abroad operating under nonofficial cover, as NOCs. The argument for operating without diplomatic cover is twofold. By now, diplomatic "cover" is paper thin; local employees in any U.S. diplomatic establishment joke about the transparency of current arrangements. What the official cover provides is not so much cover as diplomatic immunity, so that the worst that can happen to a CIA case officer if he or she is caught spying by the host government is a quick expulsion from the country, as occurred in the French case. If cover is to be serious, it requires operating outside diplomatic cover, as business people or NGO representatives.

The other argument for operating with nonofficial cover is the changed targets of espionage. During the Cold War, when the DO's targets were, first, Soviet officials anywhere, and second, officials and politicians from the local country, the diplomatic cocktail party circuit was not a bad place to troll for recruits. As former DCI Gates put it: "In the Cold War, if you wanted to recruit an East German or a Pole,

20   This is also the conclusion of the Twentieth Century Task Force on which I sat. See p. 14 of the Twentieth Century Fund report, *In From the Cold,* New York: Twentieth Century Fund Press, 1996. For a cogent statement of the counterargument, see Richard Kerr's dissent, pp. 21–22 of the same report.

the vehicle for that contact was the diplomatic cocktail circuit or the tennis court. None of the guys you're interested in now are on that circuit. None. You're not going to recruit a rogue nuclear scientist at a cocktail party."[21] Nor are Hizbollah terrorists or Colombian drug cartel leaders likely to be frequent guests on the diplomatic circuit. Getting at such targets is not easy in the best of circumstances; starting with an official U.S. connection is a handicap. In Gates's words, the

> biggest challenge [is] . . . how to move the clandestine service away from the embassy to a more independent status, without the protection of diplomatic cover or a diplomatic passport. That represents a fundamental revolution in the way CIA has conducted itself. Your whole training program, your language program, the way you pay salaries has to change. The risks are different and much higher. You no longer want people who can do tea and cookies in the afternoon. You have to look for a new kind of personality — different from the vast majority of the spies, who are primarily white middle-class guys. You need a guy walking into Tripoli or Pyongyang who doesn't look like he just left Iowa.

The disadvantages of nonofficial cover are that it is expensive and time-consuming to implement, and given the lack of diplomatic immunity, it is potentially dangerous. CIA officers operating under official cover already are distracted to some degree by the need to do the diplomatic cover job they are supposed to have in addition to their espionage work. The more convincing they try to make their cover, the greater the distraction. For officers with nonofficial cover to be convincing, they need actually to do their cover businesses or other pursuits. Even if they do it well enough to be convincing, few will do it well enough to be profitable, so they will cost the United States probably considerably more than CIA officers operating under official cover.

The NOCs are less productive, at least in the sense of having less time to devote to espionage. All espionage is a patient calling; relying on nonofficial cover will call for special patience. In current practice, NOCs also require considerable support from the local CIA station, so their value is limited. Yet to get at the targets of interest, case officers will have to abandon the familiarity of the embassy circuit. There is no alternative to NOCs, either ones operating from the United States or in a foreign country.

---

21   This and the next Gates quotation are from Tim Weiner, "The CIA's Most Important Mission: Itself," *New York Times Magazine*, December 10, 1995, p. 67.

Finally, the future mission of the clandestine service will be less spying to collect information than facilitating its collection by technical means. The service will gather secrets less through what its own spies hear than through the sensors those spies can put in place. It will have a particular role with respect to SIGINT. As chapter 3 discusses, the bulk of funding for SIGINT goes for satellite-based collectors, but most of the take comes from ground stations, many of them clandestine. Indeed, the proportions are almost a mirror image. At the same time, while the precise details are secret, the United States probably breaks more codes by stealing code books from foreign communications facilities than by breaking the codes with NSA supercomputers and brainy mathematicians. Already, the DO is more of a code breaker than is NSA.

In the future, as chapter 3 outlines, SIGINT will need to get closer to the signals in which it is interested. During the high Cold War, the Soviet Union sent many of its phone calls through microwave relay stations; since private telephones were relatively few, intercepting those conversations yielded important insights into economic production and sometimes military movements or lines of command. American intelligence built an impressive series of satellites with orbits designed to intercept those microwave signals — the KH series.[22] Now, though, with hundreds of communications bundled into fiber optic lines, there is less for satellites to intercept. If SIGINT is to intercept those signals, it will have to tap into particular communications lines in specific places.

The same imperative of getting close to sources will hold true for other collectors. Imagine the value of collecting straight from a personal computer's keystrokes, before software encrypts the message. Or implanting sensors to monitor movements, or hidden cameras to check identities of, say, drug traffickers at particular meetings. Technology will soon make it possible to monitor foreign leaders' heart rates through small sensors embedded in clothing. Getting these collectors close to their targets will be a critical mission for a reshaped clandestine service.

For these risky roles, the DO with its foreign assets will continue to be preferred to the U.S. military, which would put the lives of American soldiers in danger. As chapter 3 indicates, the lack of intelligence that is precise enough is one reason why specialized military units, such as the

22   See Jeffrey T. Richelson, *America's Secret Eyes in Space*, New York: HarperCollins, 1990.

Delta force, are so seldom employed in the war against terrorism. But the risk to U.S. lives is another reason, one that is more than a little callous but is nonetheless a fact of life: For many of the riskiest missions, such as smuggling sensors into terrorist camps, it is too risky to send an American; better to send a foreigner on the DO payroll than a U.S. military special operator.

SPYING FOR MONEY

Economic espionage — for instance, spying to gain an advantage in trade negotiations — poses special concerns for a reshaped clandestine service. In 1995, President Clinton signed Presidential Decision Directive (PDD) 35, which spelled out the case for intelligence support to economic policy: "Economic intelligence will play an increasingly important role in helping policy-makers understand economic trends. Economic intelligence can support U.S. trade negotiators and help level the economic playing field by identifying threats to U.S. companies from foreign intelligence services and unfair trading practices."[23] For the clandestine service, the particular issue is how much the United States should spy on friends for economic purposes.

Young DO case officers echo in private the more public qualms about their trade. They grumble that they were prepared to manipulate relations with foreigners, their "cases," to entice people to betray their countries during the long Cold War against the Soviet Union. Those cases often became their friends, or, if not, the case officers acquired responsibility for the fates of those they sought to target. But that was acceptable so long as national security was plausibly at stake. The same is not the case if the purpose of the spying is economic gain. Then, the manipulation seems crass, so some of the best younger officers leave the clandestine service. The preferences of younger CIA officers are hardly the sole indicator of American national interest, but they are one such indicator.

For the CIA to spy on foreign countries or their companies for the benefit of American companies would be, in the categories of chapter 4, "offensive" and "private." It would be "tactical" if the secrets passed to the companies were an occasional thing, a spillover from the CIA's

---

23   Samuel D. Porteous, "Looking Out for Economic Interests: An Increased Role for Intelligence," *The Washington Quarterly*, Autumn 1996, p. 193.

spying for the purpose of government policy. If the clandestine service consistently targeted agents to find secrets of value to the company, then the activity might be labeled "strategic."[24] Successive DCIs wisely have ruled out both the tactical and the strategic forms of spying for private advantage. Gates put it most colorfully, stating that the CIA "does not, should not and will not" spy on behalf of American business.[25]

The current approach is the right one for several reasons. For one thing, private U.S. companies are not exactly clamoring for help. Sure, many of them wouldn't mind a valuable tidbit from the government if it were available. But because the essence of business is repetition, information that is here today but not tomorrow has less value. And most companies, especially big ones, invest money in a whole range of ways of finding out what their competitors are up to, from market research to a little spying of their own.

In the world of the market state, moreover, deciding what is an "American" company is a more and more vexing choice. Today, in most cases the choice would be tolerably clear: Boeing would be favored over Airbus, our General Electric over Britain's. But the choice is getting harder: Should the government favor the company headquartered in the United States over one headquartered abroad but with large operations and many employees here?

For these reasons, a flat prohibition now makes sense, but both intelligence's growing economic role and the nature of the market state will make it harder to sustain that clear ban. As intelligence collects more economic information for the purposes of government policy, it will inevitably acquire more bits that have commercial value to private companies, so the temptation not simply to leave those bits on the cutting-room floor will increase. Now, intelligence agencies pass those bits of information to another department, usually Commerce, leaving its officials to decide whether or not to pass the information on to a private

24   Loch K. Johnson distinguishes between "microeconomic intelligence" for benefit of business and "macro" for government. *Secret Agencies: U.S. Intelligence in a Hostile World,* New Haven: Yale University Press, 1996, pp. 147–149. See, also, *Worldwide Intelligence Review,* Hearings before the U.S. Senate Select Committee on Intelligence, 104 Cong., 1 sess., 1995, p. 126.

25   Cited in Loch K. Johnson, *Secret Agencies: U.S. Intelligence in a Hostile World,* New Haven: Yale University Press, 1996, p. 153.

company or citizen. Over a longer time period, as the market state changes the definitions of both the public and the private sector, and forces the two together more intimately, new forms of cooperation by intelligence with the private sector will arise, and in the process, intelligence may share more information with private colleagues.

Now, though, the issues are spying and eavesdropping for the purposes of the government. In chapter 4's categories, these clandestine activities would be "offensive" or "defensive" depending on their purpose. For instance, tipping U.S. negotiators off in advance to their foreign counterparts' position would be offensive and tactical. Tactical help is secrets-rich, for economics just as it would be if the negotiations were about arms control.

It is true that while Washington can buy models of Japan's economy if it needs them, there is no market in the specific negotiating positions of trading partners. It is also true that U.S. negotiators virtually always like knowing what those officials on the other side of the table will say. But spying for economic advantage runs against the American grain. Moreover, because spying is inherently a target-of-opportunity enterprise, negotiating positions that a spy can provide today, he or she may not learn tomorrow. So counting on espionage to produce the missing puzzle piece is risky.

If whether to spy, often on friends, for economic purposes is an issue, so is whether to eavesdrop or otherwise intercept their communications. Those intercepts may be less a target-of-opportunity enterprise than is spying, because a line tapped or a code broken today probably will still be available tomorrow. Instead, the risk is that the more the intercepts are used to gain a tactical advantage, the greater the chances that those intercepted will suspect what is going on. So the practical question again becomes whether the take is worth the risk of embarrassment should the source be disclosed.

For instance, in October 1995, press accounts described U.S. eavesdropping on Japanese officials during sensitive negotiations with Japan the previous spring, negotiations conducted under the looming threat of sanctions to cut off Japanese luxury car imports to the United States.[26] Each morning a small team of intelligence officers gave Mickey Kantor, the United States trade representative, and his aides in-

---

26   The story had been reported earlier by the *Los Angeles Times*, but it was the *New York Times* story that captured Japan's attention. See *New York Times*, October 15, 1995, sec. 1, p. 1.

side information gathered by the CIA's Tokyo station and by NSA's electronic eavesdropping equipment, then sifted by CIA analysts in Washington. Kantor received descriptions of conversations among Japanese bureaucrats and auto executives from Toyota and Nissan who were pressing for a settlement, and he read about the competing pressures on Japan's trade minister, Ryutaro Hashimoto.

The information in this instance apparently was useful, unlike the economic spying on France, which seems to have produced little more than what could have been easily learned from public sources. Yet the risks still seem too high. In this case, the eavesdropping was also a target-of-opportunity enterprise. The trade ministry, MITI, and the foreign ministry perennially fought over turf, and as a result, MITI officials in the negotiation refused to communicate over secure equipment that was the property of the foreign ministry. Instead, they talked over open phone lines. If the U.S. eavesdropping was easier in this case, the risk of disclosure was greater, because the subject was economic and thus the American officials concerned were less accustomed than their politico-military colleagues to handling sensitive intelligence.

In the event, the Japanese reaction to the disclosures was relatively restrained, perhaps because they suspected the United States of spying or eavesdropping all along.[27]   The United States rebuffed Japan's ambassador, refusing to confirm or explain the published reports. Japan labeled the response "unsatisfactory," but both sides seemed determined not to let the frosty exchange diminish the warmth of a rare visit by a U.S. president to Japan, scheduled for three weeks later.

Economic spying or eavesdropping for defensive purposes seems less objectionable than for this offensive purpose and also, probably, more necessary. Foreigners, including friends, will indeed not advertise the bribes or side payments they make to win contracts. Moreover, defensive purposes — for example, countering the efforts of foreign intelligence services, including those of friends, to penetrate American governmental institutions or firms — almost by definition requires clandestine operations. A 1995 survey by the State Department and the newly created National Counterintelligence Center (NACIC) of 173 companies found 466 incidents of theft, many of them directed at technologies that are regarded as critical for the nation's economic future. Only 58 percent of the companies involved, however, reported

27   See *New York Times,* October 28, 1995, sec. 1, p. 4.

the thefts to the U.S. government. Those companies noted "the low probability of finding the culprit and bringing him or her to justice."[28]

That said, it is easy to overstate how much U.S. friends spy on us and how successful they are in doing so. Celebrated cases of foreign spying make splashy news.[29] It is often charged, for instance, that Japan spies on the United States for economic purposes; in fact, what Japan does is what the United States should do better, and that is to assiduously mine open sources and open contacts. The French case at the beginning of this chapter underscores the costs of such U.S. spying operations when they are blown. There would be less temptation to reach for covert sources if the State Department were equipped to do a better job of reporting on economics — on the economic institutions of major economic powers and on international financial institutions.

Periodic reviews of ongoing collection operations, both within the executive branch and with congressional overseers, are imperative to making sure the reward justifies the risk. At least one recent blue-ribbon panel explored the idea of reciprocal understandings to limit spying in countries friendly to us. In the end, those seemed unworkable. But the point of periodic reviews, outside the DO, would be to impose a broader standard of risk. Does the information gained really justify the potential risk, conceived broadly?

HIRING LOOKERS

The changed world calls for a much more focused clandestine service, because so much of the world of the 21st century will be open despite the lethal and secretive dangers that will remain. Economics exemplifies the possibilities of that more open world. During the Cold War, it was necessary to spy; now, in most of the world, even in those areas that used to be closed, it is possible to simply *look*. There is little need to spy on, for instance, the European Central Bank or other foreign economic institutions. In principle, diplomats or other trained lookers could report on them in the usual way. Better yet, economic experts — analysts — inside government could be in touch both with published sources and with their colleagues on Wall Street and elsewhere interested in the same issues.

---

28   John J. Fialka, *The Washington Quarterly*, Autumn 1996, p. 181.
29   See, for example, a reported French intelligence paper that targeted U.S. industry. Discussed in *Sunday Times* (London), April 11, 1993, p. 3.

More generally, there would be many ways to do the looking once the need for it was acknowledged. Some of these ways would cost money, but money is not the main obstacle. Rather, the main obstacle is that looking would require the U.S. government, and intelligence in particular, to do business in very different ways, ones that run against long-established organizational patterns and that conflict with American practices of, for instance, government-business relations.

At first blush, it is tempting to wish that the long decline of the State Department could be reversed. This most fundamental improvement in "intelligence" would be one apparently not to do with intelligence at all. It would be arresting the long decline of the State Department, which once produced first-rate political reporting abroad and political analysis at home. It now does little of either, and the nation suffers for it. Nothing, it seems, would be as cost-effective in improving our nation's intelligence in foreign affairs, conceived broadly, as reviving the State Department.

Admiral Bobby R. Inman, a career intelligence officer who had been both director of NSA and DDCI, was poignant on that subject in testifying before the Aspin-Brown commission:

> What I find . . . substantially different from the . . . Cold War is the is-
> sue of openly available information, where what you need are observers
> with language ability, with understanding of the religions, cultures of the
> countries they're observing, where one does not need the cost of the pro-
> cessing tied to the denied collection. . . . In the world ahead of us there is
> no diminishment in the need for in-depth analytical activity with world-
> wide coverage . . . [and] we have to rethink how we go about assembling
> the vast array of information that is openly available to observers who
> have the competence to understand what they're doing. . . . The best way
> to go about that would be a very substantial rebuilding of the Foreign Ser-
> vice.
>
> I go back to my early years as an analyst, and reflect on the enormous
> use both for daily briefing and for detailed activity that turned to the re-
> porting from bright political, economic, cultural affairs, commercial at-
> taches, legal attaches, military attaches, with language ability. The coun-
> try began to draw down those numbers in 1967. . . . Additional require-
> ments for consular, visa activities further diverted the capabilities within
> the State Department. A number of us argued these issues in the early
> eighties when the rebuilding began, and wanted the State Department

budget put in the same national security arena to be examined the same way.[30]

The foreign service has never thought of itself as in the "intelligence" business; in fact, it shuns the label. But surveys again and again record that foreign service reporting is the basic wherewithal for intelligence analysis. According to studies conducted for the Aspin-Brown commission, 80 to 90 percent of the information collected by the clandestine services arises from open sources of information. In the commission's words: "In some areas, such as economic analysis, it is estimated that as much as 95 percent of the information utilized now comes from open sources."[31]

Even if that figure is high, it is wasteful for clandestine collectors to gather so much publicly available information. The trouble is, strained for funds and stretched by new countries to cover, the foreign service does less and less serious reporting. More and more, it is a landlord for other agencies, a stamper of passports, and a tender of official foreign office channels. The anecdotes are humorous but telling. The U.S. embassy in London houses some 600 people, but only six of those are State Department political officers; there are more people in U.S. military bands than in the American foreign service serving abroad. There were reports that because the State Department lacked the money even to open embassies in the newly independent states of central Asia spawned by the collapse of the former Soviet Union, it had to depend on the intelligence community resources. If those reports were true, diplomacy became the tail of intelligence — just the reverse of wise foreign policy.

Yet, tempting as the vision of a State Department renaissance may be, it is not going to happen. It was a sadness of recent political seasons that good arguments about the need to reshape the State Department were hijacked by those who wanted to slash the department, not reform it. No secretary of state within memory has paid much attention to the department's capacity as an institution. Warren Christopher commendably came to do so, but he and the Clinton administration came late and lamely. His successor, Madeleine Albright, mostly tried to make the best of the changes Congress had forced on the department. That

30   Aspin-Brown Commission, *Preparing for the 21st Century,* Washington, D.C., March 1, 1996, appendix at www.fas.org/irp/offdocs/reform.htm.
31   Aspin-Brown Commission, *Preparing for the 21st Century,* Washington, D.C., March 1, 1996, p. 88.

Congress is not now likely to shift money from intelligence to the State Department.

Moreover, the explosion of information technology and a more open world mean that a reshaped State Department would not resemble today's version. The U.S. government can simply buy much of the basic economic and political reporting on particular countries; it does not need to produce that information itself. *The Economist* is a pretty good start, and it can be bought on the newsstand. Beyond it, the sources range from Oxford Analytica to Bloomberg, with new entries to the burgeoning market all the time. It would make little sense for the State Department to reproduce a capacity it can now acquire elsewhere.

Under the threat of terrorists, moreover, today's embassies have become virtual fortresses, not relaxed bases for reaching out into local society. Each blue-ribbon panel after each terrorist event urges that they become more so. That was the case after terrorists bombed American embassies in Tanzania and Kenya in 1998. Admiral William Crowe, the former chairman of the joint chiefs of staff, called for the nation to at last fund the new structures and other security measures that previous such panels had recommended.[32] The funding never happens, but still the embassies are daunting; those foreigners who need go there for visas run the gauntlet. They have no choice. But today's embassies hardly serve as bases for either espionage or reporting.

An alternative to the fortresses would be "diplomats without embassies."[33] Danger lurks almost everywhere in today's world, but it is routinely present in only a few places. In many locales, diplomats could live and work without embassies. They would represent themselves as what they are, and they would talk openly with local politicians, officials, and others of interest. Most of their reporting could be done openly over unclassified channels of communication, but if need be, the same Radio Shack encoders that cause NSA such trouble could work for the diplomats as well.

My model for diplomats without embassies is a British foreign service officer I met in South Africa in the turbulent days of 1986. He was assigned to London, to the Foreign Office's Research Department, a kin

---

32   Report of the Accountability Review Boards on the Embassy Bombings in Nairobi and Dar es Salaam on August 7, 1998, January 1999, available at www.state.gov/www/regions/africa/accountability_report.html.

33   This idea was suggested in a conversation with former U.S. Ambassador to Moscow Jack Matlock.

of State's Bureau of Intelligence and Research (INR). A bachelor, he spent part of most years on temporary assignment in South Africa. When the South African government moved from Pretoria to Capetown, as it then did each year, he would take a leisurely drive between one and the other, stopping in black townships along the way. He was known and welcomed in almost all of them, the result of many years of working the same account.

He had no visible ax to grind, and British policy mattered enough to make him worth the time of township leaders. He was worth their time for another reason: He was simply as well informed as anyone about what was going on in the townships during a time when communication was not that easy. As a diplomat, he was not likely to be hassled by South African officials. Local township leaders, and my white activist friends, sought him out as a source of information and a carrier of messages.

His kind are not easy to reproduce, because his success depended both on his personality and the South African circumstances of the time. Yet his experience does suggest attributes to pursue. Most notably, lookers need to be experts; intelligence's traditional separation of collection from analysis, never as sharp at it was described, is breaking down. The easiest way for collectors to know what to collect is to collect it for their own analysis. The CIA has made considerable use of "analysts in station," often doing work that in better days for the State Department would have been done by the foreign service. The analysts as lookers, though, are hampered by the need to take direction from the CIA station.

Perhaps to send diplomats abroad without embassies is to expose them needlessly to danger, hostage taking or worse. The concern is a fair one even though in many places the danger is relatively small. Instead of reporting themselves, State Department political reporters might become circuit riders for strings of unofficial Americans — or foreigners. Like many of my colleagues, I have often had the experience of visiting a U.S. embassy, in an official capacity or merely as an outside analyst sharing notes, to find that the local employees were the most interesting. To be sure, their roots in the local reality may give them stakes or biases, but they also give them a richness of context that it is hard for American foreign service officers to duplicate.[34]

34   Morton Abramowitz, former assistant secretary for INR and ambassador to Turkey, makes this point strongly about his time in Ankara.

Those stringers, students, business people, academics, or others might be paid a retainer or simply compensated for particular reports. Their work would be "unclassified looking," not spying. Some people might be leery of this kind of association with their government, but most would not; they would find it a nice focal point for their own research or observations, not to mention a source of pocket money.

The CIA's National Resources Division (NRD) tries to debrief Americans who travel to or reside in foreign places of interest. But it is triply handicapped in this task. As part of the DO, the NRD doesn't exactly advertise its presence. Americans who might be prepared to help their government may still be put off by the thought of working with the CIA. Finally, the NRD officers are all-purpose debriefers, not experts, so their sense of whom to seek out and what to ask is haphazard. It takes experts to debrief experts. It is much more rewarding to talk with someone who already knows a lot about your work — a fact that expert journalists use all the time in their conversations with senior officials.

The Army has experimented with officers who are both open reporters and, when needed, more surreptitious collectors. They conduct their basic reporting, like other military attachés, openly with their counterparts in the country where they are stationed. If the subject requires, they can turn the communication into a secure one, which would then be carried out with all the caution of espionage's usual tradecraft, which is designed to protect the collection activity and its connection to the United States.

Yet the liabilities of such multipurpose officers are more apparent than their virtues. The idea may have some appeal for military attachés, who are clearly identified and whose mission in reporting on foreign armies is well known. Used more widely, however, it would tar all civilian political officers as spies, thus compounding the problem that already afflicts all official Americans working abroad.

In fact, a series of blue-ribbon panel recommendations and congressional actions have been moving the Pentagon in the other direction, toward relinquishing its spying to the CIA. In 1992, the Pentagon was given the authority to establish commercial fronts for its own spying.[35]

35   See Tony Capaccio, "CIA Coaches Pentagon on Setting Up Commercial Spy Fronts," *Defense Week*, January 8, 1996, p. 3, and "Senate Bill Transfers Pentagon Spies Function to CIA," *Defense Week*, May 6, 1996, p. 3.

The Defense Department first moved to consolidate the espionage done by the various military services in a single Defense Human Intelligence Service (DHS). Wisely, though, in 1996, Congress directed the Pentagon to transfer its spying to the CIA. If the United States is to spy, it needs a single point of accountability.

LAW ENFORCEMENT

The 21st century will thrust the most traditional part of intelligence, the solving of puzzles with secrets, into the arms of law enforcement. By custom and law, national intelligence and law enforcement have been very separate activities. The 1947 National Security Act prohibits the CIA from having domestic law enforcement powers (recall that at the time there was fear of creating a gestapo). Executive Order 12333, signed by President Reagan, allows the CIA to "participate in law enforcement activities to investigate or prevent clandestine intelligence activities by foreign powers or international terrorist or narcotics activity." Connecting intelligence and law enforcement is not without precedent. But the connection will become much more intimate.

Intelligence and law enforcement agencies use the word *intelligence* in very different ways. For the CIA and its colleagues in the national foreign intelligence business, intelligence means puzzle solving or mystery framing that is good enough for action. The goal is policy. The context is a blizzard of uncertainty, often one that cannot be melted into clear contours. And the standard is "good enough to act": If the choice is between some action and none, or between several courses of action when doing something seems imperative for reasons either substantive or political, on which side does the evidence and inference weigh most heavily? Where can evidence and inference be marshaled into arguments convincing enough for those inside government — and plausible enough for those outside?

By contrast, for the FBI and other law enforcement agencies, intelligence is instrumental in another sense, not for policy but for cases. Intelligence means tips to wrongdoing or leads to wrongdoers. The goal is convictions. The context is individual cases. And the standard is that of the courtroom. It is beyond a reasonable doubt.

Because intelligence is careful not to reveal its sources and methods, intelligence officers try hard to stay out of the chain of evidence so that they cannot be asked to testify in a court of law. As a practical matter, that means that intelligence's role is limited to tipping off other agencies. When CIA or other "intelligence" officers help, they typically go into the field in teams with FBI, Drug Enforcement Agency (DEA), or other "law enforcement" officers.

These differing approaches to intelligence run through the processes of national intelligence and law enforcement. Intelligence for policy usually begins in secret. It does not always remain so: Skeptical publics have to be convinced, and so do still more skeptical foreigners. But the sources and methods of intelligence usually can be clothed in secrecy, even if politics bares the thread of the clothing. The presumptions of law enforcement are different. To the extent that intelligence is only tip-offs, it may remain secret. Beyond that point, however, evidence becomes part of the judicial proceeding. It is subject to disclosure. Sources rarely can be protected.

The tensions between intelligence and law enforcement were visible in the Clinton administration's investigation, in 1993, of alleged Iraqi plots to kill President George Bush.[36] The official conclusion was that key suspects in an aborted assassination plot against the former president were recruited by an officer of the Iraqi intelligence service. Based on that conclusion, the United States launched 23 Tomahawk cruise missiles against the Iraqi intelligence headquarters. U.S. intelligence agencies had turned up no direct evidence that Iraqi President Saddam Hussein was personally involved. Instead, the U.S. charge of Iraqi involvement was based on three types of evidence — forensic analysis linking a bomb smuggled into Kuwait by suspects in the case to other known Iraqi terrorist devices; incriminating statements made by the two main suspects, who admitted they had been recruited by the Iraqis; and other "classified intelligence sources" corroborating Iraq's masterminding role.

Bush had wanted to visit Kuwait soon after the U.S. victory in Desert Storm, but he did not manage a visit until after his own electoral defeat. The would-be assassination plotters never came near him during his triumphal visit, April 14–16, 1993, and the bomb was discovered on the eve of his visit. Insiders said that when measured against the standard

36   See reportage in *Washington Post*, July 1, 1993, p. A18, and June 29, 1993, p. A14. Philip Heymann, who as deputy attorney general was a participant in the episode, describes it in his elegant and sensible book *Terrorism and America: A Commonsense Strategy for a Democratic Society*, Cambridge, MA: MIT Press, 1998, p. 71ff.

the Justice Department in particular wanted to apply — that of the courtroom — the forensic evidence tying the bomb to other bombs made by Iraq was extremely strong. CIA analysts traveled to the Middle East to collect pieces of Iraqi bombs that they concluded were made by the same person who made the bomb found in Kuwait. The FBI's forensic analysis included a close examination of the soldering technique in the various devices, which amounted to a "signature" linking them to a specific designer. CIA and FBI officials made a second trip to reexamine the forensic evidence from the bomb.

This crossing of intelligence and law enforcement was not new. Intelligence long has been used to make the case for action in the court of public opinion. Recall Ambassador Adlai Stevenson brandishing U-2 photos before the UN during the 1962 Cuban missile crisis (as though anyone but a trained photo interpreter could have discerned anything meaningful from the blurry images!). What was different about this Iraqi case, and suggestive about the future, was the standard of proof that seemed required and the intense interaction of intelligence and law enforcement that was employed to reach it. It became clear that evidence good enough for policy was not nearly good enough for law. Intelligence is accustomed to inhabiting a world of uncertainty, but that uncertainty could not be taken into a court of law where "beyond a reasonable doubt" is the prevailing norm.

The argument over policy thus was related to this dispute about evidence. Should the United States ask Kuwait to extradite the suspects for trial in the United States? Or was a more immediate and direct response called for? By involving Justice and the FBI, the president had in effect asked for a second opinion to that of the foreign intelligence agencies, an opinion using different methods, evidence, and standards of proof. In the end, Attorney General Janet Reno's report concurred with that of DCI R. James Woolsey, and the decision to strike was taken.

The same difference over standards was apparent in CIA analysis relevant to the UN war crimes proceedings in Bosnia. A careful 1995 analysis of ethnic cleansing was puzzle solving at its best, combining refugee accounts with satellite photos.[37] CIA analysts concluded that 90 percent of the cleansing had been done by Serbs against Muslims. Was that assessment good enough as a guide for policy? It surely was. But the assessment was classical foreign intelligence, which discerned

37   This analysis is described in *New York Times,* March 12, 1995, sec. 4, p. 2.

patterns rather than pointing to individuals. On the question of most interest to the UN tribunal — how complicit were Serbian leaders in the ethnic cleansing? — intelligence could only say there was no conclusive evidence pointing to their involvement. Yet "the systematic nature of the Serbian actions strongly suggest[ed]" that they "exercised a carefully veiled role in the purposeful destruction and dispersal of non-Serb populations." Thus, UN officials in a new kind of law enforcement process were treated to the kind of fudged language that often has policy officials pulling their hair.

THE BUREAU AND THE AGENCY

Intelligence for policy purposes seems likely to become less important while intelligence for law enforcement becomes more so. With communism's collapse and the rise of the market state, the world is more open but also more infested with wrongdoing, for all the reasons outlined in chapter 2. As a result, the FBI is much more engaged abroad than it used to be. For instance, in 1994 the Bureau had under way some 50 investigations involving Russian crime figures.[38] By 1996, that number was 200.[39] In 1996, the FBI had 70 senior agents operating in 23 nations. During 1995, these attachés handled 11,200 issues. FBI Director Louis Freeh called the attachés the "single most significant factor in the Bureau's ability to detect, deter and investigate international crimes in which the United States or its citizens are the victims. . . . [It] expands the nation's perimeter of law enforcement protection."

In Freeh's words, "Another very powerful tool is training: the FBI places a high priority on assisting our foreign law enforcement counterparts through training courses here and abroad. And just a year ago we took a major cooperative step with other federal agencies and other foreign nations with the creation of the International Law Enforcement Academy in Budapest."[40] The Academy's eight-week professional de-

38   See *Washington Post*, December 14, 1994, p. A28.
39   This and subsequent numbers in this paragraph and the next are from Statement of Louis J. Freeh before the Senate Appropriations Committee, Subcommittee on Foreign Operations, Hearings on International Crime, March 12, 1996, available at www.fas.org/irp/congress/1996_hr/s9603.
40   The quotations in this paragraph and the next are from the Statement of Louis J. Freeh before the House International Relations Committee, Hearing on Russian Organized Crime, April 30, 1996, available at www.fas.org/irp/congress/1996_hr/h960430f.htm.

velopment program is similar to that of the FBI's national academy at Quantico. Two hundred foreign officers graduated in 1996, and in all, some 27,000 foreign counterparts had attended FBI training programs by 1996.

Freeh cited the effectiveness of these programs of international cooperation: "In a major move against a growing Russian organized crime structure in the United States, the FBI last year arrested Vyacheslav Kirillovich Ivankov, allegedly one of the most powerful Russian crime leaders in this country. . . . The arrests in New York followed an intensive FBI investigation that was aided greatly by the Russian Minister of Interior and the Royal Canadian Mounted Police and made possible because of our legal attachés and the relationships that have flowed from cooperation abroad."

Coordination across the intelligence–law enforcement divide has long been problematic. In 1992, for instance, five separate law enforcement agencies had responsibility for some piece of monitoring drug smuggling into the United States by air. There is now a Joint Intelligence Community–Law Enforcement (JICLE) working group, established in 1995. However, neither the CIA nor NSA accepts "tasking" from law enforcement agencies. Both adhere to a "principal purpose test," accepting only those taskings that are primarily intended to produce foreign intelligence. NSA is more restrictive than the CIA, which will accept tasking so long as the subject has some foreign intelligence value.

The combination of a demoralized and perhaps declining DO with an FBI that is extending its mission to new places, ones that were once the preserve of CIA spymasters, raises the risk of reopening the legendary turf battles between the two that characterized the early postwar decades. In the 1960s and 1970s, the directors of the CIA and FBI, Richard Helms and J. Edgar Hoover, respectively, did not speak to one another, and their agencies dealt with each other as sovereign powers, at best. By the 1990s, that history seemed buried, but it was in fact alive just beneath the surface. Tensions between the two were evident during the Aldrich Ames case. Bureau officials went out of their way to "background" the press on CIA mistakes — for instance, the lax CIA administration of Ames's polygraph in 1991 — and were equally careful to draw attention to the FBI's own role in catching him.

Yet the aftermath of the Ames affair did have a positive side, one that was most evident in counterintelligence but was not limited to that activity. The two agencies created the joint NACIC, located at the FBI. Senior FBI officials abroad began meeting with CIA station chiefs to discuss joint work against terrorists and other criminals — meetings that would have been all but unthinkable two years earlier. The two agencies began exchanging personnel in a way that also would have been unthinkable earlier, including at the top of counterintelligence and counterterrorism operations.

Equally important as the advances in counterintelligence is the fact that the FBI, which had been notoriously proprietary about its information (usually justifying its practice by the requirements of legal cases that were not yet public), became much more open to sharing information, and not just with the CIA. The result was impressive in the campaign against terrorism, which is much easier to talk about publicly than is counterintelligence. In a 1996 speech, for instance, DCI John Deutch argued that the CIA was recruiting agents with access to terrorist cells at an unprecedented rate. The agency had, he said, helped foreign governments arrest suspects five times in the previous two years. He specifically cited the 1995 arrest in Pakistan of Ramzi Ahmed Yousef, who was convicted of plotting to blow up a dozen U.S. commercial airliners and who stood accused of masterminding the 1993 World Trade Center bombing.[41]

For the foreseeable future, "pure" intelligence, as John Le Carré would label it, will cede ground to tactical operations, law enforcement in particular. Law enforcement is to HUMINT what support to military operations is to SIGINT and imagery — the new mission with appeal in the body politic, now that communism is gone. In those circumstances, the reasons why intelligence's modern founders kept the CIA, and thus the DO, out of law enforcement a half century ago will come under pressure but are still worth sustaining. The result will be continued skirmishing over turf and continued losses by the DO to its competition abroad, not just the FBI, but also the DEA and others. On the whole, though, that state of affairs will be better than trying to retarget the DO on law enforcement. A reshaped, smaller DO would still have plenty to do — focusing on dangerous weapons, rogue states, and terrorists — while playing a distinctly supporting role against drug trafficking and crime.

41   As reported in *New York Times*, September 6, 1996, p. A2.

THE QUESTION OF COVERT ACTION

The focus of this book is the gathering and use of information by intelligence agencies, so in this chapter, which deals with clandestine operations abroad, the concentration has been on spying to acquire information, not on covert action. Covert action, though, is important enough to merit a concluding word. And, as this chapter indicated at the beginning, while espionage and covert action are conceptually different, in fact they have much in common.

In particular, when the United States makes secret connections to foreigners through the CIA, it becomes implicated in those foreigners' purposes whether or not those purposes were the original reason for making the connection. This impossibility of separating purposes runs through all secret relationships. It was the case with the CIA and the Guatemalan military in the 1980s and 1990s. The CIA could try to support the military only in order to fight Central American radicals; in my experience, the limitation probably was sincerely intended, especially by the Washington officials who established it. But it could not stand. The colonels had purposes that ran beyond those for which the CIA supported them, and, sooner or later, the United States could not escape becoming implicated in those purposes. To traffic with "bad guys," even for good purposes, is to become tarnished with their badness.

The impossibility of limiting purposes is harder still when the United States wants foreigners to act, not merely provide information. Trafficking with bad guys is explicit in covert action, and it should be undertaken sparingly, only as a last resort when no other means will do. Events of the last decade have only reinforced the conclusions I drew when I wrote at length about covert action a dozen years ago.[42] The guidelines I outlined then are still the right ones. Their value is reinforced every time they are violated.

They are worth restating. Covert action should never be deemed routine. Hence, routine Cold War propaganda operations should be terminated. Covert action should be undertaken only in support of publicly articulated policy and only when overt means are unavailable, insufficient, or judged too costly in human life. Even then, it should be undertaken on the presumption that it will become public knowledge,

---

42   See my *Covert Action: The Limits of Intervention in the Postwar World*, New York: Basic Books, 1986, especially chapters 5 and 6.

probably sooner rather than later and perhaps well before the action is over — the *New York Times* test.

To say that covert action should be undertaken only as a last resort when other means will not do is not to imply that it should be used only *after* all else has failed. That almost surely consigns the covert action to failure. Covert action means providing foreigners with arms or money or encouragement and training. It is not likely to achieve dramatic purposes, and surely not late in the day. This test of means is analytic, not temporal: Is there no other option and, in particular, no other overt option?

The Clinton administration's blind eye to Iranian arms transfers to the Bosnian Muslims is an intriguing case in point. On the whole, the policy has to be regarded as a reasonable success. Beginning in the spring of 1994, the American ambassador in Croatia, Peter Galbraith, ostentatiously refused to object when his Croatian interlocutors raised the possibility of allowing Iran to transship arms through Croatia to the Muslims.[43] The Croats were hardly acting as philanthropists: Because Bosnia is landlocked, and its capital, Sarajevo, was under siege, the airport as a practical matter could be opened only with Serb acquiescence, so weapons for the Bosnians had to come in through Croatian territory. For Croatia, the benefits of the transshipment were considerable: It could exact a hefty "tax" in the coin of weapons for itself, while currying favor with the United States and keeping control of the arms spigot to its ally-enemy, the Bosnia Muslims. It was a neat trick all around for Croatia.

The U.S. action was probably about as open as it could have been. The administration, and the president in particular, were committed publicly to "arming the Muslims" in order to level the playing field in their conflict with both Serbs and Croats in Bosnia. America's British and French allies, however, were dead set against the arming. They had UN peacekeepers on the ground and feared that to arm the Muslims would only increase the violence in Bosnia and, with it, the risk to those peacekeepers. In the circumstances, letting the Muslims be armed while not actually doing it was fairly sensible. It probably met the *New York Times* test for covert action: Would the administration still favor the covert course it had chosen once the action appeared on the front page of the *Times?*

---

43   Of many accounts, see the one in *Los Angeles Times*, December 23, 1996, p. A14.

Surely, the arming was an open secret. I flew into Sarajevo in the autumn of 1994 while still a government official. I had not been privy to the internal discussions about the arms flow or Galbraith's role in them. But Zagreb, Croatia, was abuzz with rumors of both. My colleagues who had stopped there en route were concerned about what was going on. I had assumed that some arms, mostly small ones, were reaching Muslim soldiers, and everything I heard in Sarajevo confirmed that impression. Indeed, I spent a frightening but fascinating day traveling with the Bosnian prime minister, Haris Silajdic, from Sarajevo to Mostar and back. He was both impressive and charming, and as the day went on our conversation became franker and franker. By the end, he was complaining about the lack of heavier antitank weapons, and I was agreeing to do what I could when I returned to make the pipeline heavier. We skipped gingerly around the word "Iran," but he knew that I knew where the pipeline started. He worried openly that the longer the war continued, the more moderate Muslims like him would lose control to the radicals — a kind of code for Iran.

In this case, the covert action passed the *Times* test but failed its counterpart, that of informing Congress. The administration held its role in the arming very tightly. Indeed, the CIA itself was cut out. The administration argued that what it had done was pure diplomacy; it was Iran and others who were providing the arms, without U.S. assistance, so the effort did not qualify as a covert action that the law required be reported to Congress, specifically to the intelligence oversight committees of the House and Senate. I am no lawyer, but my guess is the administration could have won its case.

In my guidelines, however, the point of informing Congress was not just to comply with the law. Informing Congress, in secret, can be a kind a surrogate for what the American people might think if they could know about a proposed covert action. Informing Congress is thus as much a matter of prudence as of law. If Congress is informed at the "takeoff," it is less likely to object at the "landing," particularly if the landing is a rough one. In this case, the landing was not especially rough — by the autumn of 1995, the Croatians were growing weary of the Iranian role, and the arms pipeline dried up by early 1996 when U.S. troops arrived as part of the reshaped and NATO-led peacekeeping operation. Some of Clinton's harshest foreign policy critics in Congress were also sympathetic to the Muslims' plight, and if the administration had asked, Congress probably would have assented to the arming despite Iran's role.

On my last several tests, the administration's score is ambiguous. The Iran-Contra affair of the 1980s drove home the lesson that if the United States is to engage in covert action, it should do so through the professional agency designed for the role, the CIA. In Iran-Contra, White House buccaneers, Oliver North in particular, got in over their heads. This time around, the operation was a State Department–White House partnership, very closely held in both. The CIA and the Pentagon alike were cut out.

Galbraith had approached the CIA in the early spring of 1994 with the idea that the United States look the other way while Croatia smuggled arms into Bosnia. Agency officials objected: Neither they nor their colleagues in Washington thought such an operation could be kept tolerably secret, and they had good reason to worry about becoming de facto allies of Iran. Galbraith reported the conversation to his superiors in Washington. From then on, the CIA was cut out. Analysts suspected that arms were flowing and, more pertinently, that Galbraith and the American embassy in Zagreb were more than idle bystanders, but, so far as I can tell, the CIA leaders did not press their suspicions on the White House.

The arming of the Muslims demonstrates the importance of review procedures, both within the executive branch and Congress. To ignore or circumvent them is to court danger. That is as true within the executive as between it and Congress. Those procedures should be strengthened, not weakened. They should include, critically, periodic reviews of ongoing actions. As part of a public discussion, the CIA should undertake a historical review and net assessment of covert action, then make the findings public insofar as possible. That would be an invaluable counterpart to the review of spying.

6

![decorative divider]

The intelligence of policy

In the autumn of 1990, my predecessors at the National Intelligence Council (NIC) predicted Yugoslavia's tragedy with a prescience that is awe inspiring.[1] The national intelligence estimate, or NIE, concluded that Yugoslavia's breakup was inevitable. The breakup would be violent, and the conflict might expand to spill into adjacent regions. The analysis could not quite foresee the horror and special evil of what came to be called ethnic cleansing. Still, providing some shape to an uncertain future is impressive enough for intelligence, and this analysis actually predicted that future. This estimate was no weasel-worded least common denominator. The footnotes that registered dissenting opinions all sought to paint the outcome as gloomier than the basic text, not less so.

Yet so far as I can tell, the document had no effect. None. The reasons are provocative for understanding the connection between intelligence and policy. The senior levels of the Bush administration's foreign policy machine were preoccupied with other issues, so being told of one more disaster lurking in the wings was unwelcome information. It was news they did not want to hear. Hoping that Yugoslavia might somehow stay together was *convenient*. That convenience was reinforced, for many at the top of government, by experience. Lawrence Eagleburger, the deputy secretary of state, had been a Yugoslav "hand" as a foreign service officer; Gen. Brent Scowcroft, the president's national security advisor, had served there as a military attaché. They had come

---

1 For a description of the estimate, still classified, see *Washington Post*, September 19, 1991, p. A21.

to believe in an integrated Yugoslavia. They had seen it work; surely Yugoslavia was better than what might ensue if it broke apart.

Moreover, item number one on the foreign policy agenda was another state spiraling down into disintegration — the Soviet Union. If a Yugoslav federation seemed convenient, sustaining a Soviet one seemed imperative. A civil war in the Soviet Union seemed a real alternative in those days of 1990, and then what might have become of all those Soviet nuclear weapons?

The process ahead in Yugoslavia was as disastrous as it was beguiling. It was hard to resist independence for Slovenia, which was small, European, and prosperous — more like Austria than the Balkans. But if Slovenia could become independent, how could the same status be denied to Croatia, whose Muslim minority might have been digestible but whose Serbian minority surely was not? At the end of the deadly chain lay Bosnia: If it was permitted independence, it would be led by the Muslims, who constituted a small plurality in Bosnia, and then a bloodbath was certain because neither Croat nor Serbian Bosnians would abide Muslim rule.

To be sure, policy officials concerned with Yugoslavia at the time recall the estimate and the episode differently. They, or some of them at any rate, recall agreeing that any breakup of Yugoslavia was bound to be violent, indeed extremely violent. Thus, for them the estimate's foreboding was on the mark but not news; it was not "aha" but rather "duh." So, too, they remember sharing the estimate's implicit policy conclusion — that only by diverting Slovenia's drive for independence into the maintenance of a loose Yugoslav confederation could disaster be averted. In their recollection, they tried for such a confederation but failed.

And so the argument becomes a familiar one in the aftermath of a policy failure related to intelligence: If, in retrospect, the intelligence seems on the mark, did the policy failure derive from intelligence unheeded, or was the intelligence heeded but either not new or not really actionable? Did policy officers choose not to act in accord with the intelligence or were they unable to do so? In this case, policy officials needed to comprehend, then be able to act upon, a complicated double message: Yugoslavia is dead, long live Yugoslavia. The Yugoslavia of Marshall Tito, the one with which many of them were so comfortable, was indeed dead beyond resuscitating, but only some form of new confederation could save the region from a bloodbath.

ANALYSTS AND POLICY-MAKERS

Episodes like the one in Yugoslavia make intelligence analysts cynical about policy-makers. If the policy officers are not fools or knaves, they are ideologues, unwilling to listen to the truth, or their views on substance are dominated by short-run political considerations. By all accounts, those policy-makers reciprocate. They find intelligence mostly not very useful to them. Intelligence usually comes with its own policy bias or agenda attached, and sometimes it takes pleasure in telling policy how stupid its ideas are.

Take, for instance, the memoirs of former Secretary of State George Shultz. Here are his descriptions of intelligence: "unreliable," "wild plans," "out of control," "faulty intelligence to the president," "intelligence pattern alarming then vague," "is the secretary cleared?" "so much for intelligence," "ridiculous imposition," "CIA botches," and "intelligence cooking the books."[2] Shultz's descriptions cover the gamut of policy reactions to intelligence: Intelligence cannot be relied upon, and its operations cause policy heartache; it warns dramatically, then whispers; it holds its crown jewels so closely no one who might benefit from them ever sees them; and it has its own policy axes to grind, with its assessments tailored to suit. Shultz leaves out only one familiar policy complaint — that intelligence delights in sticking its finger in the eye of policy.

It is true that there is a conundrum at the core of relations between intelligence and policy. Not only are intelligence analysts and policy officials members of different tribes, most of the time intelligence cannot be directed by policy. By the time policy knows what it needs to know, it usually is too late for intelligence to respond by developing new sources or cranking up its analytic capacity. Thus, the essence of intelligence is anticipating what policy will want. It is building collection and understanding for what it thinks will be atop the agenda, based on what hints it can glean from policy. It must do so while recognizing that many of those efforts will be wasted because the issue for which intelligence prepared never will become hot.

This need to prepare for contingencies, many of which will never occur, is one of the ways in which the making of government policy is

---

2 See his *Turmoil and Triumph: My Years as Secretary of State*, New York: Charles Scribner's Sons, 1993. The quotations are, respectively, from pp. 50, 297, 307, 312, 425, 492, 493, 544, 595, and 619.

distinguished from decision-making in the private sector. Private sector analysts generally have a limited number of factors to watch — technology, commodity prices, strategies of immediate competitors, and the like. For intelligence, by contrast, the post–Cold War world is particularly shapeless, and the range of factors to watch, and for which to develop the analytic capacity for understanding, is in principle almost limitless.

This shapelessness of intelligence's task cannot be entirely eliminated. The U.S. government, though, makes the problem harder by so sharply dividing intelligence from policy, by centralizing analytic capacity in the CIA, and by drawing a line between foreign and domestic. There were good reasons for all those choices at the beginning of the Cold War, and some of those reasons linger on. But all three need rethinking now that first principles are again on the table.

Intelligence analysts and those policy officers they seek to help are indeed members of different tribes. The tribes do overlap, and people do move from one group to the other. The tribal markings are not entirely predetermined; because the roles themselves are so powerful, people bend somewhat to fit into them. Yet people do not choose to become intelligence analysts by accident. As one of them in an executive program I was teaching once put it: "If I'd wanted to sell shoes, I'd have done that. I became an analyst because I wanted to reflect, not hawk my wares in downtown Washington." Most analysts chose their profession because they wanted to think, not act, and to understand, not shape. Their temperaments are mostly professorial. They want to be left alone to understand Berlin's politics or Mexico's economics better and better. Asking them to be entrepreneurs in finding ways to get policy-makers to pay attention to their analyses is, for the most part, going against the grain.

Policy officials are different in almost every way. That is especially true of those policy officials who have been elected, but it also holds for those officers, mostly not career civil servants, who work for them. While intelligence focuses on "there," countries abroad, policy officials are absorbed in "here," Washington. They go to Washington from Wall Street or academia in order to act, to make something happen. Their tenures and thus their time horizons are short, not long; the average tenure of assistant secretaries is only a little over a year — not much time in which to signify. They are tempted to overstate how much difference Washington's actions, not to mention their own, can make.

By contrast, intelligence analysts tend toward a long view and to take the world as a given. They are steeped in the myriad of historical and cultural reasons why China's politics are what they are — and thus are likely to remain, never mind what Washington or anyone else does. Because they are so immersed in the "local," they are by profession believers in the adage attributed to former U.S. Congressman Tip O'Neill that "all politics is local politics."

Given their perspective, intelligence analysts can easily fall into thinking that part of their job is to protect overeager policy officials from their own enthusiasms. Of course, those policy officials see just the reverse: They see intelligence as perennial naysayers, eager to stick a finger in the eye of policy. There is some truth in both these stereotypes. In the first years of the Clinton administration, there was an internal debate about whether to lift the arms embargo in place against the Bosnian Muslims. Most of the executive branch was against doing so, for good foreign policy reasons: The United States had joined the embargo as an international undertaking, and U.S. allies were against lifting it because they feared that the Serbs would retaliate against their peacekeeping troops on the ground in Bosnia. However, President Clinton had spoken in favor of the idea, as had Republican members of Congress. And there was a certain undiplomatic logic to the proposition that, in the long run beyond the attention spans of international peacekeepers, the Bosnian Muslims could survive in a nasty neighborhood only if they could defend themselves.

The NIC did a special analysis on the consequences of lifting. While not wrong, the resulting paper was just the sort that irritates policy officials. It was what might be called "tour de force argument," where all the causal arrows point, improbably, in the same direction. Its effect was to leave policy with two messages, neither of which was very helpful: "Boy, is this a dumb idea," and "Nothing else will be any better." In this case, the paper implied that there was hardly any human condition, from peace in the Balkans to the common cold, that would not be made worse by lifting the embargo.

Policy officials see foreign policy issues through the prism of their own domestic stakes. While intelligence draws a bright line between foreign and domestic, that is not the case for policy officials. Because their focus is Washington, they see foreign policy issues as inseparable from the politics of governing. Those politics are Washington politics; the overseas dimension matters only as it gets reflected in those politics.

Indeed, the Washington politics can become so consuming that the ultimate purpose, affecting foreigners and foreign realities, almost fades from view. Each issue has its own substantive merits, but each also bears on who is up and who is down, who is building the stature to act and who may be losing it. Policy officials tend to see intelligence through the same prism; to them, it is not disinterested information, but rather part of the argument in the policy contest.

Intelligence is changing but is still a written culture, while politics, especially at the top, is mostly oral. I recall briefing Vice President Walter Mondale early in the Carter administration when he was about to take an official trip to Spain and Portugal. Like many politicians, he liked oral give-and-take, trying out his lines on his briefers. He began: "Let me see if I've got this right. Portugal is not a member of NATO, so we'd like to nudge them in that direction, building military-to-military cooperation." At this point, some temerarious soul (not me) said, "Um, Mr. Vice President, that's Spain, not Portugal." Mr. Mondale replied cheerfully: "Well, other than that, have I got it right?"

Given their stakes, for policy officials the standard is "good enough to act," and their time horizon for information is always yesterday. By contrast, for intelligence analysts, the professional standard is truth, and they are bound to want more time to build their analyses. The pressure of time can hardly be overstated. Much of the time the pressure is artificial. Issues will bumble along for weeks or months and then suddenly come to boil, for reasons more bureaucratic than real. But, for policy officials, the bureaucratic *is* the real, and it does intelligence little good to plead for just a little more time.

Indeed, it is an intriguing paradox of the post–Cold War period that national security in Washington has become, if anything, more frantic while the "real" world outlined in chapter 2 affords the United States what is, relatively speaking, a lull from the most dangerous threats to the nation. The reasons for the frenzy merit a book of their own. The immediacy of the media, the "CNN factor," is part of the answer. When the print media dominated public affairs, a "no comment" was not news. These days, though, a "no comment" uttered in the full glare of cameras can look as if the government is ill prepared, is caught by surprise, or even is trying to hide something.

Yet it may be the very shapelessness of this world that does not contain an overarching threat that makes for official Washington's frenetic pace. During the Cold War, any happening on the globe could, as a first analysis, be calibrated in its relation to the Soviet threat. Some of those judgments, like the worries in the 1980s that tiny Grenada's airport might become a staging point for Soviet jet transports, look odd in retrospect, but at least they provided some shape to the deliberations inside government. Now, lacking the Soviet threat as a reference point, almost any event must be assessed on its own merits: Is it trivial or important, and to what is it connected? Thus, an Albanian crisis or a run on the Thai currency eats up an enormous amount of official time, and so do a hundred other "crisis-lets" that turn out to be flashes in the pan. It is little surprise that members of the policy tribe may have a clear idea what they want to work on over the next year but almost no idea what will be in their in-box next Tuesday.

Intelligence lives in a world of secrets, so classified information is normal and codeword reports — the special compartments beyond top secret that are used to restrict access to intelligence data — are familiar. In an important sense, classified is better than nonclassified, and codeword is best of all because it maximizes the special advantages of intelligence. If intelligence is a priesthood, codeword constitutes its sacred scrolls. Policy officials are not immune to the allure of secrets, but for many of them, handling codeword material is a nuisance. Most of the State Department is not, for instance, a SCIF (special compartmented intelligence facility), so officers can keep "secret" documents in locked safes, but they cannot store codeword in their own offices. They can see intelligence documents only when a courier brings them by to be read while the courier waits or when they leave their office and go to a SCIF.

Given these differences in approach and operating style, it is less surprising that intelligence and policy misconnect than that they ever connect at all. The points in the policy process when policy is interested in intelligence or information are out of phase with the points when intelligence has something to offer. Intelligence usually gets better over time, with regard to both puzzles and mysteries; more time lets it target its collectors and refine its analyses. To simplify, the contribution of intelligence might be thought of as a continuous process of improved analysis, as in Figure 4.

To simplify again, policy officials are likely to be interested in intelligence at three points during an issue's history, but for very different reasons. Early on, if they are prescient and see an issue coming, they may be interested in gaining some sense of its size and shape. Is it important

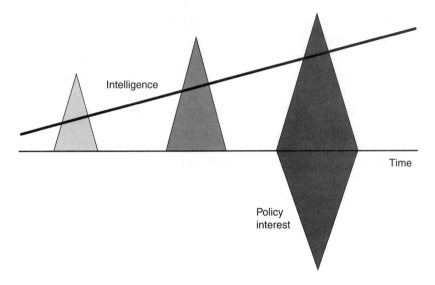

Figure 4. Intelligence Analysis and Policy Interest

or trivial? What is it connected to? Where are the levers for addressing it? And so on. The rub is that at this point, intelligence is not likely to have much to say; that will be the case unless intelligence has been unusually prescient itself, or unless policy officials have shared their own foreshadowings with intelligence, which is not a frequent occurrence in the American government. So, at this first point, intelligence will be just beginning to understand the issue.

Policy's interest will be engaged again when the issue is ripe for decision. At this point, though, policy officials will want intelligence only as it bears on the consideration of alternatives. Those officials need to decide; the time for acquiring a general understanding of the issue is past. Often, however, at this point intelligence is still at the stage of policy's first interest. Now, intelligence could make a real contribution in helping policy understand the shape and importance of the issue. The trouble is, however, that at this point policy is no longer interested in such an understanding, and intelligence is likely neither to have refined its analysis to the point where it bears on concrete choices nor to know exactly what those choices are. At this second point, the "face" of the issue for decision will be inseparable from domestic politics and may change day by day, even hour by hour.

Finally, policy officials tend to welcome intelligence at a third point, after they have made up their minds. They welcome it, though, *only* if it supports their view. Indeed, from intelligence's perspective, they may be *too* interested if the intelligence analysis supports their policy view, as they overstate or distort the intelligence to make their case. At the same time, they will be absolutely *un*interested, even hostile, if the intelligence does not support their view. That commentary is not necessarily a cynical one about policy, because interesting policy issues are hard debates over close calls. If they were easy, they wouldn't be so interesting, and most of the time they would not be much debated.

Lifting the embargo against the Bosnians, for instance, which the United States ultimately did in connection with the Dayton agreements of 1995, was not such an easy call as most of official Washington made it in 1993 and 1994. In the short run, the worries of America's European allies were on the mark; but in the longer run, Muslim Bosnia would not survive as a rump entity if its relative military might did not improve. The Muslim federation with the Croats in Bosnia was paper-thin at best; at worst, it was pure fiction. As one European diplomat put it to me at the time, for both Serbs and Croats, the Bosnia Muslims were "in the way." In the short run, the Muslims might be able to rely on UN and other international support; in the long run, though, when international attentions had shifted elsewhere, their own force of arms would be decisive.

This third point in the policy process, though, when intelligence is too welcome if it suits the preference of the policy official and entirely unwelcome if it doesn't, is a very uncomfortable one for intelligence. Intelligence conceives of itself as a teller of truth, but at this point in the process, its analyses are seen though the lens of the policy debate. The NIC analysts thought they were being objective in assessing the arms embargo. Policy officials downtown, however, saw the analysis as reflecting a policy preference: Those intelligence types are against lifting the embargo.

THE MESSENGER AND THE MESSAGE

Politicians live in a world of people, not analysis. A few politicians are analytic, but that is not what got them where they are in politics. It was their people skills. For them, calibrating the messenger is as important as understanding the message, often more so. Seeing and calibrating the expert can be compelling, while reading a paper or hearing a briefing seldom is.

The confidence that policy officials, especially elected ones, have in their people skills also makes them hardest to influence where they say they need most help — discerning the intentions of adversaries or partners. In the case of allies or friends, those policy officials will have frequent face-to-face contacts with their counterparts, so they will have both information and insight that intelligence lacks. Given their success in their own system, they can fall prey to the temptation to believe they are better at understanding what moves their counterparts than they actually are. With friends, in particular, policy officials are bound to say, in effect if not fact, that if so-and-so has a problem with what they want to do, he or she would just say so. To persuade them otherwise, intelligence must explain both the particular foreign leader's politics and the reasons why he or she might not be frank about those politics with American counterparts. The case has to be persuasive to U.S. policy officials who regard themselves as experts in politics.

With regard to adversaries, the challenge for intelligence is that policy officials may carry in their heads analogies or images of foreign leaders, mind-sets of which intelligence is likely to be ignorant. For instance, Lyndon Johnson and his colleagues in 1965 knew the World War II history of strategic bombing.[3] The vast bombing campaigns of the adversaries had brought neither industrial Britain nor Germany to its knees; quite the contrary, it had stiffened the backs of both Churchill and Hitler, and German industrial productions continued to rise until the war's end. That history was relatively close at hand, and intelligence might have used it explicitly in estimating the chances for success of the bombing campaign against North Vietnam, which was a poor country with few tempting industrial targets.

Yet Johnson also seems to have had in his head another analogy, this one of North Korean leader Ho Chi Minh, one that likened him to a recalcitrant U.S. senator. If Johnson could find just the right combination of carrots and sticks, expressed with the right combination of bluster and flattery, surely Ho would see reason. And so the bombing campaigns were accompanied by extravagant promises of public works projects that the North might receive once it made peace. For intelli-

3   On these deliberations, see Richard E. Neustadt and Ernest R. May, *Thinking in Time: The Uses of History for Decision Makers,* New York: The Free Press, 1986, chapters 5 and 8.

gence to realize that Johnson carried that analogy would have taken serious thought about his personal history and his formative experiences as Senate majority leader. Once it realized the analogy, providing more detail on Ho's own history of struggle might have challenged it. A man who had spent his entire adult life fighting for Vietnamese nationalism was not likely to be much swayed by promises of dams and electrification.

During my own stint on the National Security Council (NSC) staff in the 1970s, I came to understand the importance of knowing and calibrating intelligence analysts. I also came to value them precisely because they had time to read. I noticed that in interagency meetings, there were several people who sat around the wall, never at the table, and who spoke rarely if at all. In time, they introduced themselves as CIA analysts working on Europe, which was my NSC beat. They were eager to help, and over time we worked out an arrangement. They would serve as my early warners, for they could read all the cable traffic and intelligence for which I had no time. When they saw something of special interest, they'd call me or leave the item number with my secretary for her to call to my attention.

In return, I became a consumer of their drafts and their ideas. We'd meet for lunch occasionally to go over the Europe agenda and their projects relevant to it. They would do their best to tailor their work to my agenda as best I could see it. And it should be said that as I came to trust them, I valued their early warning on what was happening in Washington as much as on what was occurring abroad. That is, I was as interested in outgoing State Department cables as in incoming, because I wanted their intelligence not just on foreign governments but also on my own. I was eager to have any signs that officers in other departments of government were straying off the reservation of the administration's foreign policy.

Calibrating the messenger is critical for another reason. Years later at the NIC, I came to worry that all the methodological purity we tried to introduce in NIEs was ultimately self-defeating. Here's why: I am told that courtroom lawyers routinely discredit opposing experts by forcing them to "explain" their judgment, where *explain* means describing the chain of logic that led them to that judgment. But experts seldom can do that convincingly. Ballistics experts, for instance, make their judgments based not on a chain of analysis but rather on something less tangible, a pattern seen in its totality, one based on a thousand previous cases. To ask them to explain their judgments is to reduce them if not to amateur status, then to middle rank. It is like asking chess masters to explain the logic of their moves. Doing so is probably helpful to a chess learner. But masters see patterns quickly in light of a richness of previous experience; for that reason, they can play a dozen games at once. To ask them to play chess by a logic they can explain is to reduce them from masters to apprentices.

I came to worry that all our methods at the NIC — being transparent about evidence and logic, for instance — would have the same effect. Those methods would reduce experts to middleweights. For those of us writing estimates, there was no alternative, because we had to produce a piece of paper. But it surely would have been unwise to think that the paper itself would have much influence. Rather, I came to think of NIEs not just as the homework we did to stay at the top of an issue, but also as calling cards that the experts, the national intelligence officers (NIOs), could use in bringing their analyses personally downtown to policy counterparts. The NIOs' real product was their own expertise.

There is another danger to conceiving of intelligence as discrete products on paper — or even as discrete flows of electrons on a computer screen. Such analyses are static and may be badly misunderstood, especially when leaked purposely. In the transition between the Bush and Clinton administrations, the CIA had done a study of Father Jean-Bertrand Aristide, the leader of Haiti who was deposed by the military in 1991 and later returned to power by an international coalition led by the United States. The report judged that Aristide had encouraged political violence in Haiti and had ordered the killing of his political opponent, Roger Lafontant, at the time Aristide was deposed in 1991. It also said he was a manic-depressive who had been treated for the illness in Canada in 1980, a charge Aristide flatly denied.[4]

Assessing a person's temperament at a long distance is a perilous art, and this report displayed some of the perils. For instance, had Aristide been hospitalized for his depression or treated outside a hospital? The difference is probably a minor one for doctors but signifies a good deal to ordinary people. More to the point, the report became ammunition in 1993 during the debate over whether Aristide should be restored to

4   For outlines of the profile and the controversy about it, see *Washington Post*, November 5, 1993, p. A34, November 3, 1993, p. A16, October 25, 1993, p. A14, October 24, 1993, p. A28, October 23, 1993, p. A19, and October 22, 1993, p. A26.

power. Senator Jesse Helms (R-North Carolina) had heard of the report from his staff, and he asked our NIO for Latin America to brief him and a group of senators that were mostly Republican and that mostly opposed the administration's policy of returning Aristide to power.

The NIO went to the Hill; we at the NIC saw no way to say no, and neither did the director of central intelligence (DCI), James Woolsey. The session with the senators was awful. It put the NIO into an untenable position, yet a position that is more and more familiar to intelligence analysts in official Washington. The NIO felt he had to remain true to the original paper because it had been an assessment agreed to by the intelligence community. Yet the report seemed to cut directly across the Clinton administration's policy.

I later spent a long evening with the analyst who had done the study. He did not think Aristide was crazy. He would have described him as unusual, but then he would have described President Clinton that way as well. What he meant was that any person with the drive to lead a nation and the persistence to make it happen was an unusual personality by definition. As I talked to him, I realized his dilemma: If he wrote the report in prosaic language, Aristide would come across like any other politician, especially when read by a politician (Why, he's just like me!). On the other hand, if he accentuated distinctive features and cast them in somewhat clinical terms, which he did, he would run the risk of portraying Aristide to the reader as a madman. The report was read, fairly enough, as describing Aristide as pathological.

If the study had been done at all, it should never have been committed to paper. At the beginning of his dealings with Aristide, Clinton would have benefited from twenty minutes with the analyst who did the study, because quite apart from any overall judgments, he had several good suggestions about how to deal with a person of Aristide's personality. As it was, though, the CIA assessment remained a static piece of paper while Clinton's colleagues acquired experience of their own with Aristide. As Vice President Gore later put it, "We have dealt with [Aristide] for nine months now. He has been reliable, he has been very thoughtful, he has been persistent in his efforts in behalf of the Haitian people."[5] Like the rest of us, senior Clinton officials were bound to trust their own observations, first hand, more than a piece of paper

5 Quoted in *Washington Post*, October 25, 1993, p. A14.

written from afar. Thus, the study came to irritate them; worse, it became a handy stick the administration's opponents could use against it.

The static quality of intelligence on paper is the liability the Aristide story has most in common with the rest of relations between intelligence and policy. Senior policy-makers may know their broad agendas over the next few months, but, day to day, their lives are driven by their in-boxes. They could not know exactly when an issue would cross their desks or what form it would have when it did. These are difficult circumstances in which to try to make a difference with written intelligence products. If senior policy-makers read such products at all, they will ask themselves, If this is the answer, then just what was the question?

A colleague of mine, Robert Blackwill, has entertained (and horrified) midcareer students in intelligence courses with his own experience on the NSC staff. When he arrived in the morning, early, he'd be greeted by a stack of paper a foot high (this was the old, precomputer days). He'd reach for the *Washington Post* and the *New York Times* first because those might carry news that he cared most about — stories his bosses would read, which would then become the day's work for him, or commentary on how well the administration was, or wasn't, doing in foreign policy.

By the time he'd opened the papers, the phone would begin to ring, and he'd become conscious of the phone list he hadn't finished from the night before. Some calls, such as those from bosses, he had to take. Other calls, such as those from his counterparts around the government, he either had to take or wanted to take because they might help him with his problems. He'd return calls from journalists, too, because they sometimes could help him, by giving him a chance to dampen or "spin" a story or by providing him intelligence of the sort he could use — what his colleagues elsewhere in the government were saying or doing.

And so eight o'clock would arrive, and the day would be in full flight. The papers would lie on his desk just opened. He might also have opened the classified *National Intelligence Daily* (or NID). If he had, it would be for the same reason he'd looked at the *Times* and the *Post*: It might have some breaking story that would frame the day's work. Perhaps he'd have had time to at least thumb through the rest of the stack — a melange of newspaper clips, classified cables to and from U.S. embassies abroad, and intelligence reports, some of them highly classified — searching for something hot, something he'd want to know before he got a call about it. The phone would begin to ring incessantly. By ten o'clock he couldn't remember whether he'd read something in the *Times* or in an intelligence source, and it didn't much matter.

In these circumstances, most of so-called finished intelligence — that is, analyses published between covers with elegant graphics (if the real essence of the State Department is moving furniture, that of the CIA is doing graphics) — would stay in the pile. With luck, later in the day he'd skim the titles and put the interesting ones aside to read when he had time. Not that he and his colleagues didn't wish they had more time to read these finished analyses. They did. But those pieces couldn't be counted on to help with the problems at hand on the day they arrived. They were nice to know but did not provide help that was imperative.

When I was at the NIC, I came to be more impressed than ever by the expertise of CIA analysts, so I pressed my colleagues on the policy side with advice I generally wouldn't have offered: give intelligence analysts a little face time. It's worth it. We all think we can learn more quickly from a paper, but if you ask the analysts to write one, the result will be thirty degrees off from the aim point you have in mind. But if you call them in, face to face, they will understand how much you know, and you'll have a chance to calibrate them. You'll learn more in fifteen minutes than you'd have imagined. And you'll also begin to target those analysts to your concerns and your sense of the issue.

QUESTIONS NOT ASKED AND NOT ANSWERED

Taking into account the professional gap between intelligence and policy, recognizing that the messenger is inseparable from the message, and finding ways to help policy-makers calibrate the messenger — these are the first three steps toward making sure that intelligence is the intelligence of policy. Yet all three are less important than asking the right questions, which is also the most difficult step. When Senator Daniel Patrick Moynihan (D-New York) suggested that the CIA ought to be abolished, he had particularly in mind its assessments of the Soviet Union and, even more particularly, its assessment of the Soviet economy in the years before 1990. If intelligence couldn't predict the Soviet Union's fall, or even the impending collapse of its economy, what good was it? While there are in that case some cautionary lessons about how intelligence does its job, the larger lesson is about how intelligence relates to policy. Questions that go unasked by policy are not likely to be answered by intelligence. If intelligence does provide the answers without being asked, those answers are not likely to be heard by policy.

In the 1950s, the CIA was little better off than universities in understanding the Soviet Union.[6] Satellite photographs did not yet exist, and the U-2 spy plane, too, was still in the future. The CIA had spies but not many of them, and there were many targets more important for those spies than ball-bearing factories. What CIA analysts, working in the Office of Research and Reports (ORR), had was the resources to pore through Soviet journals, looking for hints about the Soviet economy that might seep through the bland prose.

These were the days of Nikita Khrushchev's shoe-banging about how the Soviet Union would "bury" America with economic growth. What Washington most wanted was a capacity second to none for understanding just how good the Soviet Union was. Hence, ORR emphasized basic research and rigorous academic standards, goals that were reinforced by continuous interchange with analysts outside government at Harvard, Cornell, The RAND Corporation, and elsewhere. In time, they were able to answer some quite specific questions. By the mid-1950s, for instance, they knew enough about Soviet industrial capacity to suggest that even if Moscow could build enough heavy bombers to produce a "bomber gap" over the United States, it still would be hard-pressed to field and support those bombers.[7]

The first cautionary lesson is that along the way, those analysts did fall in love with their analytic creation, their model of the Soviet economy. It was what they had, and it was impressive. In capitalist systems, prices are determined by supply and demand and therefore are rough surrogates for value. Yet since the Soviets set ruble prices administratively, Soviet prices meant nothing as measures of value and thus were of no help in measuring Soviet growth or gross national product (GNP). After throwing a good deal of theory at the problem, Abram Bergson of Harvard developed "adjusted factor costs" — a way of using

---

6   This is drawn from "Sunshine and Shadow: The CIA and the Soviet Economy," Case C16-91-1096.0, Kennedy School of Government, Harvard University, 1991.

7   John Prados, *The Soviet Estimate: U.S. Intelligence Analysis and Russian Military Strength,* Princeton: Princeton University Press, 1986, p. 46.

elements of Soviet pricing to produce a proxy for value that most analysts accepted.

Then, Soviet emigrés began arriving with tales of toasters produced by Soviet industry that were as likely to catch fire as to brown bread, or of televisions as likely to blow up as to show what passed for the nightly news. These anecdotes did not come as a surprise to the CIA analysts, but they did glance off the analysis. They were anecdotes, not data; they were subjective assessments about quality, and the model did not easily incorporate them. There was no way to coax implications about consumer preferences or welfare out of Soviet prices, since the pricing never was intended to reflect them. Besides, the CIA analysts already knew that the Soviet defense industry was a thing apart from the rest of Soviet industry; it produced quality goods, they judged, by a combination of brute force and special procedures. It was no surprise to them that it floated uneasily on a sea of shoddiness. Still, the lesson is that looking for your lost key under the lamppost is not a bad opening tactic, but it isn't a complete approach. What is unknown or, if known, hard to measure, may matter more than what is known or easily calibrated.

A second caution concerns the relationship between insiders and outsiders. Work on the Soviet economy looked like a model collaboration. Insiders were in constant touch with outsiders, and sometimes they exchanged places. Through the mechanism of Congress's Joint Economic Committee hearings, the insiders had the chance to publish their work openly and let it be judged by their academic peers. These "green books," as they were known because of the color of the committee's covers, did not acknowledge the analysts' affiliation with the CIA, and the analysts' license to publish waxed and waned with the sensitivities of successive DCIs. Still, everybody in the academy who mattered knew where the analyses came from, and over time, the inside analysts had the opportunity to present the body of their work for outside scrutiny.

Yet what looked like a model of open collaboration became in fact a closed club. Instead of serving as friendly critics, the outsiders became insiders. Perhaps it was destined to be so. Data were a monopsony of insiders, and the model belonged to them, too. As a result, analyses became a monopoly of the club. The criticism from outsiders to insiders was gentle, and the assumptions of the model came to be shared, not challenged.

The central lesson of the case, however, is about questions asked and unasked. Had the CIA's economists been asked to rate the chance of the Soviet economy collapsing, they could have given, for all the limits of their model, an arresting answer. The few times they were asked, they did so. The CIA's first-ever press conference in 1963 had publicized ORR's conclusion that the Soviet harvest was so bad that economic growth that year was near zero. Khrushchev's boasts of overtaking the United States were idle.[8] By the late 1980s, the CIA economists were reckoning that the chances of a collapse were pretty high.

But they were seldom asked whether the Soviet economy was collapsing. They continually were asked another question: Can the Soviet economy support x percent increase in defense spending again this year, where x is four or five or even more? To that question, the answer always was yes. In the 1960s and 1970s, with the Soviet economy growing at 3 to 5 percent, the state of that economy was a footnote to the yes answer. In later years, a yes answer only meant that long-suffering Soviet citizens would tighten their belt a notch further. Indeed, the answer might still be yes but for the arrival on the scene of Mikhail Gorbachev, that limited genius who knew his system had to be reformed but had very little idea how to do it. The Soviet economy was bound to collapse, but it wasn't bound to collapse in the decade between 1985 and 1995.

Suppose the question about the Soviet economy had been answered without being asked. CIA analysts during the high Reaganism of the early 1980s might have put the evidence together and concluded that a collapse of the Soviet economy did impend. Their conclusion would have been, in the nature of things, iffy, for they could not have predicted collapse, only that the chances of it were rising. If, then, they had taken that conclusion downtown, to an NSC staff that was working overtime on how to respond to the Soviet "evil empire," imagine the analysts' case: Actually, you shouldn't be worrying so much about Soviet power; you should be worrying more about Soviet collapse. Those analysts would have found themselves counting submarines on Kamchatka Island!

---

8   See Ray S. Cline, *Secrets, Spies, and Scholars: Blueprint of the Essential CIA*, Acropolis Books, 1976, p. 204.

It was only with the arrival on the scene of Gorbachev and his reforms that attention shifted in earnest to the state of the Soviet economy. By the end of the 1980s, Henry Rowen of Stanford and Charles Wolf of RAND had put together analyses (in particular those of Anders Aslund, a Swede who had lived in the Soviet Union) arguing that Soviet national income, then thought to be about half that of the United States, was in reality only about a third. If that was true, then Soviet defense consumed not 15 percent of GNP but more like 25 percent (in contrast to 6 or 7 percent for the United States at the time).[9] If that was so, then sustaining defense spending was not just an exercise in belt tightening. Gorbachev's reforms then looked like a last-ditch attempt to rescue a very sick system.

With the benefit of hindsight, though, it is worth noting that Gorbachev's problem was not those exploding toasters or other indicators of consumer welfare. It was that the Soviet Union's crown jewels, its defense industry, were in danger of sinking into the sea of shoddiness. Isolated, the defense industry simply couldn't keep up as more and more of the West's military technology, particularly in information, began to come from the commercial sector. In that sense, while the Reagan defense buildup of the 1980s didn't "spend the Soviet Union into collapse," it did underscore, for Gorbachev and his politburo colleagues, how dynamic the Western economies were. It signaled yet another round of defense technology with which Moscow would have to struggle to keep up.

QUESTIONS ASKED

Despite superficial similarity with the case of the Soviet economy, the instance of intelligence about Soviet missiles stands in sharp contrast. For missiles, too, data were an intelligence monopsony; everyone inside and outside government worked off the same numbers. Yet unlike in the case of the economy, the arguments over missile estimates were heated. The debate, one in evidence since the late 1960s, was a wide one; it was not the province of a closed club.

The apparently arcane subject of whether the Soviet SS-9 missile carried multiple warheads that could be targeted separately became the

---

9   Henry S. Rowen and Charles Wolf, Jr., eds., *The Impoverished Superpower: Perestroika and the Soviet Military Burden,* San Francisco: ICA Press, 1990, p. xiii.

object of wider political controversy in early 1969. Then Secretary of Defense Melvin Laird, a former member of Congress, testified to Congress that the missile signaled a Soviet intention to try for a capability to wipe out the U.S. deterrent at a single blow. The huge SS-9s, he testified, did carry what were called multiple independently targetable reentry vehicles, or MIRVs. Without MIRVs, the SS-9's multiple warheads were like a shotgun; they could do a lot of damage but could only kill one target. If, by contrast, the warheads could be targeted separately, each missile could kill several targets, so a relatively few SS-9s would pose a threat to America's land-based nuclear deterrent, the Minuteman system. For Laird, the remedy was clear: The United States needed to deploy anti-ballistic missile (ABM) defenses against the Soviet SS-9s.

For the intelligence community, the SS-9 had been a puzzle from the time it had first been detected, about 1964. It was huge and hugely expensive. Why had Moscow built it? By 1969, the community's consensus, reflected in an NIE, held that the SS-9 was not MIRVed, at least not yet.[10] That conclusion, though, was a judgment. The intelligence was not airtight, so the case turned on interpretations of technical data — telemetry and the like, which shed light on the SS-9's accuracy and the "footprint" that its warheads made, all of which were judged by the light of interpretations of Soviet intentions.

The not-yet-MIRVed assessment was primarily the property of the CIA. But there were other players — the Defense Intelligence Agency (DIA), the Air Force, and the Pentagon's Director of Defense Research and Engineering (DDR&E), then the redoubtable John S. Foster, Jr. Foster, in particular, was both close to Laird and convinced that the SS-9 was MIRVed. U.S. intelligence data gathered on Soviet tests of the new system in the spring of 1969 appeared, at least at the time, to give credence to Foster's view.[11]

Henry Kissinger, then the president's national security adviser, appointed a special NSC group, dubbed the MIRV panel, in an attempt to keep the debate within the administration. Given the widening debate, though, the MIRV panel's deliberations spilled into public, as had the

10   For this case, see Kristen Lundberg, "The SS-9 Controversy: Intelligence as Political Football," Case C16-89-884.0, Kennedy School of Government, Harvard University, 1989.

11   Lawrence Freedman, *U.S. Intelligence and the Soviet Strategic Threat*, Princeton: Princeton University Press, 1986, p. 139.

NIE that outlined the tenuous intelligence community consensus. The MIRV panel's report to the administration in May hedged but leaned toward Foster: It could not be ruled out that the Soviets were testing a MIRV.

In July, the full Senate held a closed, classified session, then only the fourth since World War II and the first devoted to an intelligence issue. The debate over ABM raged on, pulling the SS-9 question along with it. In August, the Senate voted by the narrowest of possible margins to fund the first phase of Safeguard, the administration's ABM system.

What distinguished the case of the Soviet missiles from that of the Soviet economy is twofold. First, there were competing analysts inside the government — the CIA, DIA, and Air Force in particular. And second, the analysis mattered, not just to the American republic in general, but also to important pieces of officialdom — the Air Force and Navy, especially, but also the budgeteers. Big U.S. weapons programs costing billions of dollars hinged on assessments of what the Soviets were up to. Given competing analyses and big stakes, the debate widened to include Congress, think tanks, retired officers, and defense contractors.

Absent comparable stakes, the circle of debate over the Soviet economy was narrow, and the competing analyses were confined to maverick emigrés and a few academics. Not that whether the Soviet economy was on the verge of collapse didn't matter, but unlike the current state of the economy or the question of whether the SS-9 would be MIRVed, it was a mystery, not a puzzle. For most of the Cold War, moreover, it was a mystery that was too hypothetical and too much for the future. It didn't matter *specifically* to anybody who had to decide anything.

THE BRIGHT LINE

In contrast to European traditions, since World War II the United States has drawn a bright line between "intelligence" and "policy," between those who might ask questions and those who might answer them. The operating agencies of government were bound, so the logic went, to favor intelligence judgments cut to suit the cloth of ongoing policies. The military services would naturally tend toward the worst case in assessing the threats they faced, which would imply their own needed forces had to be larger and of higher quality. This kind of conservative professional prudence was not malfeasance but rather, in an important sense, what the military was paid to do. For similar reasons, the State Department was almost bound to favor assessments that suggested a wide scope for diplomacy. Separating intelligence from policy would serve as a check on these natural tendencies.

Given this logic, intelligence should not get too close to policy lest it be "politicized" — that is, risk having its objectivity tainted by the stakes of policy and policy-makers. It should not "get on the team" if doing so means losing detached objectivity. Given the current norms and arrangements, intelligence analysts pay little price for being irrelevant. They do, by contrast, pay a price for "politicization," for being seen to cross — or be pushed — across the line from objectivity to argument, for "joining the policy team."

The sensitivities about politicization were vivid in Robert Gates's confirmation hearings to be DCI in 1991.[12] Those hearings were something of a first because they gave considerable attention to intelligence *analysis*, not just to espionage and its disgraces or to big-ticket collection systems. A number of Gates's former colleagues and subordinates testified, and several senior officers made or agreed with charges that he had politicized intelligence — most notably, Melvin Goodman, a former analyst in the deputy director for intelligence's (DDI's) office of Soviet affairs, and, more tellingly, Harold Ford, a widely respected former vice chair of the NIC.

Particularly at issue was a 1985 paper, commissioned by then DDI Gates after a meeting with the DCI, then William Casey. Casey had expressed his view that the Soviet Union had been behind the 1981 attempt to assassinate the Pope. Others who were present disagreed, and Gates commissioned the paper, which was to assemble all the evidence the CIA had that supported the argument that Moscow *was* behind the assassination. This kind of paper was unusual but not unprecedented in intelligence. It hearkened back to the method of one of the century's best intelligence analysts, the French Deuxieme Bureau before World War II. The Deuxieme Bureau would set out a hypothesis, or *hypothèse*, then assemble evidence to try to validate or disprove it. In this

12   See *Nomination of Robert M. Gates to be Director of Central Intelligence,* Report of the Senate Select Committee on Intelligence, 102 Cong., 1 sess., 1991, p. 98ff. For a thoughtful description of those hearings and the issues they raised, see James Worthen, "The Gates Hearings: Politicization and Soviet Analysis at CIA," *Studies in Intelligence,* Spring 1994, pp. 7–20.

case, the CIA was asking how good a case for Soviet complicity in the assassination it could assemble.

Inevitably, though, the form of the question looked as if Gates was trying to doctor the books in favor of a yes answer. And the paper eventually was sent to members of the NSC with a cover memo that did not include a scope note describing the nature of the project; a quick reader could thus have inferred that this was the CIA's complete analysis of the issue. Gates did not draft but did sign the cover memo. Contrary to Goodman's charges, however, the paper's drafters later indicated that any changes Gates made in the key judgments of the paper qualified the judgment about the Soviet role, rather than reinforcing it. Gates ordered a critique of the paper well before the confirmation hearings.

The episode demonstrated the ambiguity surrounding what is "politicization." What one person regards as sharpening the analysis can easily be seen by another as politicizing it. Gates pushed the system but did not disfigure it. He was a prodigious reviewer and editor of his directorate's projects, and in the process he managed to step on the prose, not to mention the egos, of senior analysts who were inclined to view their language as holy writ. When Gates's editing criticized analysis as slipshod analysis, the process could be regarded by bruised authors as pursuing an agenda.

My sympathy for Gates increased when, early in the Clinton administration, I tried to manage an NIE on heroin and cocaine. The purpose was to assess the global production of both drug crops and to estimate the flows of drugs into the United States. This was intelligence, not policy analysis, so its purpose was not explicitly to grade the performance of U.S. policy or its antidrug operations. Yet it was hard to comment on drug crop production without implicitly judging the success of U.S. eradication policies, and to the extent that flows of crops or drugs into the United States could be assessed, the assessments surely said something about U.S. efforts to interdict those flows. What *was* clear is that the policy agencies in charge of eradication and interdiction took the estimates as implicit judgments about their performance.

From the start, the enterprise was hampered by its motley shape, as reflected in the bureaucratic rivalries among the official participants. The Coast Guard and Border Patrol, for instance, were duly proud of how many drug shipments they were seizing en route to the United States, while much of the rest of the drug control community was skeptical that the seizures really did much to staunch the flow, hence raise the prices, of drugs for sale in the United States. The Drug Enforcement Agency (DEA) was more concerned with making cases against drug traffickers than in seizing their traffic. Meanwhile, analysts suspected that given America's open borders and open commerce, no actions aimed at supply would make much difference. However, successive waves of politicians and their staffs, especially in Congress, continued to find the superficial appeal of "cutting off drugs at the source" — in or near the crop-raising countries — compelling.

In doing the estimate, I was amazed that the agencies concerned could say precisely how many drug cargoes they had seized but could not offer any estimates of how many they had missed. But, I said, the point of interdicting drugs is not to increase seizures for their own sake, but rather to reduce supplies in the United States. That reduction would in turn drive up prices and discourage consumption.

I suggested that we use wholesale drug prices in various American entry cities as surrogates for the effectiveness of interdiction: If seizures were reducing supply, prices should be rising. The method was rough to the point of crudeness; I suggested it only for lack of any other. It brought forth cries of "politicization" from the agencies. I was seeking to advance my own policy preference, they charged; I sought to discredit interdiction. Nuts, I wanted to answer and almost did, to record seizures but disregard what got through was just lousy analysis.

Not to keep up the suspense: Wholesale prices mostly had drifted down as seizures had gone up, so the case that interdiction was working was a weak one, although there were some puzzlingly suggestive spikes in prices.[13]   The pattern supported a common-sense hypothesis: Concentrated efforts at seizure could temporarily dry up particular supply routes to given cities, but traffickers would adapt by finding new channels. Overall, interdiction's successes in the 1980s in the Caribbean had driven supply channels westward through Mexico.

There is something to be said for the credo of separating intelligence from policy, but in U.S. practice, the doctrine is implemented to the point that intelligence often is not in a position to be of much help. Intelligence analysts at State's Bureau of Intelligence and Research (INR) may benefit from some doctrinal separation from policy precisely be-

---

13   The estimate's conclusions are noted, though without attribution, in *Washington Post*, September 16, 1993, p. A1, where the fuss over them is also described.

cause their organizational position entangles them with policy officers. When I taught executive programs on intelligence at Harvard, those programs were composed entirely of officers from the various intelligence agencies, and the officers from other agencies tended to look on their colleagues from INR as surrogates for policy officials. Those INR analysts worked in the same building with the rest of the State Department and so could have lunch with a policy counterpart without spending a half day to do so. At least INR was left in no doubt about who it worked for, and its officers could walk down the hall to check assignments or agendas with policy counterparts. So, giving INR a little doctrinal protection from the preferences of State's operators is no bad thing.

By contrast, for the CIA's Directorate of Intelligence (DI), detachment from policy has disconnected it from policy. Especially now that the organization is large and increasingly bureaucratic, getting papers approved within the building can be consuming. The idea that the papers are not written for their own sake, but rather to help someone with concrete choices to make, can easily be lost. Moreover, because in theory the DI works for everyone, it can in fact wind up working for no one. It is perpetually on the hunt for customers, which surely is not a bad thing but can make for haphazard connections to policy. Its most natural connection is to the NSC staff, which always feels shorthanded no matter how large it becomes. Yet there, the DI has plenty of competition, the NIC in particular, and, more important, busy NSC staffers are not likely to take many intelligence officers into their confidence.

For the CIA, physical separation compounds the separation from policy. Going downtown for lunch with a policy colleague can be a half-day's endeavor. With a car and driver at the NIC, I could make it downtown for lunch in fifteen minutes, a little less if my luncheon companion and I compromised on a Georgetown restaurant. Had I depended on the CIA shuttle buses or on my own car, it easily could have taken an hour each way.

In this and other ways, bureaucratic geography in Washington matters a lot. One reason among several why NSA is not much of an analytic player and why its products are not well understood is its isolation from Washington. Getting downtown or to the Pentagon from NSA headquarters in Fort Meade, Maryland, takes nearly an hour in the best of times; with traffic, it can take hours. When, at the NIC, I sought to hire NSA officers on rotation, invariably the ones that applied were those who for family reasons lived closer to Langley, Virginia, than to Fort Meade.

For its part, the DIA also hangs in some organizational limbo, in its case between the office of the secretary of defense and that of the chairman of the joint chiefs of staff. Its analysts, though, know the range of their customers, a knowledge that is reinforced by military staffing procedures that produce a stream of taskings.

COMMANDERS AND ASSESSMENTS

If, on the civilian side of intelligence, irrelevance is more of a problem than politicization, on the military side a form of politicization seems more of a problem. This risk of "getting on the team" derives, in one way, from the services and their intelligence organizations and, in another way, from where the joint intelligence centers (JICs) are, who they work for, and how those commanders relate to Washington-based military intelligence.

Given their remaining roles in training and equipping forces — often called their Title 10 responsibilities after the act that specifies them — the service intelligence agencies do have a considerable role in military research and development (R&D). As a result, the services are doing, to a considerable extent, the threat assessment on which their own weapons programs will be justified.[14] As with the Air Force and Soviet missiles in another era, it takes no dark view of human nature, nor of command relationships, to worry that service intelligence chiefs will feel pressure to justify what their operating colleagues are planning to acquire. Nor is it much surprise that in these circumstances, DIA and the services have disputed who should control the basic force assessment centers — ground, air, and navy.

At the grander, more strategic end of assessing threats, there are other intelligence players, DIA and CIA in particular. Air Force intelligence will not be alone in judging the threat that future U.S. air forces will confront. But the futures that matter for building weapons are distant, and so they are very uncertain. In these circumstances, it is only prudential for intelligence to be cautious by making worst-case estimates of the future. That is true even if, for the near term, the U.S. Air

14   For a thoughtful discussion of these issues, see Russ Travers, "The Coming Intelligence Failure," *Studies in Intelligence*, pp. 27–34.

Force has no competition except itself, with the partial exception of close U.S. allies!

Many of the judgments on which weapons decisions turn are, moreover, much less grand, and they will not attract much competitive analysis from the various Washington agencies. They will still, however, drive major decisions involving billions of dollars. For instance, a relatively small increase in the capacity of imagined opponents to pierce the armor of future U.S. tanks would push the design of those tanks toward more armor or more expensive armor — in either case, with big implications for the size and cost of the resulting tanks.

For their part, the JICs work for commanders who have plain stakes in threat assessments that will affect their own claims on budgets, manpower, and new weapons. Like all reforms, the Goldwater-Nichols reforms of 1986 created some problems while solving others. The great achievement of Goldwater-Nichols was real jointness — providing incentives to create military forces whose commanders actually thought about fighting together — and making that change real took a decade once the measures were enacted.

The same reform empowered the joint war-fighting commanders, or CINCs. It did so on the same argument that motivated the reforms — to foster real jointness — here by giving more authority to those who would actually field or command joint forces in battle. In one sense, that change was long overdue. Those CINCs are responsible for preparing war plans and fighting wars. By contrast, the services only train and equip forces; it is the CINCs that put those forces together for combat.

Yet empowering the CINCs meant empowering their perspective, which is understandably biased toward worst cases over a short time horizon. The CINCs are acutely aware of how bad it could be tomorrow if war broke out in their areas of responsibility, so they always want more capacity now. The CINCs would not be doing their job if they didn't foresee how bad it could be very soon; for that, we taxpayers pay their salaries. By contrast, the services had, and to some extent still have, the virtue of thinking long term.

The problem is that the intelligence centers, the JICs, work for the CINCs, not the services, so there is reason to worry that the intelligence analysis will not be objective. As with the service intelligence organizations, it takes no crude presumptions about direct pressure to fear that junior intelligence analysts working for senior operational commanders will tend to fashion their estimates to suit the interests of their superiors. Guarding against that was, after all, one of the reasons for creating the CIA in the first place.

In principle, the risk of this form of "politicization" runs to the top of the military hierarchy. The director of DIA is a three-star flag officer and thus is outranked by the CINCs, who wear four stars. However, the DIA chiefs are not likely to become four-star officers; they have reached as high as an officer whose specialty is intelligence can aspire to go, and given that fact, they have little to risk by standing up to their senior officers.

Still, in my experience at the NIC, who wore how many stars did sometimes matter, or seemed to. We were doing an estimate of Iraqi military capabilities in the several years after Desert Storm. At issue was the question of how far into the Arabian peninsula Iraqi forces could strike with surprise. All the Washington agencies, DIA included, held one view, but CENTCOM, the "CINCdom" with responsibility for the Gulf, had a different, more alarmed, view.[15]

CENTCOM was keenly interested in the estimate. I welcomed that interest, for CENTCOM was both a principal consumer of the estimate and also a possible producer of analysis of interest. Because the command had an interest, however, I wanted its view to be plainly visible. I suggested a "CENTCOM view" box in the estimate. That would have suited my purposes all around: By including the command view, it would have enriched the estimate; yet by labeling it as such, it would have made plain the operational stakes of the command that was making the assessment.

CENTCOM, however, would have none of it. For the CINC, to be isolated in a special box was to be marginalized as a special pleader — which was, to be fair, more or less what I intended. The CINC flew to Washington from his base in Tampa and, whether through the power of his argument or the number of his stars, persuaded the DIA director to assemble a single military view. That view was just what I'd hoped to avoid. It was muddy and ambiguous, a least common denominator that neither fully validated nor firmly rejected the threat of an Iraqi strike.

15 Detail has been deleted here.

CHANGING THE CULTURE

Over the last decade, the civilian agencies, especially the CIA, have acquired new customers and become more tactical. In the process, some of the separation of intelligence from policy has begun to break down — a trend particularly associated with Robert Gates, first as DDI, then DCI. Gates, an intelligence careerist, had ample opportunity to see which intelligence was helpful and which wasn't during several stints on the NSC, and ultimately as President Bush's deputy national security advisor. He had come to know how different the intelligence and policy cultures are and how valuable it could be for intelligence to get close to consumers.

Gates and his successors sought to change the DI culture through a number of measures. One was sending DI analysts more frequently to serve on rotations in policy agencies — State, the NSC, the Pentagon, the U.S. trade representative, and elsewhere. While on such rotations, they are all-purpose staffers who happen to have intelligence expertise, just as other staffers might be lawyers or economists. They acquire a feel for the pace and rhythm of policy, as well as personal contacts within the policy world that can be acquired no other way. The effect of those rotations on intelligence officers is striking, all the more so because many DI analysts have spent years trying to help policy without ever serving among those who try to make it.

In contrast to the DI officers on rotations, the permanent intelligence liaison operations that exist in many smaller agencies — Treasury and Commerce, for instance — are often less a part of the solution to the divide between intelligence and policy than a part of the problem. The liaison operations are composed of paper-passers, not experts. At best, they can tune the flow, if not the substance, of intelligence coming to their agency's senior officials. In many cases, however, they become overly tactical, eager to "scoop" the intelligence agencies in providing the latest secret tidbit sooner than anyone else if they can. Jealous of their prerogatives and skeptical of their former colleagues — many of them are long-term exiles from their original agencies, most often the DI — they can hinder, rather than facilitate, contact between their seniors and relevant experts in intelligence agencies.

While the DI is still a "publish or perish" culture, that, too, is changing. Surely, rising analysts need to be judged on their written analytic outputs, but too much of what they write is "published" — that is, put between covers and distributed to large numbers of officials with appropriate clearances. In fact, most of what they write they are really writing for themselves, in order to build their own expertise. The DI culture has begun to reward, and promote, analysts who are entrepreneurial in seeking contacts with policy-makers. Not that policy types feel besieged by intelligence, quite the contrary. But there has been perceptible change in the old attitude that said: "We're in the business of telling the truth. If policy doesn't listen, that's their fault." No longer does providing intelligence mean simply tossing papers over the transom. Ten years ago, venturesome DI analysts spoke of "marketing" their products; now, they realize that marketing isn't the right metaphor, because their products need to be designed from the beginning with a clear eye to the detailed needs of those they would assist.

The DI's role with respect to the National Economic Council (NEC) in the first Clinton administration is an example of the change. A DI manager was assigned, full time, to the NEC deputy director, Bowman Cutter. Cutter had been the associate director of the Office of Management and Budget (OMB) for national security in the 1970s, and as a result he knew the intelligence community well. The DI officer met with him briefly several times a week, giving her a sense of his agenda. Out of these conversations grew the *Daily Economic Brief*, a CIA publication organized around his concerns. On occasion, she would bring teams of analysts to meet with NEC staffers. For his part, Cutter's insight was that you do indeed get what you pay for, and on the policy side of the government, you pay with the time you spend alerting intelligence to what you need.

The NIC's national intelligence officers (NIOs) traditionally have been critical connections between intelligence and policy. They are senior specialists on regions or functional issues from inside or outside intelligence, and their job keeps them in constant contact with what intelligence has to offer. Their stature usually gives them access to senior counterparts on the policy side. I thought good NIOs should spend half their time out of the building, downtown, with policy officials. In a way, that is truer for them than for most intelligence analysts; they contribute more through what they *say* in meetings or less formal conversations than in what they *write*.

Getting closer to policy officials can help intelligence do better at knowing what question to ask. As the Soviet economy cases suggested, getting the question right is absolutely critical and not at all trivial. [16] Too many intelligence papers are of the "whither Uganda?" variety, and policy-makers are almost never interested in such broad questions. Their questions are more specific and more operational, but policy-makers aren't always very clear in their own minds what the real question is, or if they are, they aren't willing to share it with intelligence. On one occasion at the NIC, the NIO for East Asia learned from his colleagues on the NSC deputies' committee what policy alternatives about trade with Japan were being considered. Alternatives are not the same as key questions but are a considerable help in framing them. For that NIE, we were able to point the analysis directly at the policy alternatives on the table — a circumstance more unusual than it should be.

One of the innovations of John Deutch's tenure as DCI was a daily morning meeting, chaired by his deputy, of the CIA deputy directors for intelligence and operations, the chairman of the NIC, and other senior officers. The meeting's purpose was to share notes not just about what had happened in the world, but also about what was going on in Washington. Its result was some planning for the day's current intelligence publications and some ideas for longer-term work. A DCI policy action staff had been proposed earlier in the 1990s. The idea behind that staff was to provide the DCI with a forum for assessing current intelligence and for foreshadowing what policy might need. The DCI could then understand what the community could do and couldn't with respect to that policy agenda and could set in motion adaptations in collection.

Another innovation designed to get intelligence closer to policy was MAGIC. It was explicitly aimed at providing better tactical support, and it envisioned a network of interactive computers on the desks of senior policy-makers. Those policy officials could then browse current intelligence as they chose, passing quickly over items of little interest and clicking for more information on others. Over time, their choices would let intelligence develop profiles of their interests, and what they received would be tailored accordingly. MAGIC would let those offi-

---

16 See my "Estimating Beyond the Cold War," *Defense Intelligence Journal,* 3, 2, Fall 1994, pp. 5–20; and Joseph Nye, Jr.'s "Peering into the Future," *Foreign Affairs,* 77, 4, July/August 1994, pp. 82–93. For the DI, see (then Deputy Director for Intelligence) Douglas MacEachin, *The Tradecraft of Analysis: Challenge and Change in the CIA,* Consortium for the Study of Intelligence, Working Group on Intelligence Reform Paper, 1994.

cials make immediate requests for more or different information, requests that would be turned around within the day, quicker if possible.

MAGIC was shelved for several reasons, money prominent among them. Because it was so expensive, it was designed to be provided only to a few senior officials. It thus suffered from an all-or-nothing character: It would have given principal policy-makers everything but their staffers nothing, and just at a time when information overload was making principals more and more dependent on processors of all sorts, prominently including their own staffs.

Still, MAGIC represents an intelligence direction for the future. It would be a clear break from information *push*, the force-feeding of officials with a torrent of factoids. It would permit policy-makers to *pull* information. With its emphasis on question asking and answering, though, it would be extremely expensive in analytic manpower, and so the number of officials who could receive full service would be limited. Its opportunity cost in, for example, more reflective, longer-term thinking would be high.

In principle, technology will permit all kinds of connections between intelligence and policy. Over time, connections like MAGIC will permit intelligence to build a profile of a particular consumer's interests and needs. Connections among teams of analysts and policy officials will let them work together intensely as problems dictate, then move on to other business after crises pass. Technology will also permit officials to be, on occasion, their own collectors. They will be able to be in direct contact with foreign service officers on the ground in Russia or with military commanders in Bosnia.

CHALLENGING MIND-SETS

Often, lines of analysis, or of policy, are based on half-buried assumptions. To counter this tendency, intelligence would need to interrogate policy about its assumptions or mind-sets, then try to validate or discredit the assumptions. In the period preceding India's nuclear tests, American presumptions were rock hard and shared throughout the government: The BJP's rhetoric about nuclear weapons was pure bluster, designed only for domestic political consumption. The party would be forced to moderate in governing; and, besides, it would be crazy for India to test.

So much of what goes down in history as "intelligence failures" result from assumptions, ones that are often derived from mirror imaging — asking what *we* would do if we were in *their* shoes. Sometimes, as in the case of the Indian nuclear tests, the assumption is shared by policy and intelligence. In 1973, Americans and Israelis, policy and intelligence officials alike, were surprised by Egypt's attack across the Suez Canal because they knew Israel would win any war with Egypt, perhaps overwhelmingly.[17] They *assumed* that no nation would start a war it could not win; surely they wouldn't.

And so they missed Egyptian president Anwar el-Sadat's calculation: If Egypt won the first battle, it might win the peace even though it lost the intervening war. A tactical victory would transform images of the Middle East situation: Arabs could defeat Israelis. Moreover, Sadat reckoned or hoped that the international community would prevent Israel from destroying Egypt's army in a counterattack and might, to boot, pressure Israel to come to the negotiating table. Intelligence and policy both could not imagine that Sadat might start a war that they, in his place, would not have begun. They were surprised because they could not fathom Sadat's logic.

Mind-sets have afflicted America's understanding of Iraq for a decade. In 1991, the conventional wisdom among Arabists, in government and out, in policy and in intelligence, was that Arabs would not attack Arabs. They might bluster and rant, and they might attack Persians, but not Arabs. Accepting this conventional wisdom, it was easy to dismiss Saddam Hussein's threats against Kuwait as economic blackmail, not a prelude to war. Had intelligence known of the mind-set but not shared it, it might have probed history or Saddam's earlier statements to build a basis for questioning the assumption that Arabs do not attack Arabs.

Later in the decade, intelligence was slow to unravel Saddam's nuclear weapons program because of assumptions about methods for building such weapons. Iraq had used a process that the United States had tried in the 1950s, then discarded as inefficient. It was a perfectly good way to build nuclear weapons, just not one that was technically respectable by American lights.

17   See, for example, William B. Quandt, *Peace Process: American Diplomacy and the Arab-Israeli Conflict Since 1967,* Washington, D.C.: Brookings Institution Press, 1990.

At other times, the root of the failure in policy is assumptions unknown to, hence unchallenged by, intelligence. This was the case in 1940. The German invasion surprised France, despite good intelligence. Once the attack was under way, French commanders were still slow to recognize what was happening, because they did not regard an attack through the Ardennes forest as possible; it was not respectable in military terms, as they calculated.[18] The indications of an attack that intelligence provided were not enough to dislodge the mind-set of those French operational commanders.

In the instance of Iraqi chemical weapons, it was intelligence, not policy, that clung to distracting assumptions. The issue became an emotional one in the context of the search for the sources of Gulf War syndrome — the cluster of mysterious symptoms that Gulf War veterans evinced. Exposure to chemical weapons was high on all lists as the cause, so this particular intelligence failure acquired a special prominence. By its own account, the CIA had information as early as 1984 that Iraq stored chemical weapons at Khamisiyah, in southern Iraq. A day before the ground war in Iraq began, in 1991, an American ambassador in the region — not identified in the CIA report but probably conveying Iranian air force information — identified the geographic coordinates for the chemical weapons depot.[19]

At the time, however, in war's midst, a CIA analyst reported that the agency could not identify a chemical weapons depot at the suspected site. American troops destroyed the Khamisiyah facility soon after they routed Iraqi forces in the ground war in 1991, but they did so in ignorance that chemical weapons might have been stored there.

In Washington's fashion, the subsequent inside-the-beltway story was less about what might have been known than about who said what was "known" and when. George Tenet, then acting DCI, had said six weeks earlier that the CIA had not identified Khamisiyah as a chemical weapons facility, and for the previous three years the CIA had been saying it had nothing to add about the Khamisiyah facility. The internal CIA report was scathing about the failure but most insightful about mind-set. During the eight years of war between Iran and Iraq, CIA analysts developed what the report's leader, Robert D. Walpole, de-

18   See Ernest R. May, *Strange Victory: Hitler's Conquest of France*, New York: Hill and Wang, 2000.
19   See *New York Times* and *Washington Post*, both April 10, 1997, both p. 1.

scribed as "tunnel vision" about Iraqi chemical weapons. The weapons they identified were stored in characteristic S-shaped bunkers, and so it was easy, particularly for newcomers, to dismiss the possibility that chemical weapons could be stored in any other kind of facility.

If getting the questions right is the first task, being clear about what is an assumption and what is a critical variable is the second. Thinking about the prospects for Castro's Cuba turns on judgments about the Cuban military. Will it hold together and hold loyal to the fidelista legacy, even to the point of firing on fellow citizens if necessary? Or does it resemble its East European counterparts at the turn of the 1990s, formidable and loyal on the surface but underneath divided and diffident about unleashing bloodshed in the service of discredited regimes? Differing judgments about the likely role of the military may contain buried assumptions. In fact, though, that role is a critical variable or linchpin for subsequent analysis.

The next key to good analysis of mysteries is framing indicators. If the Cuban military, its role and cohesiveness, is identified as a critical variable or linchpin, then what indicators should we watch for? How, in fancier words, would we have reason to believe that the world was moving from one set of possible Cuban futures to another? Indicators about the military's role might come from how it exercised, whether it deployed only special units in Havana or other cities, whether it moved local recruits to units far from home, whether there were spy reports of dissidence in the ranks, and so on.

ERASING THE LINE?

In the 1980s and 1990s, the intelligence community created several functional centers designed to better connect intelligence not just to policy but also to operations, including law enforcement. These centers, for counterterrorism, counternarcotics, and nonproliferation, all are in the puzzle-solving business. The counterterrorism center is perhaps the most successful of the centers and also the most operational, hence tactical. As one of its directors told me: "As a citizen, I might care about the roots and sources of terrorism. But not in this job. Here, I just want to know how to deter or catch terrorists."

The counterterrorism center has a clear and popular mission and agreed-upon targets. It benefits from the opprobrium of terrorism almost everywhere and thus enjoys good links with fellow military and police services around the world. The positive climate in which it operates also means that foreign states more often agree to extradite or, in the evocative language of the trade, to "render" suspected terrorists (simply let U.S. officials take them away without benefit of formal extradition).[20] In 1993 and 1994, only two terrorists were tried in the United States, and since then, a further ten have been brought to this country to face trial.

At the other end of the spectrum, the nonproliferation center is in the more traditional intelligence business of supporting policy. It, too, is very tactical, with a focus on where sanctions against proliferation are being evaded, and how. While it does aid operations, including law enforcement (for instance, when it discovers companies selling proscribed technologies abroad), its cases are mostly tried before Congress and the court of international opinion. For instance, it might seek evidence that will convict China of selling missiles to Pakistan that are too capable.

The counternarcotics center falls somewhere between the terrorism and nonproliferation centers. It is connected to the hodgepodge of agencies involved in the war against drugs, so its dominant role is supporting their activities. Yet it is also the repository of solved puzzles about the nature of the narcotics trade, viewing it as a business and asking where the profit is and where the profit centers, channels of distribution, and marketing are. The experience I described previously regarding a heroin and cocaine estimate illustrates the ambiguity of the center's position. The writing of the estimate caught the center's best analysts in an awkward bind: On the one hand, they needed to keep good working relations with the operators, so belittling their success was impolitic; yet those analysts knew better, on the other, than to accept the claims of the operators.

These centers have begun to erase the line separating intelligence and policy and to bring the two groups together. But their focus is still on intelligence; they are "the DCI's" centers. The British counterpart to the U.S. NIC, the Joint Intelligence Committee (JIC) — not to be confused with the joint intelligence centers (JICs) that work for the American CINCs — illustrates a more dramatic erasing of the line. The context is very different because it operates in a dramatically smaller gov-

---

20   See "Extraditions/Renditions of Terrorists to the United States — 1993 to 1998," available at http://www.state.gov/www/global/terrorism/terrorists_extradition.html.

ernment than Washington, so most of the major players are within a ten-minute walk down Whitehall; analysts can easily meet with policy counterparts in defense, the foreign office, or the treasury. Moreover, there is in London nothing approximating Washington's stream of current intelligence — that huge pile of papers, now replaced by screens of messages, that framed my NSC colleague's day. JIC papers are the main intelligence analyses in town. They are usually read and known to be read by the prime minister and so have a cachet that American NIEs very seldom achieve.

In several respects, though, JIC procedures could serve as a model. Usually chaired by a foreign service officer on secondment, the JIC works from the cabinet office. Its staff is drawn from both intelligence and policy agencies, from MI6 and MI5 but also from the policy offices of the treasury and the foreign office. And policy officials sit in on all the JIC's deliberations from drafting to meetings of the JIC itself. The obvious risk in this arrangement is politicization, for those policy officials have their own stakes and preferences. In my experience, however, the advantages greatly outweigh the risks, for at each stage, the process is animated by a sharper sense of what the real issues are and what information or analysis might be helpful when they come up for decision. Such participation improves the chances that intelligence will be useful when alternative courses of action are debated.

So, too, in a world where both structures and U.S. interests are up for grabs, might American policy-makers be better served by intelligence brokers close at hand, down the hall, not out at Langley. In this confused world, Sen. Daniel Patrick Moynihan may be half right but for the wrong reasons.[21] Perhaps the CIA should be not abolished but dispersed, its analytic pieces assigned to State, Treasury, Commerce, and elsewhere around official Washington.

INTELLIGENCE FOR WHOSE POLICY?

The policy that intelligence tried to help during the Cold War was that of the United States, and most of the time its consumers were a limited group of officials with responsibilities for politico-military issues. Both those facts are changing, and U.S. intelligence support to in-

21   See his "Our Stupid But Permanent CIA," *Washington Post*, July 24, 1994, p. C3.

ternational peace and humanitarian operations, usually run under UN auspices, illustrates the change. Those operations have an important military component, but they are also multilateral and often run well beyond strictly military purposes to try to rebuild shattered nations. They thus mix old intelligence agendas and new, old and new consumers.[22]

Yet these operations also foreshadow a new era in the sharing of intelligence and, ultimately, in determining the parties for whom intelligence works. Peacekeeping threatened existing concepts of holding back rather than sharing, in which glimpses of the crown jewels were doled out sparingly, mostly to English-speaking services that were partners of the DO or NSA and that provided something in return. Peacekeeping imposes operational needs to share information, so sharing cannot easily be avoided. The next step in sharing will be conceiving of intelligence strategically, as a means of helping others see a set of issues the way the United States does and so facilitating the building of coalitions.

When new possibilities for peacekeeping opened up at the end of the Cold War, the UN had almost no institutional peacekeeping capacity. Indeed, it was said, alas truthfully, that after office hours at UN headquarters in New York, there was no one to take phone calls from far-flung peacekeepers. The Clinton administration's Presidential Decision Directive 25, issued in May 1994, recommended that the UN establish an information and research unit, linked to field operations, "to obtain and provide current information, manage a 24-hour watch center, and monitor open sources material and non-sensitive information submitted by governments."[23] For its part, the United States would "share information, as appropriate, while ensuring full protection of sources and methods." Those words codified the halting movement of American intelligence from a primary concern about security toward the recognition that getting U.S. information into the hands of, or U.S. interpretations into the heads of, foreigners could also serve America's purposes.

The United States designed the Joint Deployable Intelligence Support System, a computer system using commercially available technology. Any UN member can hook into the system to provide whatever it

22   Richard A. Best, Jr., "Peacekeeping: Intelligence Requirements," Congressional Research Service, May 6, 1994.
23   United States National Security Council, "The Clinton Administration's Policy on Reforming Multilateral Peace Operations," May 1994, pp. 7, 9.

chooses. Little by little, *intelligence,* which had been a dirty word at the UN (*information* was the politically correct term) became less so. Kofi Annan, then assistant UN secretary-general for peacekeeping and later UN secretary-general, was, perhaps ironically, much less nervous about the word *intelligence* and about materials with American provenance than had been his predecessor, the Briton Maurice Goulding.

In practice, the defense intelligence community became the focal point for sharing once it was authorized for use in the Somalia, Bosnia, or Cambodia missions, for example. Assessments were provided to the U.S. Mission to the UN, then to be handed to the UN Operations Center or other peacekeeping officials. When U.S. military forces were involved, as in Somalia or Bosnia, there was in effect a second channel for intelligence through the U.S. chain of command. Tactical U.S. commanders could then pass the reports on to their non-American UN colleagues. Having U.S. "friends" as the senior UN representatives on the scene facilitated the arrangement: In Cambodia, the UN representative was an Australian, and in Somalia, it was an American, former admiral and NSC official Jonathan Howe.

Beyond these recent developments, U.S. intelligence had thought of sharing as a one-way activity, letting a few trusted friends see some of the crown jewels. It had been a grudging and an explicitly tactical act: When immediate coalition operations required it or as part of building institutional relationships, the gems would be passed along from intelligence service to fellow intelligence service. Building relationships will still be an important reason for sharing, but in the future, the partners will be much more varied — not just intelligence agencies but also NGOs, and not just foreign offices but also foreign companies. And the sharing will be two way, not one. In the world of the market state, a world that is not fully open everywhere but is not very closed anywhere, humanitarian NGOs will know more about many African countries than does the CIA, and oil companies will be as expert on Indonesia.

7

A reshaped intelligence

Suppose the international environment remained a relatively benign one for the United States over the next decade-plus, the period between now and 2015. That doesn't seem a bad bet. No military peer of the United States will emerge, though the shadow of a future such possibility might conceivably fall over the latter years of that decade. The major alternatives to a benign world for intelligence are two, each with very different implications for intelligence. The first would be a series of terrorist attacks on the United States with biological weapons or other weapons of mass destruction. The damage from those attacks could be truly fearsome; even if it were not, the attacks would be likely to frighten Americans well beyond the real damage.

That world of direct threat would push intelligence back in a Cold War direction: National purposes would become paramount, and secrets would loom larger, as would what the government itself collected. Cooperating with foreigners in fighting terrorism would probably be just as necessary in that world as it is now, but actually accomplishing the cooperation would be harder. In a climate dominated by national purposes, intelligence would be seen as a way to get a leg up on others. And if the military seemed frustratingly awkward to bring to bear against terrorists, and so lost favor in Washington's budget wars, intelligence would still be regarded as invaluable. Its budgets could rise as the military's fell. Indeed, bringing the military to bear would depend precisely on what intelligence alone could offer — precise location of foes and precise information on the area of battle. The lack of that precision is what often accounts now for decisions *not* to use special military units such as the Delta force.

The other alternative to a relatively benign world would be a prolonged global economic collapse. In the emerging world of the market state, the collapse would probably discredit the private sector more than government or intelligence. Intelligence was modestly criticized for not predicting Mexico's peso crisis of 1994 but was not similarly chastised for not foreseeing Asia's debacle a few years later. Why, after all, should intelligence have done better than big banks with huge stakes or international organizations with relevant mandates? A prolonged economic crisis, like the terrorism future, would also increase the role of government, and it would also turn Americans more nationalist. Beggar-thy-neighbor policies would be on the agenda; how to insulate America against globalization's evils would supplant how to take advantage of its pluses.

Yet if intelligence were a beneficiary of this future, it would only be a modest one. The most tempting economic policies would be autarkic, inward-looking ones, which would not depend on any precise calibration of foreigners or their actions. If intelligence could provide an advantage in negotiations or steal useful industrial secrets, that would be all to the good. But neither, and especially not the second, has been a strong point of intelligence in the past, at least not reliably.

Suppose, though, continued fair weather. Suppose Washington became less a military capital in hot war and cold and moved toward becoming the capital of the globe's most important market state. Over a decade, that world would defy all the old distinctions on which intelligence has been based — analyst versus collector, information versus intelligence, secret versus open, foreign versus domestic, and public versus private. Another decade of economic and political opening would probably spell the end for most of the remaining closed states: Imagine North Korea unified with the South, Iraq autocratic but opening, and Cuba all but the fifty-first U.S. state.

In that world, competition in information would be intense, but the competition would not depend very much on who held the secrets. Secrets would be transitory. Rather, small teams would compete intensely to see which could assemble information in useful ways the fastest or get innovations to the marketplace the quickest.

The competition would look much more like where Silicon Valley seems to be headed, not where the United States and Soviet Union were during the Cold War: Small teams would form and dissolve, with ideas and information swirling, and no single bit of information would be either decisive or held secretly for long.

(The debate over Chinese nuclear spying on the United States in 1999 obscured an important foreshadowing of what "keeping secrets" will mean in the future. So long as would-be spies had to steal documents or microfilm them, spying was a "retail" enterprise. The secret documents themselves could be protected, and the vast apparatus of physical security that intelligence developed made some sense. Now, though, a spy with a few minutes of access to the target's computer Zip drive can steal material wholesale; such a spy could acquire quickly more material than his intelligence service could process in a year. In these circumstances, physical security is much less effective. What will be required are processes, perhaps akin to those in the private sector, that depend on the fleeting nature of most secrets. Security will need to derive not from protecting any particular bit of information, but rather from its rapid obsolescence.)

Intelligence agencies themselves would do much less work in-house; they would instead depend much more on a wide range of outside consultants. Conflict-of-interest laws and practices would be radically reshaped, so experts would move easily among the CIA, Wall Street, and British Petroleum; indeed, consultants might work for all three on successive days.

The agencies would also be dispersed, in order to be much closer to consumers, colleagues, and "sources." Much of the time, the teams could be virtual, not real, so the CIA might, for instance, become a dozen or so small regional centers located to reach all three. Being physically close would be necessary in order to calibrate other experts and to be calibrated by policy-makers. It would also matter in the way it seems to matter in Silicon Valley: For all the technology, there still seems something special about face-to-face interchange, especially in pursuit of creativity.

Consumers, colleagues, and sources would often be the same. For example, a CIA analyst might on one day debrief a nongovernmental organization (NGO) official just back from a trip to Africa, then the next day find him- or herself sharing information with that official while trying to put together a coalition, under the umbrella of the Organization for African Unity, to meet a humanitarian emergency in West Africa. Nike might be a "customer" one day as the U.S. government seeks to assemble a coalition in support of international reforms of child labor, but a source the next, when a company executive just back from Indonesia meets with a CIA analyst to discuss conditions there.

Consumers would multiply. For the U.S. government, the task would be to build broad coalitions of countries, companies, and other private actors. Traditional diplomacy, with its focus on foreign offices, would be more and more irrelevant. While the Treasury's Office of the Assistant Secretary for International Affairs (OASIA) is not small, with a staff of about 200, it is still striking that it is only a tenth the size of the CIA's Directorate of Intelligence. And OASIA would pale, for better or worse, by comparison to the thousands of bankers, almost all of them private citizens, who would exercise public authority without quite realizing it.

This change in who intelligence worked for would be the most momentous. As the territorial state faded and the U.S. government was more and more in the business of assembling "coalitions of the willing," information would be critical. It would be an important part of what the government could offer would-be coalition partners, in addition to whatever legitimacy the government retained as an intermediary. To be valuable in coalition building, however, information — and intelligence — would have to be shared, not held closely. That intelligence might derive from secrets, but its consumers would not all, or mostly, be from the U.S. government or indeed from any government at all.

Collection, too, would be radically transformed. For one thing, there might not be much clandestine collection of human intelligence (HUMINT). Technology for identifying people quickly through the irises of their eyes or their fingerprints would be widely in use and would make it much harder to create false identities for spymasters. Those technologies, however, would be much more prevalent in the rich countries than the poor, and the rich countries would be mostly beyond spying on each other anyhow. Spying would still continue, but mostly in the places where it has always been difficult — in the lands that harbor terrorists or terrible weapons.

The emphasis for intelligence would be on processing, not collecting. Voice recognition and translating technologies would, on the one hand, make processing easier, but the sheer volume of information, on the other, would be daunting. Traditional secrets would be fewer and transitory; rather, the challenge would be assembling information from many sources and authenticating it, and doing so faster than others. Moving information around would be child's play because enormous bandwidth would be installed everywhere, so anybody could be in touch with anybody. In the process, layers of bureaucracy could continue to disappear, but at the cost of also eliminating layers of processing. The art for designing organizations would lie in deciding who should see what, when, and how much.

Much more imagery could be bought, and thus nations would literally be more transparent: They could see what they looked like to other nations. For signals, strong encryption would mean the end of signals intelligence (SIGINT) as it has been practiced. To be sure, crises would lure people into carelessness, and some less sophisticated targets of U.S. intelligence might be eavesdropped upon. But SIGINT would become traffic analysis, and even that might become nearly impossible as packeting and other techniques sent vast streams of data down single communications lines.

At the same time, microsensors — ranging from "brilliant" rocks and artificial gnats to, ultimately, smart molecules — would be able to detect everything from movements and heat to heartbeats and blood pressure. Getting these sensors into position might not be very hard in a more open world. Again, however, many of the targets of these special collectors would not be other democracies; rather, they would be the havens of terrorists and remaining autocrats. With regard to those targets, getting special sensors in place secretly and, still more, getting their take out without the knowledge of those being monitored would be harder.

RETARGETING THE COLD WAR LEGACY

The world as it is now undercuts all the attributes of the old intelligence paradigm, and another decade or more of change would do so even more dramatically. The reshaping of intelligence that is needed is a sweeping one. That reshaping has organizational implications, but profound as those are, they matter less than the transformation in how intelligence conceives of its business. To talk of a shift in the paradigm of intelligence sounds hackneyed, but intelligence confronts nothing less as it begins the 21st century. This chapter briefly recapitulates the strands of that shift, then turns to its organizational implications.

The United States, which was a latecomer to the idea of a permanent intelligence service in peacetime, has known but one intelligence paradigm. That paradigm was based on a single foe, depended on secrets, and was mostly designed to solve puzzles. In the circumstances, collection and analysis were separate tasks done by different people. Analysis and collection were relatively centralized, the first in the CIA, the second in the various INT stovepipes. During the Cold War, intelligence's consumers were officials of the U.S. government, for the most part those engaged in a fairly narrow range of political and military issues. For reasons more of doctrine than of necessity, the government drew a sharp line between intelligence and policy, and for reasons rooted in history and the U.S. Constitution, it walled off domestic from foreign.

That was not a bad way to organize the business of intelligence then, but it is a bad way now, when intelligence has many targets, not one, many customers, not few, and when secrets do not provide it a monopoly.

With intelligence during the Cold War aimed at a single principal foe, the Soviet Union, lesser foes, and friends too, claimed attention. For the most part, however, those other targets were lesser-included cases: The capacity to understand them was a by-product of what was needed to assess the main enemy. Intelligence's franchise depended on secrets because that main enemy was a closed society. So intelligence became used to operating in a world where it "owned" its information, and where that information, from satellite images or spy reports, was limited and deemed reliable. More often that not, and particularly about the Soviet Union, the problem was that there was too little information.

Because intelligence obtained its limited information through sources that were, if less and less secret as the Cold War progressed, at least unusual or technical, collection and analysis were separate tasks, and they were done by distinct groups of officials. What was collected needed to be processed, and the processing was analysis of a sort — those satellite photos used to make America's cases in the court of public opinion from the Cuban missile crisis onward didn't mean much to other than trained photo interpreters. Yet on the whole, those who collected and did the first processing of information worked in "stovepipes" that were separated from those who did the ultimate analysis.

National Security Agency (NSA) officers felt that their products were underappreciated because their art was so arcane, but the agency did not think of itself as in the business of analysis. Nor was it regarded that way in Washington — its mission was collection. That was the case despite the value of the capsule summaries of SIGINT that NSA published and, more important, despite the accumulated understanding of those who did the listening. Nobody understood the nature of conflict in a given country better than those who had been listening to the communications of the various groups. By the same token, few understood foreign communications better than those officers, both listeners and translators but not "analysts," who had listened to them at all times of the day and night. Yet that repository of wisdom was seldom tapped, because it was collection, not analysis.[1]

The centralization of intelligence was purposive, deriving from a reading of Pearl Harbor's lesson. The surprise attack had underscored the dangers of dispersed analysis: America's prewar intelligence had collected a number of signals that Japan was preparing an attack, but those signals remained dispersed in the various U.S. intelligence agencies. The puzzle pieces were there, but they were not assembled to solve the puzzle, at least not in time. Preventing another Pearl Harbor, especially when the warning time of a Soviet nuclear attack might be minutes, not days, seemed to call for a centralized processor of those puzzle pieces — first the Central Intelligence Group (CIG), then the CIA.

The assembling of collection into the stovepipes was more haphazard, as agencies carved out missions when new technology made new forms of collection possible. The military services long had been engaged in SIGINT, and a loose consolidation of those efforts under military auspices, in NSA, was a natural evolution. By the summer of 1946, barely a year after the Office of Strategic Services

1   Detail has been deleted here.

(OSS) was disbanded, a clandestine espionage service had been re-assembled in the CIG's Office of Special Operations. It took the CIA's entrepreneurship, by comparison to the Air Force's dubiety, to create the U-2 and so take America into photo reconnaissance from near-space. Later, though, when satellites came along, imagery intelligence (IMINT) became too big a task for the CIA alone, and besides, neither the Air Force nor the Navy, both of which had stakes in estimating the nuclear forces of the preeminent Soviet foe, was willing to yield reconnaissance on that foe to a third agency. The National Reconnaissance Office (NRO) was the result.

For reasons more of doctrine than necessity, the United States drew a bright line between intelligence and policy. The origin of that separation is also more obscure than that of the centralization of analysis; it was imposed more by ourselves than by our stars. In part, Pearl Harbor's intelligence failure suggested the virtue of a cen-tralized intelligence agency that was divorced from the stakes of pol-icy: Intelligence that was too close to operators was not likely to sound the tocsin when the warning, iffy by nature, required opera-tors to take actions that were costly or inconvenient.

The separation also resulted, though, from the creation of peace-time civilian intelligence agencies, the CIA in particular, when the premier foreign policy agency, the State Department, was some-where between standoffish and hostile in its attitude toward intelli-gence. Given that attitude, it was only with the emergence of the National Security Council (NSC) as an independent player that the CIA acquired a real policy "customer" — and then one that was meant to be, and often was, a coordinator and ring holder, not an advocate. The NSC did, however, provide a focal point for intelli-gence through its staff and its processes, including some sense for the agenda and a legitimate way to get to NSC consumers not just at the NSC but at State and Defense and later other agencies as well.

Neither Pearl Harbor nor the Cold War decreed, however, that the line between intelligence and policy would forever be the right solution. Nor did they forever enshrine the virtues of centralization. Policy operators and intelligence analysts inhabit such different worlds that it is more surprising that they ever connect than that they so often do not. The United States has made the situation worse by reinforcing the separation with principle. Given that prin-ciple, intelligence and its people sometimes have paid a price for crossing the line and becoming "politicized" — that is, abandoning the canon of objectivity to "get on the policy team." They have not paid any comparable price for being irrelevant. And so, intelligence is often interesting but not so often useful. Too often it reads like op-ed pieces in the *Post* or the *Times*. As a reader, you wonder, If this is the answer, just what is the question?

What information was passed to policy depended on the secrets intelligence had to offer. In any case, because senior policy-makers had neither time nor prescience to be very coherent about what they would need, whether their flow of intelligence was a trickle or a rush was usually decided by intelligence. Intelligence was provided, in today's language, by "push," not "pull." Consumers might ask questions, but most of the time, what was put before them was pushed there by intelligence, not pulled there by the stakes and agendas of those policy-makers.

Finally, if politics was supposed to stop at the water's edge, so was intelligence. In creating a peacetime intelligence community, the United States enshrined twin distinctions — between "foreign" and "domestic" and between foreign intelligence and law enforcement. The distinctions had not been so sharp before: The wartime FBI had run clandestine intelligence operations in Latin America. The distinctions, and thus the creation of civilian intelligence agencies in the "foreign intelligence" business, were an effort to balance a recognition of the grave foreign threat with the requirements of the Constitution. The United States was not above worrying about communists in its midst, but the Cold War consensus had located the security threat abroad, particularly the Soviet Union. Intelligence followed that focus.

In combatting the Soviet Union, the distinction between home and abroad became a sharp one. In principle, the threat justified almost any means abroad. There, any limits were those of prudence. Our allies sometimes worried that we might become as nasty as our enemy, and they were sometimes tempted to locate themselves "equidistant" between the two superpowers, but these bouts of ethical fretting never had much currency in the United States. Americans and American soil were quite another matter. The intelligence investigations, especially those of the mid-1970s, found evidence of abuses of the rights of Americans, and no one doubted that those were abuses. The abusers mostly came from the FBI, not the

CIA. Spying on Americans had, with narrow exceptions, to be justified by the standard of "probable cause" in reference to possible crimes; national security wiretaps for intelligence purposes without such a probable cause could be applied only on foreigners. In the war on terrorism, U.S. allies broadened the range of police powers available for use against their own citizens, but, with small exceptions, the United States did not.

A NEW PARADIGM

All of these premises of intelligence since World War II have been overturned or cast into question. There are now many targets and many possible missions, the world is open, and we are witnessing the rise of the market state. Yet the demise of the Soviet Union does not merely convert one large threat into many small ones, and the task for intelligence is not simply to convert old capacity to new purposes. It is to change fundamentally how the business is done.

The multiplicity of possible targets for intelligence is real. There are now few lesser-included cases. To be sure, the satellite systems that were originally bought to keep tabs on the Soviet Union are pretty good now at supporting military operations abroad, but choices about the next generation of sensors will call for decisions about precise targets and capabilities. Intelligence will have to decide what to do and what not to do, when to build capacity in-house or buy it outside should need arise, or when to let it go altogether.

In money terms, these choices about missions will bite hardest in the competition for new technical collection systems. It will always be possible to do just a little better in supporting military operations by locating that foe "over there." The United States will continue to confront particular bad people or bad forces whose precise location it would dearly love to know. The price tag for the improvements will be enormous, and perhaps worse still, the cost to national intelligence can be high as the priority shifts to the mission of supporting America's warriors. The cost will be high because those who frame mysteries will also benefit from access to secrets. Even if more and more of the information required to address strategic mysteries will be openly available, not all of it will.

The second dramatic change in the world of intelligence is the diminished value of secrets and the multiplying of information that is available, if not fully openly then not entirely secretly either. What has gone — probably but not ineluctably forever — is the closed state. Some such dinosaurs survive, and we cannot be certain that more will not emerge, or revert. But we can be sure that at this stage of the global economy and technology, would-be autocrats will face what is, for them, a Hobson's choice: They can close themselves off to global commerce and technology, and to the political forces that come with them, and remain impoverished; or they can seek to become rich but only at the price of opening up. They can be closed or prosperous, but not both. They cannot become wealthy enough to be powerful while remaining closed.

To be sure, poor closed states still may threaten the United States: North Korea, an utter failure, managed enough bluster and military hardware to tie down tens of thousands of U.S. soldiers and to preoccupy America's national leaders. Syria and Libya, smaller still, could threaten Americans with the weapons of terror; so can groups that do not control states. These states or groups will not advertise their activities, and states that are not so closed will also hide some of what they do. Collecting secrets thus will remain a function of intelligence.

Yet so much more of the world is open, whether it intends it or not. What used to have to be photographed from miles up can now be observed on the ground. And the World Wide Web spews out a stew of fact, fiction, disinformation, and fancy. If closed states have gone, it is this open world that has arrived.

Openness is at the heart of the change in the paradigm of intelligence: Intelligence's world used to be one of finite amounts of information deemed reliable (satellite photographs and spy reports), but now it is one of a surfeit of information of very uncertain reliability. The change cannot be overstated. Its implications run from the balance between collection and analysis, to how analysis is done, to the culture of the organizations involved.

In this world, the business of intelligence is information, not secrets. Intelligence can no longer concentrate on secrets, for the wherewithal for understanding many of the most portentous issues confronting the United States is not to be found there. To say intelligence will be in the information business is not to say it should produce all the information itself, far from it. In the words of former Deputy DCI Richard Kerr, intelligence "has to learn that it no longer controls its own sources."[2] It will have to conceive of its world as a torrent of information to which it may add from its own sources but only at the margins. For some issues, tactical puzzles about secretive adversaries, that margin will be important. For many strategic mysteries, by contrast, it will be negligible.

Intelligence has been dominated by collection, but now the pendulum needs to swing toward processing and analysis. Collection will continue to consume the lion's share of intelligence's funding because it is expensive and analysis is relatively cheap. Analysis may not remain as cheap as it has been in absolute terms if, for instance, intelligence tries to hire economic analysts who are the equals of their colleagues on Wall Street. Now, the restrictions of the civil service system make such analysts essentially unobtainable. Hiring and, still more, keeping them would require dramatic changes in the way the government hires, deploys, and compensates its officials. Moreover, the processing that lies ahead will require expensive high-powered computers, and connecting analysts to consumers will be facilitated by sophisticated networks, ones that will also be expensive, to make two-way communication easy. On the whole, though, and despite these changes, intelligence's people will remain cheap relative to its technology that is deployed in space or in complicated ways on earth.

In these circumstances, a doubling or trebling of resources allocated to analysis would only take its share to a fifth or a quarter of the total intelligence budget.[3] A shift of that magnitude is not likely to happen soon, in part because there are no lobbies for analysts but there are lobbies for expensive technical systems. But the required direction is clear. The world ahead requires more processing and analysis, not less. Over the past 20 years, the intelligence budget has grown by over 50 percent relative to the defense budget, and

2   Quoted in Mark M. Lowenthal, "Open Source Intelligence: New Myths, New Realities," *Defense Daily Network Special Reports*, November 12, 1998, p. 2.

3   This was a main recommendation of the Twentieth Century Fund panel. See p. 7 of *In From the Cold*, New York: Twentieth Century Fund Press, 1996.

virtually all that relative growth has resulted from more, and costlier, collection systems.

Over the longer term, doing better at looking, not spying, would help. In this area, too, the question the government faces is how much to buy its own "lookers," in particular new ones, and how much to make better use of the lookers that already exist. There were, for instance, plenty of lookers inside the U.S. government in 1999 who knew where China's embassy was in Belgrade, but they were not well enough connected to either the photo analysts in intelligence or the bomb targeteers in the military. By the same token, it would be nice for intelligence to hire a cadre of inexpensive stringers in, say, Russia, but a better first step would be to find ways to take better advantage of Americans and others who already travel or reside there. The idea would not be to "collect" better from co-operating citizens and other people, but to put analysts in touch with them. Doing so will require both new habits and new or revamped institutions.

In the world that lies ahead for intelligence, openness will not just be desirable, it will also be imperative. Intelligence will need to reach out in a hundred directions through a variety of means. The climate surrounding intelligence is changing, so it is much easier to reach out. In 1999, the National Intelligence Council (NIC) published a glossy brochure listing its officers, their portfolios, and phone numbers. Indeed, intelligence will find it easier to engage willing colleagues outside government — in the universities, think tanks, and NGOs — than to adjust its own personnel practices. Analysts will need both license and encouragement to think of themselves as their own "collectors" by meeting with colleagues among private-sector counterparts and NGOs.

For at least some of those analysts, intelligence will need to provide working conditions akin to those of universities — freedom to publish in their own names, to attend conferences and, perhaps most important, to specialize in particular countries or topics, in some cases for entire careers. It used to be that people could build careers in intelligence while working on a fairly narrow range of problems, but that time is no more. The analytic organizations, especially the Directorate of Intelligence (DI), came to reward managing over analyzing and flexibility over depth. Intelligence needs to change those practices, at least for some of its analysts.

In addition, the world ahead will require intelligence, like the military, to become much more hospitable to lateral movements from outside to inside, including temporary ones. Just as the U.S. Army will not be able to compete with the private sector for the information specialists it wants in its enlisted ranks, intelligence cannot compete with Wall Street for first-rate financial analysts. But it could attract those people for limited periods when they are curious about another perspective, or want a change of pace, or, happily, seek to serve their country at the end of long careers.

THE RISE OF THE MARKET STATE

The third broad change that is undercutting the Cold War paradigm of intelligence is no less dramatic than the Soviet Union's demise and the world's opening, but it is less appreciated. It is the sum of the trends outlined in chapter 2, amounting to the demise of the territorial state and the rise of the market state. There is nothing new about this change, for it has been under way a century or more; it was obscured in this century, though, by the special and specially fearsome territorial states, first Germany and Japan, then the Soviet Union. The long transition toward the market state, one that is now more and more apparent, is the backdrop for America's engagement in the world and for how intelligence assists that engagement.

The driving forces of international politics are now economic, not the politics of relations among states. Armies, territory, and sovereignty: None of these is irrelevant, but all are slowly being depleted of meaning. The process is uneven across the globe; the 18th century conflicts in Bosnia and Kosovo under way at the dawn of the 21st century testify to that. Still, what will drive global politics is how people within states engage the fast-moving international economy, not how nation-states engage each other. The implications are far-reaching, though they will be perceptible only gradually.

Neither the United States nor intelligence can afford to stop paying attention to the military forces of the powers that might be threats. They are not hard to name. The point, though, is that in the world of the market state, their military potential cannot be evaluated in isolation from their economic paths. Understanding the military potential of the Soviet Union was a bean-counting exercise, though the beans were easy neither to find nor to sum up.

(Had a war come, too, we might have found that the sums were badly wrong because of all the things we couldn't count — the morale of military organizations, the proficiency of their soldiers, and the leadership of their commanders. Fortunately, we never had that test.)

Then, however, it was possible to make tolerable estimates of Soviet military potential by counting what could be seen. Those estimates could be abstracted from Soviet politics and economics. Political choices surely mattered, but we knew so little about those, and the chain between our actions and their outcomes was so tangled, that those choices didn't seem to matter much to the immediate business at hand. Former Defense Secretary Harold Brown is credited with the line that captures that fact: "When we build, the Soviet Union builds; when we stop, it builds." Soviet citizens, we came to know, would suffer the privations necessary to fund military increases; at least that was a safe bet from one year to the next. So the estimating of Soviet military potential was a technical task, not a political or economic one.

That is not the case for market states. For them, including the most formidable of America's possible military foes, economics will be decisive. Russia, for instance, faces the choice outlined earlier: It can be rich and friendly or hostile and poor. In any case, whether it could again become a serious military threat to the United States will turn entirely on whether its economic engagement with the world will give it the economic muscle to support a 21st century military establishment.

The same is true for China. Whether it becomes America's principal military rival — a "peer competitor" in the Pentagon's language — will turn to some extent on U.S. policies. But mostly it will turn on the course of China's politics and economics. If the country remains a unit and grows at anything like its recent rate, it will become a formidable military power, if not necessarily an enemy, simply through the compounding of economic growth. Yet a thousand political possibilities lie between that forecast and its coming true. China might fragment, or economic decentralization might proceed to the point that, in traditional military terms, the whole state is less than the sum of its parts. Or a center that is jealous of its prerogatives might act in ways that throttle economic growth.

Two implications of the market state for intelligence stand out. The first is that *foreign* and *domestic* are losing their traditional meanings. Market forces do not respect national sovereignty, and while nations, including the United States, may still try to separate home from abroad, it will be harder and harder to do so. In the short run, this blurring of the line between foreign and domestic will push intelligence analysts where they ought to be going in any case — toward paying more attention to the "domestic" side of foreign policy issues. They usually will be able to do so with open sources: witness the national intelligence officer in touch with Wall Street analysts of Mexico. She understood that the United States, in this case less the government than the financial sector, was a powerful determinant of Mexico's future, and her sources were telephone calls, not secrets.

However, the foreign-domestic divide will put more pressure on how intelligence does its collection. Terrorism and law enforcement do so already, but so far intelligence has gotten better at working with law enforcement agencies while still staying out of the chain of evidence. Over time, however, if international law enforcement continues to rise on the agenda of the market state, traditional intelligence runs the risk of seeming less and less useful if it sustains its existing role.

So far, terrorism has not pushed intelligence toward the domestic side of the foreign-domestic divide — that is, collecting on Americans — as much as might have been expected. The reason is twofold: International terrorists are seldom Americans, and criminal prosecution or other law enforcement is only one among a number of U.S. policy responses. Intelligence that is not good enough to bring a case in a court of law, in the event that the perpetrator could be captured, may still be good enough for a policy decision to apply what a counterterrorism specialist called "TLAM therapy" — cruise missile attacks on suspected terrorist bases abroad.

The more immediately troublesome frontier would seem to be domestic terrorism. If such terrorism is on the rise, won't combatting it require collecting more intelligence on Americans? Perhaps not, because if there is any good news in the difference between domestic and international terrorism, it is that the state retains powerful advantages with regard to the former: If the government and intelligence are more constrained in their information-gathering options for citizens at home than for foreigners abroad, that disadvantage is more than outweighed by their control of the territory and of punishments, and the lack of the need to cooperate with other states. Domestic terrorism may put less pressure on the role of intelligence than might seem to be the case.

In pursuing cases designed to level the playing field of international commerce, intelligence will indeed confront a more and more tangled web of the foreign and domestic. Suppose, for instance, that an American company had complained a decade ago that it was being unfairly competed against for the acquisition of a Slovak arms manufacturer, part of the legacy of the Soviet Union's decision to site arms industry in then Czechoslovakia. In the first analysis, the U.S. company's complaint might have seemed on the mark: European competitors were seeking unfair advantage. On second analysis, though, it might have turned out that the would-be American acquirer also had dirty hands, for it sought the Slovak company at least in part to evade U.S. restrictions on arms sales to Iran.

The other dramatic change engendered by the market state is the widening of intelligence's consumers. Those consumers already include economic officials who now look to intelligence for staff work, if not for analytic insights. Peace and other contingency operations have made foreign governments into consumers of U.S. intelligence, and if U.S. intelligence agencies have been reluctant to share their take in principle, they have been creative in fact. Intelligence was used throughout the Cold War to make America's case in the court of world public opinion, but the use was mostly tactical, not strategic. Given secrecy, it did not come naturally to intelligence to ask how it might get its analyses into the heads of foreigners and so build support for U.S. perspectives on world events.

That strategic use is beginning to occur; it is impelled in part by the plain fact that other nations and groups, and their information sources, can be valuable. During my time on the NIC, I sometimes had occasion to meet with representatives from other intelligence services. Of those, the most enlightening were with one service that was the most open.[4] Not only did they take the craft of intelligence

4   Detail has been deleted here.

seriously, their approach to their nation's security was intriguingly open-minded. On one visit, they left behind a "nonpaper" listing security challenges or possible conflicts, circa 1995. The threats ranged from a nuclear power accident or fishing wars in the region, to escalating conflict between Russia and its neighbors leading to Russian intervention. If getting our perspective into their heads was valuable, so was getting theirs into our heads. Similarly, the NGOs, CARE and the like, that we at the NIC invited to shape the national intelligence estimate (NIE) on humanitarian emergencies had more experience on the ground in the most likely crisis locales than did the U.S. government.

Sharing intelligence with those private groups will be even harder than sharing with foreign governments. After a visit to Bosnia in 1994, I stopped in Geneva to visit the UN, Red Cross, and other international relief agencies. What quickly struck me about those agencies — and struck their officials, too, in our conversations — was that we were in the same business! I sat behind walls of security in the CIA building, and they, careful about their private status, were often edgy about getting too close in cooperating with governments, but we faced the same challenge. For all of us, achieving warning of impending crises was often not so hard; for the relief agencies, particularly, famines are pretty predictable, even when those famines are created by politics. What was harder for all of us was getting the warning paid attention to by relevant political actors — the U.S. government in my case, the UN and the international donor community in theirs.

For all of us, inducing the targets of our warning to act required getting them to make preparations based on "iffy" arguments; it was a bother, perhaps an unnecessary one. My problem was overloading an American government that, for all its capacity, seems hard-pressed to deal with more than one crisis at a time. The counterpart problem for the relief agencies was "donor fatigue." Afghanistan might still be on the verge of a humanitarian disaster, but it was no longer in the headlines; it had been "solved" by the Soviet withdrawal and had returned to obscurity.

The next step for intelligence will be sharing its information and analyses with NGOs and then with private individuals and companies. Now, the sharing of information with firms is episodic, and it is mostly driven by particular abuses in international commerce or by specific threats from foreign intelligence services. The CIA debriefs business people who have had travel or contacts of interest, but that process is pretty haphazard. Intelligence analysts sometimes share notes with Wall Street counterparts, but, again, doing so is unusual, not normal. Indeed, intelligence agencies ask private think tanks such as RAND to undertake projects on international economic topics precisely because RAND analysts have easier access to the World Bank and International Monetary Fund (IMF), not to mention private bankers.

In the world of the market state, the comparative advantage of the U.S. government will be less its ability to compel than its opportunity to convene. The government exists, with taxpayers funding lights and secretaries. It is a logical convener, and it may be that private institutions will cooperate with or through it in ways they would not directly cooperate with competitors. Shell and Exxon might share information with or through the U.S. government, at least for some purposes, that both would be reluctant to share directly with each other. (The limits to this sharing with the government are also present. Shell apparently uses U.S. intelligence as a test of its own corporate security; the operative question is, Can NSA break into the Shell communications system?) The NGOs that helped us at the NIC frame the estimate on humanitarian emergencies overcame their skepticism about intelligence mostly because it was welcome that someone, anyone, was paying attention to *their* issue. But they may also have found it easier to attend a meeting called by us, a neutral party, than by one of their number.

Information, or intelligence, will be a critical part of what the government can offer would-be coalition partners. That will be the case for issues of concern to the market state, just as it has been for peace operations in the early years of the post–Cold War world. Using information to build those future coalitions will require, though, both new ways of sharing intelligence products with private actors and, probably, new institutional arrangements to do the sharing.

THE ROLE OF THE DCI

The missions for intelligence in the future suggest a very different organizational shape for America's intelligence community than the Cold War legacy that still exists. It would be open, not closed; decentralized, not centralized; organized more around "pull" than around "push." It might take as its organizational model the director of central intelligence's (DCI's) centers that already exist, but make the centers virtual ones, not physical sites, and extend them to the policy world. Doing so would acknowledge the existence of overlapping sets of intelligence collectors, analysts, and consumers, usually organized by issue, sometimes fleetingly (as with Albania or Kosovo in the late 1990s) and sometimes more enduringly (as with North Korea). To do this, it would be necessary to fashion an intelligence community that would permit, even facilitate, those virtual centers — no easy task.

The first conundrum facing intelligence for an age of information is what to do about the DCI. DCIs are tugged in three directions — overseeing the community; managing the CIA, which in practice means watching over the Directorate of Operations (DO); and serving as the president's chief intelligence officer — causing most of them to be torn apart. Robert Gates's reputation was tainted by his earlier association with the William Casey regime, but he was still unusually effective, especially as intelligence advisor to a president, George Bush, who cared about intelligence. Moreover, while the legacy of earlier clandestine misadventures (arms sales to Iran and CIA support for the Central American contras in particular) hung over Gates's tenure, he was lucky enough not to have fresh scandals to clean up.

Gates's successor, R. James Woolsey, never got close to his president, Bill Clinton, and so devoted his efforts to the community, particularly to securing its budget. There, bad chemistry between Woolsey and the Senate committee chair, plus Woolsey's own dedication, turned the selling into the appearance of overselling, damaging Woolsey's relations with the Hill. Then Woolsey was overwhelmed by a mighty tug in the third direction, managing the CIA, when it was badly shaken not by scandal this time, but through treason, Aldrich Ames's. John Deutch's tenure as DCI was brief and almost accidental; he did not really want the job, and his lack of interest in intelligence, at least beyond the needs of the military, was visible to all. He did try hard, too hard, to extend the writ of the DCI, and he did, surprisingly, begin to develop some standing in Clinton's inner circle, though not enough to secure the job Deutch did want, that of defense secretary.

George Tenet came to the job with political savvy, from both the Hill and the NSC staff, and with a real interest in intelligence. Yet he paid little attention to the community, preferring instead to concentrate on managing the CIA, a choice that fit with his apparent conception of intelligence as narrow and tactical, focused on secrets. To be fair, he served a president who, though a reader of intelligence, seemed to care most that intelligence not bring the administration major scandals or flaps. Moreover, Tenet reported to congressional intelligence committees that were both less weighty than some of their predecessors and more scattered in views.

There is no easy escape from the DCI's conundrum. One part of refashioning the DCI's role is obvious and ought to be easy but is not. It is time to divest the DCI of responsibility for managing the clandestine service on a day-to-day basis. Jim Woolsey and John Deutch were not the first DCIs who saw their broader goals frustrated by the need to spend the bulk of their time cleaning up the DO's broken crockery. Past DCIs, however, resisted relinquishing control of the DO for fear that they would lose their connection with the collection community. Just as they have wanted to keep a hand in technical collection, they have been loathe to abandon espionage, "real" intelligence, to become leaders merely of analysts.

A deputy to the DCI, confirmed by the Senate, might become the day-to-day manager of the clandestine service, elevating that deputy director for operations (DDO) in form as well as fact to something more than *primus inter pares* among the DCI's deputies. Or, better, mimicking early Cold War arrangements, the DDO, who heads the clandestine service, might report to a committee of the DCI, and the secretaries of state and defense. Reporting to a committee is always perilous because it usually means reporting to no one, but in this case the arrangement would have two virtues. By including the defense secretary but not the treasury secretary, it would also underscore the clandestine service's tight focus on foes, terrorists, and awful weaponry, not economics.

The arrangement could also serve as a countervailing weight against the State Department's distaste for intelligence, and so it could at long last begin to make possible some sense for the comparative advantages of political reporting and espionage. It could mute the competition for information, even sources, that now occurs between State's political officers and the CIA's case officers abroad. A series of intelligence committees under the DCI has tried to coordinate HUMINT tasking but without any meaningful participation from the most important government source, State Department political reporting.

If DCIs were somewhat removed from the daily management of the clandestine service, there would still be the puzzle of how to make them the president's senior intelligence officers. In particular, how could they be effective focal points for national and strategic intelligence missions, not military and tactical ones, without becoming mere special pleaders? On the one hand, the logic of the collection stovepipes and of supporting military operators in harm's way does suggest that there should be an overseer of intelligence collection, and that the overseer should be not the DCI but the secretary of defense (as a practical matter, the deputy secretary, who usually serves as the Pentagon's chief operating officer). On the other hand, almost all observers worry, with reason, that a DCI shorn of any authority over the technical collectors would become nothing more than a special pleader. As a practical matter, there is no alternative to some form of joint management by the DCI and the secretary of defense (and the deputy secretary). That joint management can be no better than are the personal relations among the principals.

In the first Clinton administration, the deputy secretary of defense and the DCI (first Bill Perry, then John Deutch and Jim Woolsey) jointly conducted intelligence program reviews. There was no pretense then, however, and there would be none in the future, that the DCI was the ultimate decision-maker; rather, he was the advocate for nonmilitary interests and consumers in a largely Pentagon-run process. The Woolsey-Perry reviews made graphic just how far the community is from arrangements that would facilitate such joint management: It was impossible then to tote up a budget across agencies by function or problem — how much was intelligence spending, for instance, on economics or on the Iraqi problem?

Those shortcomings demonstrated just how much need there is for more shape to and "jointness" in the joint management by the defense secretary and the DCI. The heads of the intelligence agencies now meet regularly in two forums, the National Foreign Intelligence Board (NFIB), to review NIEs, and the DCI's executive committee, to discuss more operational issues. What is lacking is a serious joint process for reviewing programs, perhaps at the level of deputy directors, backed by something akin to the Pentagon's policy analysis and evaluation (PA&E) office and empowered to examine major intelligence choices. The existing community management staff (CMS) has little analytic capacity to look across agencies in framing trade-offs, and it is hampered by the fact that its officers are on secondment from the various agencies and so are bound to take the interests of their home agencies into account in doing analyses. Making the CMS director a full deputy director of central intelligence would help solve the problem, as the congressional committees long have favored, but that step is only a start.

Intelligence last tried to establish a systematic approach to analyzing program priorities the last time it faced declining budgets, in the latter 1970s. The record of that attempt is not encouraging but is hardly an argument against trying again. As budgets declined in the first half of the Carter administration, the DCI, Admiral Stansfield Turner, secured agreement from President Carter that he would have, in the words of Executive Order 12036, "sole and exclusive authority" over the intelligence budgets, and he was determined to exercise it.[5] Alas, as other DCIs have discovered, reaching to make that authority real was overreaching, and Turner paid a high price in terms of his relations with the defense secretary, Harold Brown.

Still, the administration's commitment to zero-based budgeting, enforced by the Office of Management and Budget (OMB), stiffened the effort's spine. The agencies were asked to group like activities and to be explicit about priorities among them. To be sure, the agencies could outsmart the system by using "Washington monument" ploys. Nearly as old as the republic, these ploys involve consigning sure winners to low priority (as the park service did with the Washington monument) while elevating more dubious projects, betting that the budgeteers would accept the more questionable "high priorities" in order to rescue the winners. Despite budget ploys and the guerrilla war with Defense, many of the DCI's choices in the 1970s held.

As is often true in government, the fact and appearance of due process made it easier for agencies to accept adverse results; at least

---

5   This account is based largely on interview sources with participants during that earlier period.

the agencies could not argue that they hadn't been heard. In addition, having one primary target — the Soviet Union — provided a structure to the process that today's shapeless world does not have. Some major decisions, about imagery systems, for instance, could be reduced almost to a formula: What is the cheapest way to ensure, with a given probability, that a new Soviet submarine would be detected within a given time? In this context, the analytic process had some coherence, and a fairly regular schedule for considering upgrades to major collection systems added somewhat more. If the central analytic staff suffered from the same obstacle under which its successor, CMS, now labors — namely, that the agencies seldom seconded their best people to it — there was one thing to be said for secondees: They could be sent back home without having to be fired.

The effort waned with the Reagan administration's surge in defense, and thus intelligence, spending. William Casey, the DCI, and, in particular, Admiral Bobby R. Inman, the DDCI, opted for a full-court press in Congress for more money, which made serious analysis about major choices less pressing; not only that, forcing hard choices was bound to engender bad feeling among the intelligence agencies. The experience does, nevertheless, suggest several lessons for the future. One is the importance of evaluation. Only if relative value is measured can sensible choices be made — for instance, between new SIGINT satellites and a greater number of clandestine ground stations. And measuring value is all the more important in today's world because the large number of scattered targets means many of the choices must be between apples and oranges — satellites with ground stations or with unmanned aerial vehicles (UAVs), espionage with analysis.

The other lesson is that reserving money for experiments or targets of opportunity is important. In the 1970s, the argument for doing so was that because the Soviet Union was gaining an understanding of the big technical collectors, investing in new ways of doing business was necessary as a hedge against nasty surprises. Today, the arguments for doing so are that experiments might lead to finding new ways to do old business, and speculative investments provide some protection against the risks inherent in an uncertain future.

THE COLLECTION "MARKET"

The second conundrum confronting choices about organization is to what extent intelligence should follow "market" signals emitted by government consumers. My colleagues and I have joked for years about what would happen if policy agencies were allocated their pro rata share of intelligence budgets. Suppose they could do what they wished with the money: buy intelligence, grant bonuses, travel more, or procure more of something else. That would be the market test of intelligence: Was it worth its opportunity cost?

During the Clinton administration, Vice President Al Gore's effort to reshape government, Reinventing Government, emphasized finding surrogates for market forces inside the government and so lent our jokes a measure of reality.[6] The effort was worthy, but it was undercut by the political failure to acknowledge that neither the government nor the private sector can have it both ways: In the government's case, procurement processes have been designed primarily to minimize chances for abuse and secondarily to pursue estimable social values, *not* to be efficient. Indeed, in some areas, such as preferences for small businesses or minority contractors, these processes are designed to be *in*efficient. No politician can be honest about *this* trade-off, and Gore was not.

A number of other issues come into play in the case of establishing a market system for intelligence. There are strong grounds, for instance, for thinking that too little intelligence would be produced, let alone used. Almost by definition, intelligence is a service; it is not at the center of any policy organization. And so at the margin, and absent visible need such as war, armies will prefer guns to intelligence, diplomats will favor more consulates, and defense officials more travel. At a minimum, the short-term nature of policy would produce a boom-and-bust cycle: In times of peace, intelligence would be starved, but in times of crisis or war, policy would reach for intelligence that had not been created.

Intelligence also suffers because it is a free good for consumers. The logic of economics suggests that consumers will consume *too much* intelligence. However, there is little evidence that this proposition applies, except perhaps on the military side — rather, a cyni-

6 For more detail and background on the Reinventing Government project, go to www.npr.gov.

cal wag on the policy side might observe that you get what you pay for! In any case, market solutions are problematic.[7] First, shaping market arrangements would be complicated. An output for one part of intelligence is an input for another, so organizing ways to set transfer prices would be no easy task. Second, writing contracts would be bedeviled by the unpredictability of intelligence: "Goods" that can be provided today may be unavailable tomorrow. Neither of these objections is insuperable, however; the private sector encounters and surmounts them.

In the end, the strongest argument against market solutions is market failure, for intelligence is, to some extent at least, a public good. Since it has been virtually free to consumers, they are likely to be predisposed to undervalue it. Given choices, they would buy too little of it, and they would buy the wrong kind. So goes the argument. Almost certainly, consumer preferences would heavily favor the short term. Given short time horizons, senior policy officials want to make their mark, and quickly. It is a rare assistant secretary who comes to Washington with a hankering to leave his or her agency stronger. They spend institutional capacity; they hardly ever build it. Even apart from their personal ambitions, it is apparent that today's consumers of intelligence, preoccupied with this week's in-box, are not necessarily the wisest choosers of the collection systems that will serve their successors a decade hence.

Thus, immediate tactical support would be favored over research intended to frame longer-term mysteries. Collection today would be preferred to capacity building for tomorrow; the test for intelligence would be, What can you do for me today? When all the pressures in Washington shrink time horizons, however, intelligence should be unfashionably "unmarket" by existing outside of the prevailing pressures. The challenge to introducing market principles will be to find ways to empower consumers through marketlike arrangements while recognizing the limits of those arrangements. Such a system would of necessity introduce competing initiatives and experiments, and such arrangements always look like duplication and waste on Capitol Hill.

As it stands, the powerful stovepipes inhibit market tests by monopolizing the menu of alternatives and making it difficult to pose

7 See Michael Herman, *Intelligence Power in Peace and War*, Cambridge: Cambridge University Press, 1996, p. 313.

trade-offs across the stovepipes. The stovepipes probably cannot be broken up soon, so the challenge will be to open them up. Little by little, the monopoly of the stovepipes needs to be ended, by a combination of competition and privatization. The challenge for the stovepipes will be to keep abreast of technology. For SIGINT and NSA, that means moving away from space and to the ground. Already, the vast majority of SIGINT comes from ground stations, while space-based vacuum-cleaner systems continue to consume the vast majority of the money. The period ahead will mean new partnerships with the clandestine service in stealing codes and placing signals interceptors close to the signals they are intended to capture.

For imagery, the challenge will be deciding what to make and what to buy. The commercial market for imagery will continue to be dominated by aircraft flying at low levels over friendly territory. For some purposes, especially wide-area imagery for mapping, the United States will be able to piggyback its sensors on commercial satellites or buy the images commercially. Buying commercially for other purposes, though, will raise questions of who controls the shutter and who receives the take. Like SIGINT, IMINT also places too much emphasis on satellite technology. Getting close to military targets, arising unpredictably in places that are otherwise not of much interest to the United States, will require cheap sats or UAVs or other sensors as yet unthought of.

At its beginnings, NRO was a technological pacesetter. Little comparable to satellite reconnaissance was going on in the civilian sector, so the technical challenge, impelled by the Soviet threat, attracted scientists and engineers at the top of their games. NRO operated with unusual freedom for a government agency, contracting out most of its work and maintaining a multimillion-dollar contingency fund. That freedom got it into trouble after the Soviet Union broke apart, and with it, the conditions that once justified NRO's exceptional practices. Now, NRO, like the rest of the intelligence community, has become more bureaucratic. It remains technically adept, but it and its contractors have become wedded to what they do best — building large, multisensor satellites, dubbed "Battlestar Galactica" by insiders.

One possible — albeit radical — way to open up the stovepipes to competition from new ideas is to abolish NRO and turn over existing and successor collection systems to the operating agencies, NSA and the National Imagery and Mapping Agency (NIMA).[8] This would break the satellite monopoly by giving the two operators both the technical wherewithal and the incentive to invest in a wider range of technologies based on their judgments about the needs they will have in the future. Yet, given the power of the satellite lobby in both these operating agencies, along with the complexity of flying existing systems, abolishing NRO might only spawn little NROs in each of the operators.

The classic reasons related to the public good for why empowering the consuming agencies to build or buy their own collectors is an incomplete solution are fully discussed in chapter 4. Briefly, under such a plan there would be a risk that systems *all* consumers might want would not be bought or built if no single consumer wanted the system badly enough to pay for it. Yet empowering consumers is the right direction to move in, just as the market-forces model remains the right metaphor for the opening up of the stovepipes. Creating new focal points for competition, as the Pentagon did in creating a separate program office for UAVs, is one approach. Giving operators or consumers more say in decisions about collection technologies is another. In collection, too, intelligence needs to be opened to competition, from both within and outside government.

THE SPLIT FRANCHISE OF ANALYSIS

On the analytic side, the purposes of intelligence in the era of the market state suggest two organizational principles. The first is to distinguish between tactical puzzle solving, on the one hand, and mystery framing, on the other. The second is the need to move much further in decentralizing intelligence in order to get closer to consumers — a process that needs to be pushed to the point that it begins to erase the line separating intelligence and policy.

Distinguishing puzzles from mysteries indicates separate organizations for separate franchises. Tactical puzzle solvers should be close to the secrets on which their franchise relies. Because the relevance of their work is easier to display to consumers, they have less need

8 Lieutenant General William E. Odom, Chair, *Modernizing Intelligence: Structure and Change for the 21st Century,* Fairfax, VA: National Institute for Public Policy, 1997, pp. 47–49 and 70–83.

to fear that their puzzle solving will be interesting but not useful to policy. The principle of keeping these analysts close to the collectors, especially the collectors of secrets, means that the idea of co-locating the CIA's analysts and operators is not a bad second-best; the clandestine service as HUMINT collector badly needs the direction to its work that analysts could provide. A first-best would be puzzle-solving teams that include representatives from all the collecting INTs. Those teams would be virtual, and they would be created and lapse as particular issues waxed and waned. While they operated, though, they would provide almost continuous feedback between what analysts need and what collectors of secrets can provide.

Such teams would have particular value as the clandestine service comes to work for NSA, in effect if not fact. Only on rare occasions would the DO be able to put some sensor into place in time to provide tactical pieces to solve the puzzle immediately at hand. But, over time, an intense connection between NSA and the DO would begin to suggest which sensors ought to be where if only a way could be found to get them there.

In contrast to the franchise of the puzzle solvers, that of intelligence's mystery framers is more tenuous. Those framers need to be experts and to be able to demonstrate their worth as such. They need to be close to consumers and in touch with a range of experts inside and outside government. For them to have any chance of influencing their policy counterparts, they must be close enough not only to be calibrated but to calibrate in turn, to understand something of the mind-sets and agendas of policy officers. The natural colleagues of this group of intelligence experts are not the collectors of secrets, but rather those who work from open sources in the universities, NGOs, and think tanks, as well as the government.

The two distinct franchises would give rise to two organizations working for the DCI — one organization close to the collectors, for tactical support and puzzle solving, and the other close to consumers and colleagues outside government, for more strategic issues and mystery framing. In my time at the NIC, we and the CIA's DI were edging toward this kind of division of labor. The DI was, and is now, more and more tactical. By contrast, we at the NIC found that our estimates, most of which tried to give shape to mysteries, were driving us toward more and more cooperation with people outside intelligence and outside government. To make this openness clear, we toyed with the idea of taking "intelligence" out of the NIC's name, changing it to "national estimates council."

The tactical organization might still be called the central intelligence agency, but most of its analysts would be dispersed, not centralized. The DI has moved a long way in sending analysts to policy agencies on rotation, but the organization's culture continues to treat those analysts as emissaries and those who remain at home as the ones who do the work. That attitude needs to be reversed: Those away from headquarters do the work, while those at home facilitate it. (Interestingly, the attitude that the DI needs to acquire is one that already dominates the other side of the CIA, the DO, in which station chiefs abroad effectively outrank the Washington officials for whom they nominally work.)

The analysts on rotation would act as all-purpose staffers in their policy agencies, ones who happened to have intelligence as their specialty, just as other staffers are experienced in law or another profession. They probably should continue to be "owned" by the intelligence agency, however. That would ensure that intelligence remained to some extent a free good. If the policy agencies owned the positions, they would be liable to turn them into operators or something closer than intelligence to the essence of the policy agency: Witness the fate of those at OSS research and analysis (R&A) at the hands of the State Department's operating desks in the late 1940s. (One of the lessons I learned in managing the NIC was that "slots" — that is, authority to fill positions — are more valuable than money; money is fungible, but slots either exist or they don't.)

The more strategic organization, perhaps called the "national estimates council" but perhaps also the "national intelligence council," would be downtown, not out in Langley.[9] It would be near its consumers at State, Treasury, and the NSC, and it would be open to

9   In the 1990s, the NIC twice had the opportunity to move into the old Selective Service building on F Street downtown, a half block from the White House, and twice squandered it. The first time money played a role, for DCI Woolsey did not want to spend even a few million renovating a building inside the beltway. The second was even sadder, for the then NIC chair wanted to move but could not persuade his NIOs, who preferred staying close to fellow analysts over getting closer to their consumers!

outside experts and outside expertise. It would reach out in a variety of ways — by hiring senior outsiders on rotation, by holding conferences and brainstorming sessions with outsiders as a matter of routine, and by forging more enduring connections with think tanks and universities, perhaps through something akin to the current FFRDCs (federally funded research and development centers).

If this organization could entangle policy officials in producing its assessments, somewhat on the model of the British Joint Intelligence Committee (JIC), so much the better. In any case, its officers would add value more through what they said than what they wrote. They should be hired accordingly. Their days should be spent not in the office but around town, sharing assessments with other experts and checking agendas with policy counterparts. One gleam in my eye while at the NIC, though one I never turned into reality, was to hire a practicing journalist as an NIO. I suspected such a person would do well. And I also wanted to see the power of example if, when an issue arose, his or her first instinct was not to log onto the computer to check secret sources, but rather to pick up the phone and begin making calls, including calls abroad.

COLLECTING WHAT IS FREE

In dealing with the other great challenge for collection, "open source" — that is, everything that is not secret — organization matters but mind-set is critical. Given the recognition that intelligence is now in the information, not the secrets, business, a variety of organizational forms could do the job. One strategy would simply be to invest in a variety of interesting experiments across intelligence. The NIC or something like it might be designated as intelligence's link to outside expertise, with budgets for conferences and exchanges to match. The NIC has moved in that direction by developing a strategic estimates program on broad mysteries, accompanied by funding for contracts to enable it to collaborate with outsiders.[10] Innovative uses of open databases, like those undertaken by the Non-Proliferation Center, would be encouraged. And money could

10 See National Intelligence Council brochure, *The DCI's Strategic Estimates Program*, Washington, D.C., 1999.

be provided for analysts to meet with counterparts in academia and the private sector.

There was an unusual hue and cry from the academic community in 1996 when John Deutch proposed to cut the budget of the CIA's most visible open source collector, the Foreign Broadcast Information Service (FBIS). Scholars have for years depended on FBIS translations of foreign press and media, so cutting its budget seemed just the opposite of what the more open world should indicate. In fact, there were good grounds for reshaping FBIS, if not for reducing its budget. It had grown stodgy. It had been slow to move into machine translation and to move away from familiar countries into new places and new forms of gray (that is, not secret but not entirely open either) communication. It had acquired its own clients, including in-house translators, and its own practices had become too expensive. As it was, it probably deserved to be cut; suitably reshaped, it could be a valuable part of intelligence's open source collection.

More ambitious proposals would earmark a chunk of the intelligence budget for new open source analytic institutions.[11] One model might be the existing FFRDCs, such as RAND and the Institute for Defense Analyses, private institutions intended to have privileged access to public agencies. These institutions could maintain closer links to scholars in academia and analysts in NGOs than intelligence will find it easy to do. They would thus be in a position both to do one level of "processing" and to reach outside for the nation's best experts when occasion arose.

Another model would be a new government agency, a kind of Congressional Research Service (CRS) for the executive branch, or the government as a whole. It would have links to but not be part of intelligence. Functioning as an important government byway on the information superhighway, it would be an open source processing and research operation endowed with its own funds and operating as a public good for the government as a whole. The little-known Federal Research Service was another era's innovation in a similar spirit. Virtually unknown, by contrast to the CRS, it was in-

---

11 Robert Steele of Open Source Solutions has made several proposals along these lines. They can be located at www.oss.net/OSS21 or at www.defensedaily.com/reports/osint.htm.

tended to be an in-house consultant, doing contract work for other government agencies. However, it never developed the standing or the expertise to compete with think tanks outside the government. Moreover, with so much free research available, especially from the intelligence community but also from CRS, it never found more than a smattering of government customers.

Similarly, there are many organizational ways for intelligence to do better at looking, not spying. At a minimum, intelligence needs to create a serious mechanism, one outside the CIA and surely outside the DO, for debriefing Americans and others who have traveled to interesting places or otherwise have valuable insights. In contrast to now, this mechanism's mission should not be collection; rather, it should be to facilitate contacts between intelligence analysts and interested colleagues in the academy, the think-tank world, and private business. If the NIC, for instance, were beefed up to be intelligence's principal contact with the outside world, it might play this facilitating role.

For the last collector, the clandestine service, the prescription is a complete reshaping, one sketched in chapter 5. As it now stands, not only is it demoralized, but its espionage runs too much risk for too little gain. If it could be abolished and recreated, that would be ideal. In any event, it needs to be shrunk and targeted on those issues where espionage can provide information that is not available in any other way — concentrating on terrorists, dangerous weapons programs, and a few threatening states, not on economics or the politics of states that are friends. Because terrorists do not frequent the embassy cocktail party circuit, it needs to operate not out of embassies but, rather, mostly under nonofficial cover or from the United States. It plainly needs to be tightly managed and held to strict standards of accountability.

POINTS OF LEVERAGE: A PRACTICAL AGENDA

Most of this book has wandered at the edges of practical politics. It did so with malice aforethought, because my aim is not to suggest what might be doable in this political season but, rather, to recommend what might be thinkable in the next or the next after that. For instance, while the clandestine service is in dire straits, there is now little stomach in the executive or on the Hill for the complete revamping that is needed. Instead, the prevailing political mood alternates between desires to protect the service from its critics and to protect it from itself. The changes described in chapter 2 still rush about us; they are too new to apprehend with any clarity. That is why the debate over intelligence has been so organizational and so inconclusive.

America has come to a junction where the choices of path are many but the destinations are hazy. In those circumstances, it is perhaps not so unwise that we have, collectively, sat down in the middle of the road to scratch our heads. What former DCI James Schlesinger called "Lewis and Clark planning" may not be so unwise for intelligence. Like those explorers, we may not know where we are going or what we will confront once we arrive, but we may nonetheless have a decent sense of what we would like to carry in our kit bag for the journey. To escape the metaphor, the capacities embedded in existing intelligence organizations are both powerful and hard to create, so caution is called for in demolishing them in favor of something new while we are yet so uncertain of the world we will confront.

The challenge, however, is not to let Lewis and Clark planning slide into the mistake of defense conversion, which wrongly assumed that institutions producing great value in the Cold War easily could be turned to produce something else afterward. Lewis and Clark planning can easily be an argument for simple inertia: What we did *was* valuable, so it must still be.

The inertia of mature organizations is powerful and, for intelligence, such vested interests as exist in the private sector mostly cut against the needed reforms. Those interests are the big contractors, which are bound to be lobbyists for more large collection platforms.

Any effort at serious reform must search for points of leverage. One of those, perhaps the most promising, is open sources. Making much more use of open sources does have advocates within intelligence. It need not be too expensive, hence wouldn't threaten to gore too many intelligence oxen. If intelligence could make the doctrinal shift from intelligence-as-secrets to intelligence-as-information, that could set in train a longer process of change. The change might be symbolized by visibly setting aside, say, $1 billion for open source initiatives.[12] Ideally, the money would be spent to hire more processors and analysts inside intelligence, to foster experiments with databases inside, and to build partnerships with think tanks and other sources of expertise outside government.

Crossing the doctrinal Rubicon by recognizing that intelligence is in the business of information, not secrets, could be accompanied by a series of modest steps:

Move the NIC downtown and perhaps rename it. The old Selective Service headquarters on F Street was to be the NIC's. It would serve well. The purposes of the move would be threefold. Most important, it would put the NIC close to its consumers at State, the NSC and the National Economic Council (NEC) (by whatever name), the trade representative, and others. Second, it would both bespeak and facilitate openness to outsiders in a way that Langley, with all the CIA's cumbersome security, cannot. For similar reasons, new names for the NIC, such as "national estimates council," might attenuate the lingering closed connotations of "intelligence." Finally, moving the NIC would underscore that the NIC, by any name, was not a CIA organization but a true integrator of analysis from whatever source, both inside and outside the intelligence community.

Open the community to real experts. The CIA has for a long time had a category of senior analysts. The effort was a worthy one, and it was well intended. But the cadre of senior analysts became less a repository of world-class expertise than a convenient place to park talented folks who did not fit the very round holes of the DI bureaucracy. A serious opening could make use of the special authorities that intelligence still enjoys within government to hire distinguished outsiders. Again, the NIC or its kin could be the focal point for such an effort.

These are wonderful times for such an initiative. As our interactions with the relief agencies demonstrated, the reticence of outsiders to be associated with intelligence is waning. We succeeded in attracting distinguished outsiders as NIOs — for instance, Ezra Vogel from Harvard, dean of the nation's east Asia specialists, and Enid Schoettle from The Ford Foundation and the Council on Foreign Relations, a premier expert on multilateral diplomacy and op-

12   Ibid.

erations. These people had a stature on the outside and thus a reach to policy insiders, especially at the top of government, that few intelligence professionals could match. And this is not to malign professional intelligence officers, for they often have contacts of their own, particularly if they have served several rotations in policies agencies. But by virtue of their career patterns and the culture of their calling, most have a low profile, more inside than outside.

Reshape existing institutions to lead the open source revolution. In their current form, neither the Community Open Source Program Office (COSPO), nor FBIS, nor the DO's National Resources Division (NRD) is in a position to play that role. FBIS remains, for budgetary reasons more than any other, part of the CIA's Directorate for Science and Technology. It is something of an orphan there, though it should be admitted that when it was part of the DI, it fared little better.

FBIS, while stodgy, is good at what it does. But there never has been much reason for it be part of the CIA: witness its cooperation with the British Broadcasting Company (BBC). And what is formally published or aired by recognized media in foreign countries is of less and less consequence, even in the poorer countries. It is as if a foreign service had continued to try to understand the United States by remaining focused on the news programs of the major television networks. So, too, in a world of looking, not spying, debriefing willing Americans through the spy service is, at least, awkward. The process needs to be open, not debriefing but, rather, putting government experts in touch with outside experience.

COSPO was dominated by technologists who worried about the technical problem of how to connect insiders who work on secrets to outsiders who don't. It was creative but within the limits of that perspective. Intelligence's problem, however, is not technology but mind-sets. Those who would make the open source revolution need to be those who see most clearly the need and the opportunity to reach out. Those people are the analysts, especially but not only those who would frame enduring mysteries.

The open source revolution needs to realize that the Web is more important than foreign broadcast media; for intelligence as for the rest of society, the future is narrowcast, not broadcast. For other countries as for the United States, it will be less important to monitor what CBS equivalents are broadcasting to the nation than what, say, right-wing militia adherents are e-mailing to each other. And facilitating contacts with people is as important as improving access to databases, because no government organization can hope to do much information processing itself. Rather, the government and its intelligence will depend on their ability to be in touch with experts quickly, even when the issue has been unfamiliar and the expertise is arcane.

Take the dispatching of analysts seriously. If the CIA's analytic capacity cannot be broken up and dispersed to the policy agencies, at least the current trend of sending those analysts on secondment ought to be redoubled. A creative DI would offer lots of officers on rotation. In time, those on rotation would come to be seen as the workers and those at home as the facilitators, instead of the current tendency to see those analysts away from home as the exiles and the homebodies as the workers.

Do substantial experiments. Experiments are cheap and often unthreatening to existing agencies and their vested interest. These experiments should especially aim to use open sources, ranging from efforts to build databases and search the Web, to discovering what can be bought, to finding ways to engage "lookers." In many of these respects, intelligence now lags behind the regional military CINCs, who have been pushed by the need to mount peace and other smaller-scale contingency operations in unfamiliar places to learn what they can from open sources. An experiment might, for instance, assemble the set of academics and NGO staffers that knows most about Burundi. The assembling could be virtual, not real, and done practically for free; most of the experts who were consulted would welcome the attention provided the connection was entirely open. Then the network might be used in a crisis game, perhaps with half of it remaining at home, meeting virtually, while the other half goes to Washington to participate in the game face to face.[13]

In conducting experiments, the intelligence community is perhaps somewhat in the position of the armed services, which are now able to benefit from traits that arguably were failings in the past. In principle, a truly efficient Cold War military might have been much more joint, perhaps even a single service. Now, though, as long as

13   This is the outline of a RAND proposal in which I for several years
      tried, unsuccessfully, to interest my intelligence community sponsors.

the United States does not have a single military service, it may not be so bad to have at least five — Army, Air Force, Navy, Marines, and special operators. During the Cold War, competition for missions may have been costly. Now that competition might make possible innovations that would not occur without it. By the same token, intelligence may be able to benefit from the collection stovepipes competing for new missions and from groups of analysts competing to serve new interests and new customers.

MAKING THE CASE PUBLICLY

In the end, the case for what intelligence the government may require can no longer be made only in secret to approved committees of Congress. It has to be made convincingly to the American people. The Clinton administration finally got around to making public in 1997 what the rest of the world already knew, namely, that the United States spent about $27 billion per year on intelligence. Despite doing so, the United States still lagged in openness behind Britain, the land of official secrets. Worse, the trend toward openness did not last long. DCI Tenet opposed revealing the 1999 budget request. He argued that revealing the 1997 and 1998 totals was acceptable because there had been little change between those years, but that revealing the 1999 request for a sizable increase "would provide foreign governments with [an] overall assessment of [U.S.] intelligence weakness and priorities."[14]

The original argument against revealing intelligence's total was that doing so would be a slippery slope: If the overall, top-line number were revealed, that would lead to pressure to make public the next level of detail and the next. The concern is fair, but the sign is wrong because intelligence should welcome some further disclosure, not shun it. The budgets of the major agencies — CIA, NSA, NIMA, and NRO — should be public, as should the major divisions of those budgets. The United States should go at least that far. Since the budgets of the agencies and thus of major functions are available anyway, there is nothing to be lost by making them of-

---

14   Quoted in Federation of American Scientists, *Secrecy and Government Bulletin*, 76, January 1999. The full text of Tenet's declaration is available at www.fas.org/sgp/foia/tenet1298.html.

ficial. As President Clinton said of making public the budget total, disclosure "will inform the public and will not, in itself, harm intelligence activities."[15]

Making public a total number for, say, espionage, and letting it be compared to SIGINT would advance the public debate with little help to foes. Would-be adversaries might be either awed by how much the United States spends on spying or surprised at how small the number is. In either case, the number they care about is how much the United States spends spying *on them* — a level of detail whose revelation would indeed help foes more than it would advance debate in the United States.

I have long been surprised by the loyalty of CIA officers, or the power of the CIA culture, because those officers should be the people most eager to have intelligence budgets made public. Every media story and every American's image conflate "intelligence" with "CIA" and so imply that taxpayers spend $27 billion on the CIA. Were I a CIA employee, I would demand either disclosure or all of the $27 billion for my agency!

Canada's recent experience with more openness is suggestive of what the United States could do. In 1991, the Canadian Security Intelligence Service (CSIS) began publishing its overall budget, and since 1994, it has broken that number down among personnel, operations, and construction; it also now provides a three-year projected budget. By the same token, the budget of Canada's Communications Security Establishment (CSE), NSA's counterpart, has been public since May 1995. CSIS now publishes *Commentary*, current analyses written by its staff on subjects such as insurgency and intervention in Algeria and the security implications of environment degradation in China. The authors are named, and their telephone numbers are provided.[16]

As it stands, U.S. intelligence is confronted with public numbers it does not acknowledge. As a result, not only does it lose the opportunity to educate the public, it looks as if it has something to hide. It should take every opportunity to show citizens what it does. Openly publishing analyses only for their public-relations value is

15   Ibid.
16   See Federation of American Scientists, *Secrecy and Government Bulletin*, 63, December 1996.

transparent, but making public as much analysis as possible and, still more, encouraging analysts to publish openly is all to the good.

When I joined the NIC, I told myself I should stay only as long as I could continue to laugh at the peculiarities of the CIA culture, such as classifying my schedule. Alas, I stopped laughing at about the time I left. This book was meant to end with the story of why I stopped laughing. It had to do with an unclassified NIC project and my effort to get the NIC, and intelligence, some public credit for their work. Alas, the CIA review of my manuscript required that story to be deleted — a deletion whose irony was not lost on the reviewers. Suffice it to say that the episode I wanted to describe seemed a lost opportunity, a small one to be sure, to display what intelligence could do. Intelligence needs to look for such opportunities, not avoid them. That proposition is, at any rate, a premise of this book. My little story's fate at the hands of the security reviewers testifies, sadly, to just how far this nation's intelligence is from sharing that premise.

Index

Abramowitz, Morton, 165n
Addressing mysteries, 127–129
  doing well at, 129–132
The Agency. *See* Central Intelligence
  Agency
Agenda for intelligence, 248–253
  making the case publicly, 253–255
Ahmed Yousef, Ramzi, 172
Air Force, 77, 197, 202, 223
Albania, 235
Albright, Madeleine, 163
Alpirez, Julio Roberto, 144
America
  changing interests in the world, 20–25
  changing public and private roles of,
    51–54
  Cold War intelligence in, 98–102
  intelligence beyond 2010, 20–61
  redefining, 56–61
  shaping the clandestine service of,
    138–141
Ames, Aldrich, 63, 137–138, 141,
  147–149, 171, 235
Ames, Bob, 147
Amnesty International, 52
Analysts, and policy-makers, 179–185
Annan, Kofi, 215
Anti-ballistic missile (ABM) defenses,
  195–197
Aristide, Jean-Bertrand, 188–189
Asia, 126
Aspin-Brown commission, 153n, 162–163
Assessments
  commanders and, 202–204
  framing, 141–145
Aum Shinrikyo group, 39
Aviation Week and Space Technology, xvii

Balladur, Edouard, 143
"Battlestar Galactica," 86, 242

Bentsen, Lloyd, 97
Berger, Samuel ("Sandy"), 30
Berkowitz, Bruce, 108n
Big Brother, 30, 42
bin Laden, Osama, 69
Biological weapons program, in Russia, 37
Bissell, Richard, 75n
BJP party (in India), 4, 17, 208
Blackwill, Robert, 190
Bloomberg, 10, 164
Board of National Estimates, 128
Bobbitt, Philip, 46n
"Bomber gap," 78, 192
Boren, Senator David, 80
Bosnia, 17, 22–24, 50–51, 54, 154,
  174–176
  Muslims in, 23–24, 181, 185
Brazil, 27, 43–44, 46, 111
The bright line between "intelligence" and
  "policy," 197–202
  erasing, 211–213
Britain, 25
British Broadcasting Company (BBC), 114,
  251
British Foreign Office, Research
  Department, 164
British Joint Intelligence Committee (JIC),
  212, 247
"Broadcasting," *vs.* "narrowcasting," 32,
  251
Brown, Harold, 238
The Bureau. *See* Federal Bureau of
  Investigation
Bureau of Intelligence and Research (INR),
  105, 120, 165
  analyses by, 127, 200–201
Burrows, William, 75n
Burundi, 154, 252
Bush, President George, 235
  plot to assassinate, 168

257

C3, meaning of, 118
Canada, 41
 Sikh community in, 2
Canada's Communications Security
  Establishment (CSE), 254
Canadian Security Intelligence Service
  (CSIS), 254
CARE, 52, 133, 233
Carter, President Jimmy, 60, 238
Casey, William, 198, 235, 239
Castro, Fidel, 21, 211
Catching criminals, *vs.* spying and looking,
  136–152
CENTCOM, 204
Central Imagery Office (CIO), 81, 121
 as imagery stovepipe, 9, 65
 analytic department, 84
Central Intelligence Agency (CIA), xiii–xiv,
  57, 78, 100, 104–113, 122–123, 138,
  153, 202–207
 analyses by, 23n, 95–96, 127, 197–198,
  210–211
 analysts from, xiii, 4, 15, 82, 142, 187,
  191–195, 205–206, 218–219,
  243–244
 authorized to engage in law enforcement,
  167
 budget of, 142, 253–254
 Cold War intelligence from, 7
 colocation of the DO and the DI,
  122–123, 125
 criticisms of, 63–64 69–70, 254–255
 Deputy director for intelligence, 146
 Directorate for Science and Technology,
  73, 251
 Directorate of Intelligence, 122–123,
  125, 146, 201, 205, 228
 Directorate of Operations, 2, 7, 63, 119,
  122–123, 125, 141–143, 146–150,
  156–157, 172, 214, 235–236
 Directorate of Plans, 141
 directors of, 14
 and the FBI, 170–172
 mission of, 136–161, 165–169, 222–225
 National Photographic Interpretation
  Center (NPIC), 81, 84
 National Resources Division, 166
 Office of National Estimates, 6
 Office of Research and Reports, 192
 Office of Special Projects, 140
 recruiting by, 153n
 Satellite and Missile Observation System,
  76
 Tokyo station, 160
Central Intelligence Group (CIG), 99, 139,
  222
 evolving into CIA, 99, 139

 Office of Special Operations, 139, 141,
  223
The Century Foundation, xi, xiv
Charhdi Kala International, 2
China, 11, 114, 230
 bombing embassy of in Belgrade, 10, 69
 controlling its citizens, 30
 deterring nuclear development by, 5
 granting most-favored-nation (MFN)
  status to, 52
 growth of, 33
 military emergence of, 25–26
 satellite tracking by, 4
 selling missiles, 11, 121, 212
 spies for, 64
Choosing systems, 84–89
Christopher, Warren, 163
Church, Senator Frank, xv
CIA. *See* Central Intelligence Agency
CINCs, 203–204
CIO. *See* Central Imagery Office
Civil War, aerial reconnaissance in, 71
Clandestine operations, xviii
 range of, 137–138
Clandestine service
 reshaping in service of NSA, 152–157
 reshaping the NSA's, 152–157
 shaping America's, 138–141
Clapper, James, 35
Clinton, President Bill, 17, 23, 30, 157,
  175, 181, 189, 253
CMS. *See* Community management staff
CNN, 10, 14, 103
"CNN effect," 30–31, 34, 116, 182
COCOM. *See* Coordination Committee for
  Multilateral Export Controls
Colby, William E., 66, 102
Cold War legacy, 1–12, 21, 34, 44–45,
  103
 from the CIA, 7
 control of reconnaissance, 74–79
 intelligence in America, 98–102
 retargeting, 65–70, 220–225
 reversing, 92
Collection market, 240–243
 free intelligence, 246–248
Colocation, of the DO and the DI,
  122–123, 125
Colosio, Luis Donaldo, 96
COMINT, 79
Commanders, and assessments, 202–204
Commentary, 254
Commerce Department, 120, 158
Communications intelligence. *See*
  COMINT
Community management staff (CMS),
  238–239

Community Open Source Program Office (COSPO), 113, 115, 251
Congress, 121, 175, 200, 239, 249, 253. *See also* House Intelligence Committee; Senate Select Committee on Intelligence
Joint Economic Committee, 193
Congressional Research Service (CRS), creating an analog of, 17, 119, 247
Contrarian approach, to intelligence, xii, 5
Coordination Committee for Multilateral Export Controls (COCOM), 111
Cornell University, 192
CORONA, 73, 76, 78
Cost of systems, 84–89
Council on Foreign Relations, 250
Covert action, question of, 173–176
Criminals, catching, 136–152
Croatia, 174
Crowe, Admiral William, 164
CSE. *See* Canada's Communications Security Establishment (CSE)
CSIS. *See* Canadian Security Intelligence Service
Cuba, 126, 142, 211, 217
Culture of spying, 145–150
changing, 205–208
Cutter, Bowman, 206
Czechoslovakia, 140, 232

Daily Economic Brief, 206
Dayton accords, 24, 185
DCI. See Director of central intelligence
DDCI. See Deputy director of central intelligence
DDI. See Deputy Director for Intelligence
DDO. See Deputy Director for Operations
DEA. See Drug Enforcement Agency
Defense Advanced Research Products Agency (DARPA), 68
Defense Airborne Reconnaissance Office, imagery department, 84
Defense Department, 7, 78, 140, 167
Defense Human Intelligence Service (DHS), 167
Defense Intelligence Agency (DIA), 4, 35, 65, 105, 121–122, 196, 202
analyses by, 127
imagery department, 84
Defense Mapping Agency, 84
Defense Support Program (DSP) satellites, 67
Defensive intelligence, 109
Delta force, 86, 157, 217
"Denied areas," 9
Deputy Director for Intelligence (DDI), 146

Deputy Director for Operations (DDO), 83, 146, 236
Deputy director of central intelligence (DDCI), 83, 137
Desert Storm, 36–37, 62–63, 67, 69, 89, 112, 204
foreshadowing future wars, 14
Designated readers, 93–135
addressing mysteries, 127–132
in America's cold war intelligence, 98–102
bringing outsiders inside, 132–134
in distributed intelligence, 104–108
estimating as process, 134–135
intelligence for an age of information, 102–104
learning to read, 113–119
national intelligence estimates, 127–129
open sources and secrets, 108–113
organizing for tactical support, 120–123
processing information, not secrets, 119–120
strategic franchise, 125–127
tactical franchise, 123–125
Deutch, John, 39n, 82–84, 172, 207, 235–237, 247
DHS. *See* Defense Human Intelligence Service
DI. *See* Directorate of Intelligence
DIA. *See* Defense Intelligence Agency
Directive 5, 139
Directive 10/2, 140
Director of central intelligence (DCI), 1, 99, 207
authority of, 89–91, 139–140
role of, 14–16, 234–239
Director of Defense Research and Engineering (DDR&E), 196
Directorate for Science and Technology (DS&T), 73, 251
Directorate of Intelligence (DI), 122–123, 125, 146, 201, 206, 228, 244–245
becoming more creative, 252
Directorate of Operations (DO), 2, 7, 63, 119, 122–123, 125, 136–137, 141–143, 146–150, 156–157, 172, 235–236, 244–245
Directorate of Plans, 141
Directorate for Science and Technology, 251
Discoverer 13, 76
Distributed intelligence, 104–108
DO. *See* Directorate of Operations
Dornbusch, Rudiger, 95n
Douglas Aircraft, 75
Drones. *See* Unmanned aerial vehicles

Drug Enforcement Agency (DEA), 168, 200
DSP. *See* Defense Support Program satellites

Eagleburger, Lawrence, 177
East Germany, 31, 142, 154
Economic and Monetary Union (EMU), 27
Economic Espionage Act of 1996, 110
The Economist, 164
Economist Intelligence Unit, 27
Egypt, 33, 45, 117, 209
Eisenhower, President Dwight D., 73, 75, 78–79, 84
Electronics intelligence. *See* ELINT
11/3 series, of national intelligence estimates, 102, 129
ELINT, 80
EMU. *See* Economic and Monetary Union
Encryption, 88
Environmental nongovernmental organizations (NGOs), 60
ESDI. *See* European security and defense identity
Estimating
  national intelligence, 127–129
  as process, 134–135
EU. *See* European Union
European security and defense identity (ESDI), 27
European Union (EU), 27, 133, 143
  Economic and Monetary Union, 27
Exchange Stabilization Fund (ESF), 94
Executive Orders, 167, 238

F-117 Stealth fighter, 90
Factions analysis, 23n
Far East, 101
FBI. *See* Federal Bureau of Investigation
FBIS. *See* Foreign Broadcast Information Service
Federal Bureau of Investigation (FBI), 40
  and the CIA, 147–148, 167–172
  intelligence claims of, 139, 224
Federal Research Service, 247
Federal Reserve, 95, 97
Federally funded research and development centers (FFRDCs), 117, 124, 246–247
Financial Times, 150
Ford, Harold, 198
The Ford Foundation, 250
Foreign Broadcast Information Service (FBIS), 113–114, 247, 251
Foreign Corrupt Practices Act, 55, 111
Fort, Randall, 109n
Foster, John S., Jr., 196
Fox, Daniel, 14n

Framing an assessment, 141–145
France, 11, 49, 111, 143–144, 154, 161, 210
Franchises. *See* Strategic franchise; Tactical franchise
Freeh, Louis J., 39n, 170–171
French Deuxieme Bureau, 198
Fukuyama, Francis, 31

Galbraith, Peter, 174–175
Gardiner, Samuel, 14n
Gates, Robert, xiv, 46, 69, 81, 146, 155, 158, 235
  confirmation hearings of, 16, 198
  impact on DI culture, 205
Geolocation technology, 14
Geopolitics, 47
Geosynchronous orbit satellites, 79
Germany, 71, 120, 186. *See also* East Germany; West Germany
Global Broadcast System, 68
Global processes, future, 28–35
Goldwater-Nichols reforms, 203
Goodman, Melvin, 198
Gorbachev, Mikhail, 194–195
Gore, Vice President Al, 46, 189, 240
Goulding, Maurice, 215
Government Printing Office, intelligence available from, 8
Governmental intelligence, 109
"Green books" on the Soviet economy, 193
Greenspan, Alan, 97
Guatemala, 64, 144–145, 154, 173
Gulf War syndrome, 210

Haiti, 50, 60, 154, 188–190
  boat people from, 29
Halperin, Morton, xv
Harbury, Jennifer, 144
Harriman, Pamela, 143
Harvard University, xiv, 192, 250
Hashimoto, Ryutaro, 160
Helms, Richard, 171
Helms, Senator Jesse, 189
HEO. *See* Highly elliptical orbit satellites
Herman, Michael, 56n
Heymann, Philip, 168n
Highly elliptical orbit (HEO) satellites, 79–80
Hizbollah terrorists, 152, 155
Ho Chi Minh, 186–187
Hoover, J. Edgar, 139, 171
House Intelligence Committee, 103
Howard, Edward Lee, 147–148
Howe, Jonathan, 215

HUMINT (human intelligence), 8, 66, 108, 125, 142, 172, 237, 244
  attribution of, 142n
  future of, 219
Hungary, 140
Huntington, Samuel P., 32
Hussein, Saddam, 38, 54, 85, 104–105, 151, 168, 209

IFOR, Bosnia, 24
IMF. *See* International Monetary Fund
IMINT (imagery intelligence), 9, 14, 65, 67, 81, 242
  choices within, 92
  competition of, 87, 103, 223
  turnaround time for, 13
Imperative, of reshaping intelligence, 1–19
In From the Cold, xi
India, 27
  American handlers of, 5
  BJP party in, 4, 17, 208
  intelligence failures regarding, 2–5
  nuclear testing in, 64, 72, 87
Indonesia, 11
"Info-warriors," 14, 62
Information processing, *vs.* secrets, xii, 119–120
Inman, Admiral Bobby R., 162, 239
INR. *See* Bureau of Intelligence and Research (INR)
Institutional Revolutionary Party (PRI), 96
Intelink, 118
Intelligence
  for an age of information, 102–104
  contrarian, xii, 5
  distributed, 104–108
  failures in India, 3–5
  governmental *vs.* private, 109
  legacy of hot and cold wars, 5–8
  of the market state, 54–56
  mission for, 63–65
  national purpose of, 91–92
  new paradigm for, 225–229
  offensive *vs.* defensive, 109
  practical agenda for, 248–253
  reshaped, 216–220
  reshaping, 1–19
  statistics about, 6n
Intelligence beyond 2010, 20–61
  changing public and private roles, 51–54
  coming of the market state, 46–51
  forms of power, 25–28
  global processes, 28–35
  intelligence of the market state, 54–56
  new-old threats, 35–43
  redefining America's interests in the world, 20–25

threats without threateners, 43–46
  what kind of America, 56–61
The "intelligence community," xiii
  community management staff (CMS), 238
Intelligence functions, 136–150
  the Bureau and the Agency, 170–172
  the culture of spying, 145–150
  framing an assessment, 141–145
  hiring lookers, 161–167
  law enforcement, 167–170
  question of covert action, 173–176
  range of clandestine operations, 137–138
  reshaping the clandestine service in service of NSA, 152–157
  shaping America's clandestine service, 138–141
  to spy or not, 150–152
  spying for money, 157–161
Intelligence of policy, 15–18, 177–178
  analysts and policy-makers, 179–185
  the bright line, 197–202
  challenging mind-sets, 208–211
  changing the culture, 205–208
  commanders and assessments, 202–205
  erasing the line, 211–213
  intelligence for whose policy, 213–215
  messenger and the message, 185–191
  questions asked, 195–197
  questions not asked and not answered, 191–195
Intelligence Oversight Board (IOB), 144–145
Interim Research and Intelligence Service, 98
International Affairs, Assistant Secretary for, 219
International Monetary Fund (IMF), 49, 53, 94, 234
International Security and Defense Policy Center, xi
Intervention force. *See* IFOR
INTs, 108, 111, 221, 243–244. *See also* COMINT; ELINT; HUMINT; IMINT; SIGINT; Stovepipes
IOB. *See* Intelligence Oversight Board
Iran, 35, 122
Iraq, 11, 25, 31, 35–36, 52, 62, 66, 69, 89, 104, 122, 124, 209, 217
Israel, 49
Ivankov, Vyacheslav Kirillovich, 171

Japan, 111
  economy of, 13, 159–161
  imports from, 29
  terrorism within, 39
Jeremiah, Admiral David, 1–2, 4

JIC. *See* British Joint Intelligence
   Committee (JIC)
JICLE. *See* Joint Intelligence Community–
   Law Enforcement working group
JMIP. *See* Joint Military Intelligence
   Program
Johnson, Loch K., xv, 158n
Johnson, President Lyndon, 186
Joint Deployable Intelligence Support
   System, 214
Joint intelligence centers (JICs), 203, 213
Joint Intelligence Community–Law
   Enforcement (JICLE) working group,
   171
Joint Military Intelligence Program (JMIP),
   65
Justice Department, 169

Kantor, Mickey, 159–160
Kaplan, Robert D., 50n
Keegan, General George, 77
Kendall, Willmoore, 12n
Kennedy, President John F., 114
Kent, Sherman, 6, 12n
Kenya, 164
Kerr, Richard, 145, 227
Kerrey, Senator J. Robert, 82, 96
Keynes, Lord John Maynard, 47–48
KH series satellites, 156
Khrushchev, Nikita, 192
Killian, James R., Jr., 75
Kissinger, Henry, 196
Korea, 11, 58, 74, 116, 126. *See also*
   North Korea
Kosovo, 22, 235
   air war over, 10, 14, 26, 63, 69, 121
Kuwait, 151, 168–169

Lafontant, Roger, 188
Laird, Melvin, 196
Lake, W. Anthony, 126
Langer, William L., 101
Latin America, 49, 101, 139
Law enforcement, 167–170, 172
Le Carré, John, 42, 138, 172
Le Monde, 143
Leahy, Admiral William D., 99
Learning to read, using open sources,
   113–119
LeMay, General Curtis, 74–75
Leone, Richard, xii, xv
Leverage, points of, 248–253
"Lewis and Clark planning," 249
Liberia, 154
Lockheed's "Skunk Works," 74
Lookers, hiring, 161–167

Looking, *vs.* spying and catching criminals,
   136–152
Luttwak, Edward N., 47

M-11 missiles, Chinese sales of, 121
MAGIC, 72, 207–208
Malaysia, 49
Market state, 46n
   coming of, 46–51
   intelligence of, 54–56
   rise of, 229–234
Marshall, George, 140
Matlock, Jack, 114
May, Ernest, xiv, 57
Medicare, 60
Meeting the Threat of a Surprise Attack,
   75
Mexico, 13, 29, 56, 58, 102, 113, 217,
   231
   debt crisis in, 93–97, 109, 118
MFN. *See* Most-favored-nation status
Militarization of intelligence, 62–92
   change or retrogression, 70–74
   controlling Cold War reconnaissance,
   74–79
   mission for, 63–65
   new missions for old systems, 79–81
   NIMA, as imagery stovepipe, 81–84
   ownership of, 89–91
   retargeting the Cold War legacy, 65–70
   serving intelligence's national purposes,
   91–92
   systems and their cost, 84–89
Milosevic, Slobodan, 69, 121
Mind-sets, challenging, 208–211
Minuteman missile system, 196
MIRV panel, 196–197
Missions for intelligence, 63–65
Mitterand, François, 49
Mondale, Vice President Walter, 182
Montreal Protocol, 52
Most-favored-nation (MFN) status,
   granting to China, 52
Moynihan, Senator Daniel Patrick, 4, 18,
   108, 191, 213
Mysteries
   addressing, 127–129
   vs. puzzles, 11–13

NAFTA. *See* North American Free Trade
   Agreement
National Counter-intelligence Center
   (NACIC), 110, 160
National Defense Highway Program,
   21
National Economic Council (NEC), 57,
   206, 250

National Foreign Intelligence Board
  (NFIB), 237
National Imagery and Mapping Agency
  (NIMA), 4, 83–84, 92, 121, 243
  as imagery stovepipe, 9, 65, 81–84
  budget of, 253
National intelligence, 91–92
  vs. tactical, 79–81
National Intelligence Authority (NIA), 99
  Directive 5, 139
National Intelligence Council (NIC), xiii–
  xiv, xvii, 22, 52, 83, 105, 117, 127,
  181, 187–189, 255
  analyses by, 95, 132, 134, 177, 185,
  201–202, 206–207
  brochure about, 228
  experiments conducted by, 126–127,
  244–245
  future of, 248
  moving downtown, 245n, 250
  national intelligence officers, 94, 102,
  109, 118, 130, 188–189, 206–207,
  245n, 250
National Intelligence Daily (NID), 103,
  190
National intelligence estimates (NIEs), 102,
  105, 119, 127–129, 150, 187, 233
  11/3 series, 102, 129
  usefulness of, 134–135
National intelligence officers (NIOs), 102,
  109, 130, 188–189, 206–207, 245n,
  250
  for Warning, 94, 118
National Photographic Interpretation
  Center (NPIC), 81, 84
National Reconnaissance Office (NRO), 9,
  65, 68, 78, 81, 87, 223, 242, 243
  budget of, 14, 253
  CIA officers in, 73
National Resources Division (NRD), 166,
  251
National Security Act of 1947, 73, 99–100,
  138–139, 167
National Security Agency (NSA), 7, 56, 65,
  105, 112, 214, 242
  analyses by, 127, 156
  budget of, 14, 89, 253
  feeling products were underappreciated,
  222
  reshaping the clandestine service for,
  152–157, 244
National Security Council (NSC), 7, 57,
  78, 104, 138–140, 151, 187, 223,
  250
  Directive 10/2, 140
National Security Education Act, 21

NATO
  air war over Kosovo, 10, 14, 26, 63, 69,
  121
  enlargement eastward, 48
  European allies in, 24, 36
  peacekeepers, 175
NEC. *See* National Economic Council
New York Times, 190–191
  test for covert action, 174–175
NFIB. *See* National Foreign Intelligence
  Board
NGOs. *See* Nongovernmental
  organizations
NIA. *See* National Intelligence Authority
NIC. *See* National Intelligence Council
Nicholson, Harold, 137
NID. See National Intelligence Daily
NIEs. *See* National intelligence estimates
NIMA. *See* National Imagery and
  Mapping Agency
NIOs. *See* National intelligence officers
Nixon, President Richard, 101
NOCs. *See* Nonofficial cover
Nolan, Janne, xv
Non-Proliferation Center (NPC), 115, 246
Nongovernmental organizations (NGOs),
  2, 52, 116, 133, 233, 244. *See also*
  individual NGOs
  environmental, 60
  reporting guerrilla events, 29–30
  sharing intelligence with, 35, 215,
  218–219
Nonofficial cover (NOCs), 154–156
North, Oliver, 176
North American Free Trade Agreement
  (NAFTA), 96
North Korea, 11–13, 35–36, 60, 85, 122,
  124, 128–129, 131, 186, 217, 226,
  235
NPIC. *See* National Photographic
  Interpretation Center
NRD. *See* National Resources Division
NRO. *See* National Reconnaissance Office
NSA. *See* National Security Agency
NSC. *See* National Security Council
Nuclear meltdowns, 33
Nye, Joseph, xiv, 11n, 126

Offensive intelligence, 109
Office of Management and Budget (OMB),
  206, 238
Office of National Estimates (ONE), 6,
  101–102
Office of Policy Coordination (OPC), 141
Office of Research and Evaluation (ORE), 99
Office of Research and Intelligence, 99

Office of Research and Reports (ORR), 192–194
Office of Special Operations (OSO), 139, 141, 223
Office of Special Projects, 140
Office of Strategic Services (OSS), 98, 139, 153, 222–223
research and analysis branch, 98, 245
Oklahoma City bombing, 38, 60
OMB. *See* Office of Management and Budget
ONE. *See* Office of National Estimates
O'Neill, Congressman Tip, 181
OPC. *See* Office of Policy Coordination
Open sources
revolution in, 93–135
using, 113–119
vs. secrets, 8–10, 108–113
Operation Desert Storm, 25–26, 52
ORE. *See* Office of Research and Evaluation
Organization of African Unity, 117
Organized crime, 42, 171
Organizing, for tactical support, 120–123
ORR. *See* Office of Research and Reports
OSO. *See* Office of Special Operations
OSS. *See* Office of Strategic Services
Outsiders, bringing inside, 132–134
Owen, David, 24
Ownership of systems, 89–91
OXCART, 73
Oxford Analytica, 10, 27, 164

PACOM. *See* United States Pacific Command (PACOM)
PA&E. *See* Policy analysis and evaluation
Pakistan, 4–5, 11, 121, 212
Palestine Liberation Organization (PLO), 147
Partnership for Peace program, 130
Pasqua, Charles, 143
The past, returning to, 70–74
PDD. *See* Presidential Decision Directives
Pearl Harbor, lessons for intelligence, 6, 18, 72–73, 100, 222–223
Penkovsky, Oleg, 142
Pentagon, 57, 79, 83, 89–92, 122
Director of Defense Research and Engineering, 196
policy analysis and evaluation (PA&E), 238
Perry, William, 83–84, 237
Persian Gulf War, 69
Peru, 50–51, 154
Plagnol, Henri, 143–144
Plus ça change, or forward to the past, 70–74

Poland, 129, 140, 154–155
Policy
decisiveness of early choices for, 21n
intelligence of, 15–18, 177–215
the messenger and the message, 185–191
Policy analysis and evaluation (PA&E), xviii, 238
Policy-makers, analysts and, 179–185
Policy questions, 213–215
asked, 195–197
not asked and not answered, 191–195
Politicization, 202, 204
Polygraph standards, 148–149
Pope, assassination attempt against, 16, 198
Portugal, 49
Power, future forms of, 25–28
Powers, Francis Gary, 75
Practical agenda for intelligence, 248–253
making the case publicly, 253–255
Preliminary Design of an Experimental World-Circling Spaceship, 75
Presidential Decision Directives (PDDs), 157, 214
President's Daily Brief (PDB), 106–107, 135
President's Summary, 135
"Priesthood" of intelligence, xiii–xiv
Private intelligence, 109
Processing
estimating as, 134–135
future global, 28–35
information *vs.* secrets, 119–120
Public advocacy, for a practical intelligence agenda, 253–255
Public and private roles, America's changing, 51–54
Purple Code, SIGINT cracking, 72
Puzzles, *vs.* mysteries, 11–13

R&A. *See* Research and analysis branch
Radio Shack, 88
RAND, xi, 75, 192, 195, 247
RB-47s, 74
Reading intelligence, 93–135
Reagan, President Ronald, 167
Reconnaissance, control of Cold War, 74–79
Red Cross, 233
"Red teaming," 38
Redefining America, 56–61
Redefining America's interests in the world, 20–25
Reich, Robert, 29n
Reinventing Government program, 240
Reno, Janet, 169
Research and analysis (R&A) branch, 98–99, 245

Reshaped intelligence, 216–220
  collecting what is free, 246–248
  collection "market," 240–243
  making the case publicly, 253–255
  new paradigm, 225–229
  points of leverage, 248–253
  practical agenda, 248–253
  retargeting the Cold War legacy,
    220–225
  rise of the market state, 229–234
  role of the DCI, 234–239
  split franchise of analysis, 243–246
Reshaping intelligence, 1–19
  aiding war-fighters, 13–15
  clandestine service of the NSA, 152–157
  failing in India, 3–5
  imperative of, 1–19
  legacy of hot war and cold, 5–8
  open sources *vs.* secrets, 8–10
  policy issues, 15–18
  puzzles *vs.* mysteries, 11–13
Retargeting, the Cold War legacy, 65–70,
  220–225
Return to the past, or *plus ça change*,
  70–74
Revolution in military affairs (RMA), 25n
RMA. *See* Revolution in military affairs
Rogue states, 35–36
Romania, 140
Rowen, Henry, 195
Russia. *See also* Ames, Aldrich; Soviet
  Union
  biological weapons program of, 37
  future of, 127, 133, 230
  launching Sputnik, 76
  terrorism within, 42
  threat posed by, 8, 12, 25–27, 39, 122,
    171
Rwanda, 50, 116

SAC. *See* Strategic Air Command
el-Sadat, Anwar, 209
Safeguard system, 197
SAMOS. *See* Satellite and Missile
  Observation System
Satellite and Missile Observation System
  (SAMOS), 76
Satellites
  for IMINT, 242
  for SIGINT, 79
  tracked by China, 4
  tracked by the Soviet Union, 3–4
Saudi Arabia, 37, 40, 111
Schelling, Thomas, 33
Schlesinger, James, 101, 249
Schoettle, Enid, 250

Schwarzkopf, General Norman, 69–70, 80,
  89
SCIF. *See* Special compartmented
  intelligence facility (SCIF)
Scowcroft, General Brent, 177
Search engines, 104
Secrets
  vs. open sources, 8–10, 108–113
  vs. processing information, xii, 119–120
Senate Select Committee on Intelligence
  (SSCI), xv, 80, 96
Sendero Luminoso insurgents, 51
Shackley, Ted, 136
Shultz, George, 179
SIGINT (signal intelligence), 8–9, 14, 65,
  67–68, 104–108, 156, 172, 239,
  242–243
  cracking the Purple Code, 72
  future of, 87–89, 125, 221–223, 254
  satellites for, 79
  turnaround time for, 13
Sikh community, 2
Silajdic, Haris, 175
"Skunk Works," 74
SMO. *See* Support for military operations
Social Security, 60
Somalia, 50–51, 55, 116–117, 122, 154
Soros, George, 13
Sources, open *vs.* secret, 8–10, 108–113
South Africa, 33, 131–132, 164–165
Soviet Union. *See also* Ames, Aldrich
  demise of, 5, 47
  satellite tracking by, 3–4
  threat posed by, 6–9, 11–13, 20–21, 26,
    64, 100–101, 120, 122, 195–197, 225
Special compartmented intelligence facility
  (SCIF), 183
Special Forces, 62
"Special operations," 140
Specter, Senator Arlen, 96
Spies, howlers received from, 119
Split franchise of analysis, 243–246
Sputnik, 76
Spying
  culture of, 145–150, 205–208
  for money, 157–161
  pros and cons, 150–152
  vs. looking and catching criminals,
    136–152
SR-71s, 73
SS-9 missiles, 195–197
  MIRVed, 196–197
SSU. *See* Strategic Services Unit
Stalin, Josef, death of, 101
Stanford University, 195
State Department, 4–5, 7, 99, 140, 160,
  165, 198, 236, 245, 250

budget of, 142
Bureau of Intelligence and Research,
    105, 120, 127, 165, 200–201
    long decline of, 162–164, 219
Statistics
    about intelligence, 6n
    about nations' growth, 33n
Steele, Robert, 247n
Stevenson, Adlai, 169
Stovepipes, 8, 65, 222
    NIMA, as imagery, 81–84
Strategic Air Command (SAC), 76
Strategic franchise, 125–127
Strategic Services Unit (SSU), 98, 139–140
Studeman, William, 137
Summers, Lawrence, 97
Support for military operations (SMO), 1,
    13–15, 64
    dominating technical collection, 89
    renewed emphasis on, 1, 15, 84–85
Systems
    ownership of, 89–91
    various, 84–89

Tactical franchise, 123–125
Tactical intelligence, 109
    vs. national, 79–81
Tactical support, organization for,
    120–123
Talon Lance system, 67
Tanzania, 164
Technical collection, xviii
    support for military operations
    dominating, 89
Tenet, George, 1, 4, 210, 236, 253
Tesobonos, 95, 97
Think tanks, 244–245, 250
Thomson, James, xii
Threats
    asymmetric, 36n
    of mass disruption, 40
    new-old, 35–43
    religion-based, 32n
    without threateners, 43–46
TIARA budget, 66, 91
"TLAM therapy," 86, 231
Tomahawk cruise missile, 90
TRANSCOM. *See* U.S. Air Force
    Transportation Command
Treasury Department, 95–97, 120
    Assistant Secretary for International
    Affairs, 219
Treaty of Versailles, 47
Treaty of Westphalia, 28, 48
Truman, President Harry, 73, 98–99, 139
Tunisia, 33

Tupac Amaru guerrillas, 50
Turkey, 16–17, 33
Turner, Admiral Stansfield, 238

U-2s, 74–76, 169, 223
UAVs. *See* Unmanned aerial vehicles
UN. *See* United Nations (UN)
UN Protection Force (UNPROFOR),
    23–24
United Nations (UN), 169–170
    peacekeepers, 23, 214–215
United States Pacific Command (PACOM),
    116–117
Universities, 228, 244, 246
Unmanned aerial vehicles (UAVs), 85–86,
    239, 243
UNPROFOR (UN Protection Force),
    23–24
Uruguay Round, 143
U.S. Air Force Transportation Command
    (TRANSCOM), 134

Vance, Cyrus, 24
Vandenberg, General Hoyt S., 100
Vogel, Ezra, 250

Wall Street, 95, 97, 113, 227, 229
Walpole, Robert D., 210
War, intelligence legacy of, 5–8
War Department, 98–99, 139–140
War-fighters, intelligence aiding, 13–15
Washington Beltway, world outside, 125
Washington Post, 107, 190
Welch, Larry, 67
West Germany, 11, 31
Western Europe, 101
Wolf, Charles, Jr., xi, 195
Woolsey, R. James, 55, 79, 169, 189,
    235–237, 245n
World Bank, 49, 53, 234
World interests, redefining America's,
    20–25
World Trade Center bombing, 38, 40, 60,
    172
World Trade Organization (WTO), 53, 96

X-2, 98

Yeltsin, Boris, 150–151
Yugoslavia, 10, 22–23, 37, 177–178. *See
    also* Bosnia; Kosovo

Zaire, 17, 50
Zapatista National Liberation Army, 29
Zedillo, Ernesto, 93